IMAGE COMICS, INC.
Robert Kirkman – Chief Operating Officer
Erik Larsen – Chief Financial Officer
Todd McFarlane – President
Marc Silvestri – Chief Executive Officer
Jim Valentino – Vice-President

Eric Stephenson – Publisher
Ron Richards – Director of Business Development
Jennifer de Guzman – Director of Trade Book Sales
Kat Salazar – Director of PR & Marketing
Jeremy Sullivan – Director of Digital Sales
Emilio Bautista – Sales Assistant
Branwyn Bigglestone – Senior Accounts Manager
Emily Miller – Accounts Manager
Jessica Ambriz – Administrative Assistant
Tyler Shainline – Events Coordinator
David Brothers – Content Manager
Jonathan Chan – Production Manager
Drew Gill – Art Director
Meredith Wallace – Print Manager
Monica Garcia – Senior Production Artist
Jenna Savage – Production Artist
Addison Duke – Production Artist
Tricia Ramos – Production Assistant
IMAGECOMICS.COM

EAST OF WEST

JONATHAN HICKMAN
WRITER

NICK DRAGOTTA
ARTIST

FRANK MARTIN
COLORS

RUS WOOTON
LETTERS

EAS

W

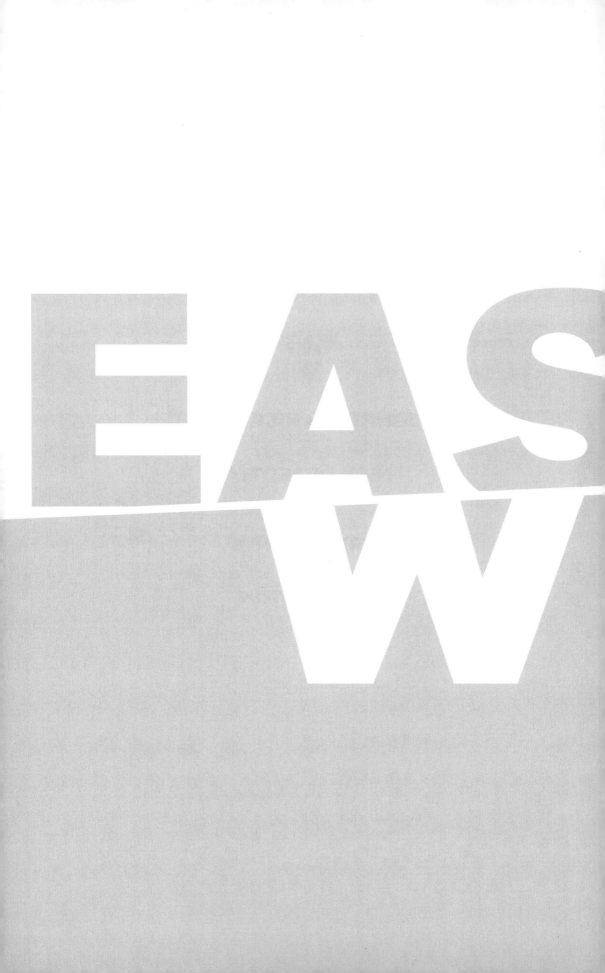

OF

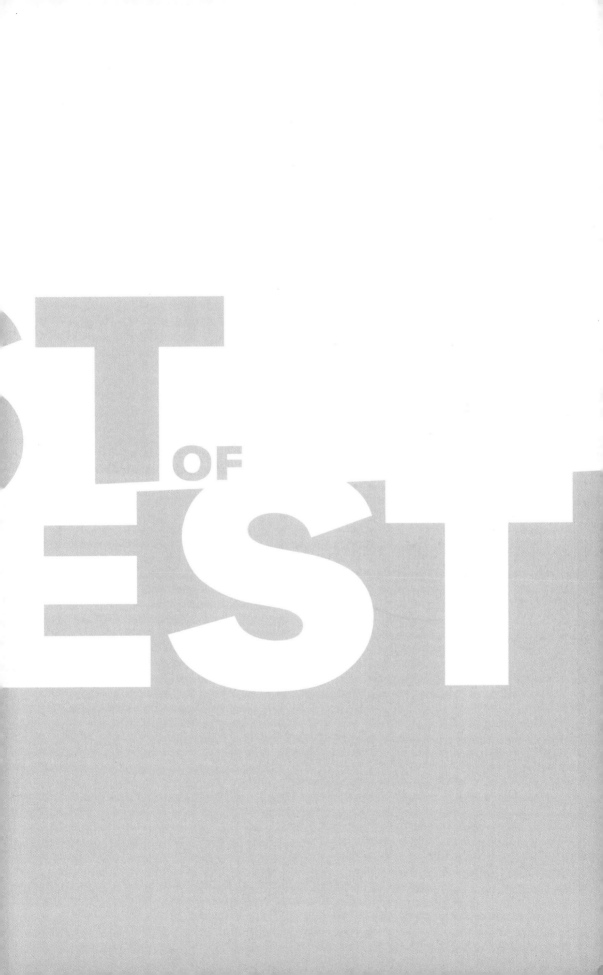

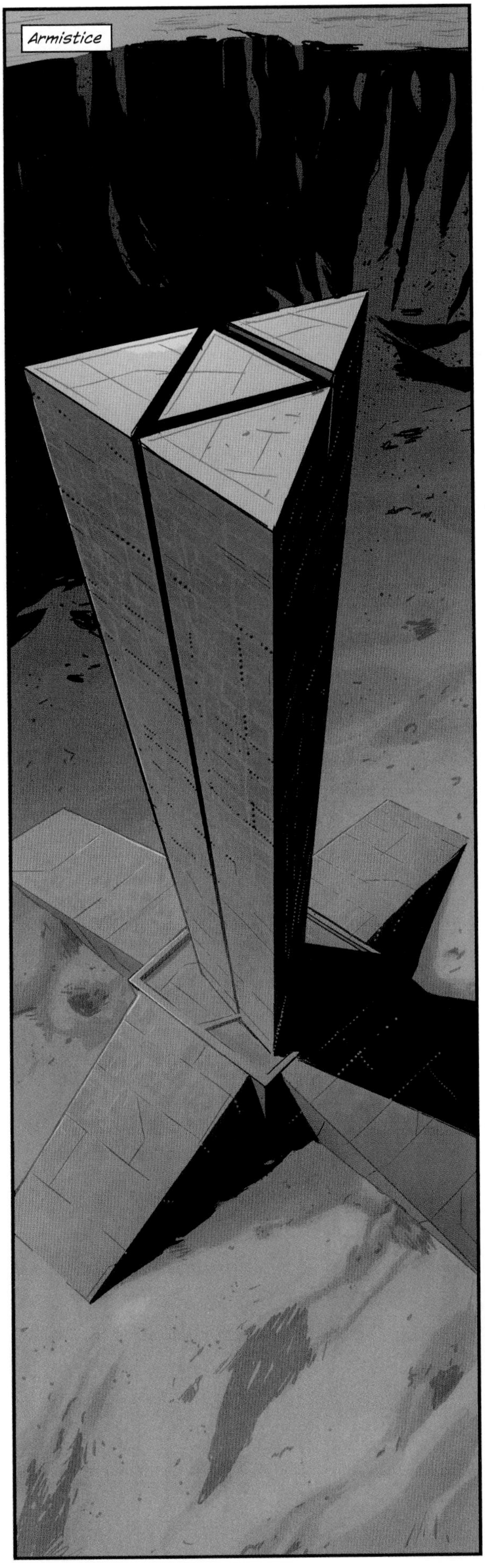
Armistice

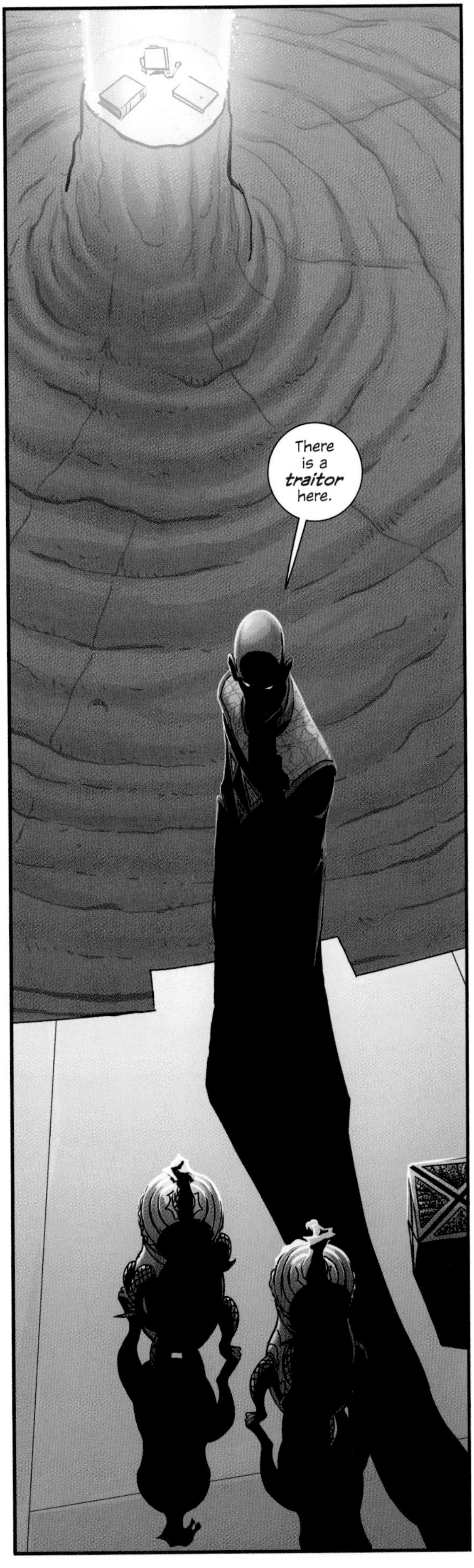
There is a ***traitor*** here.

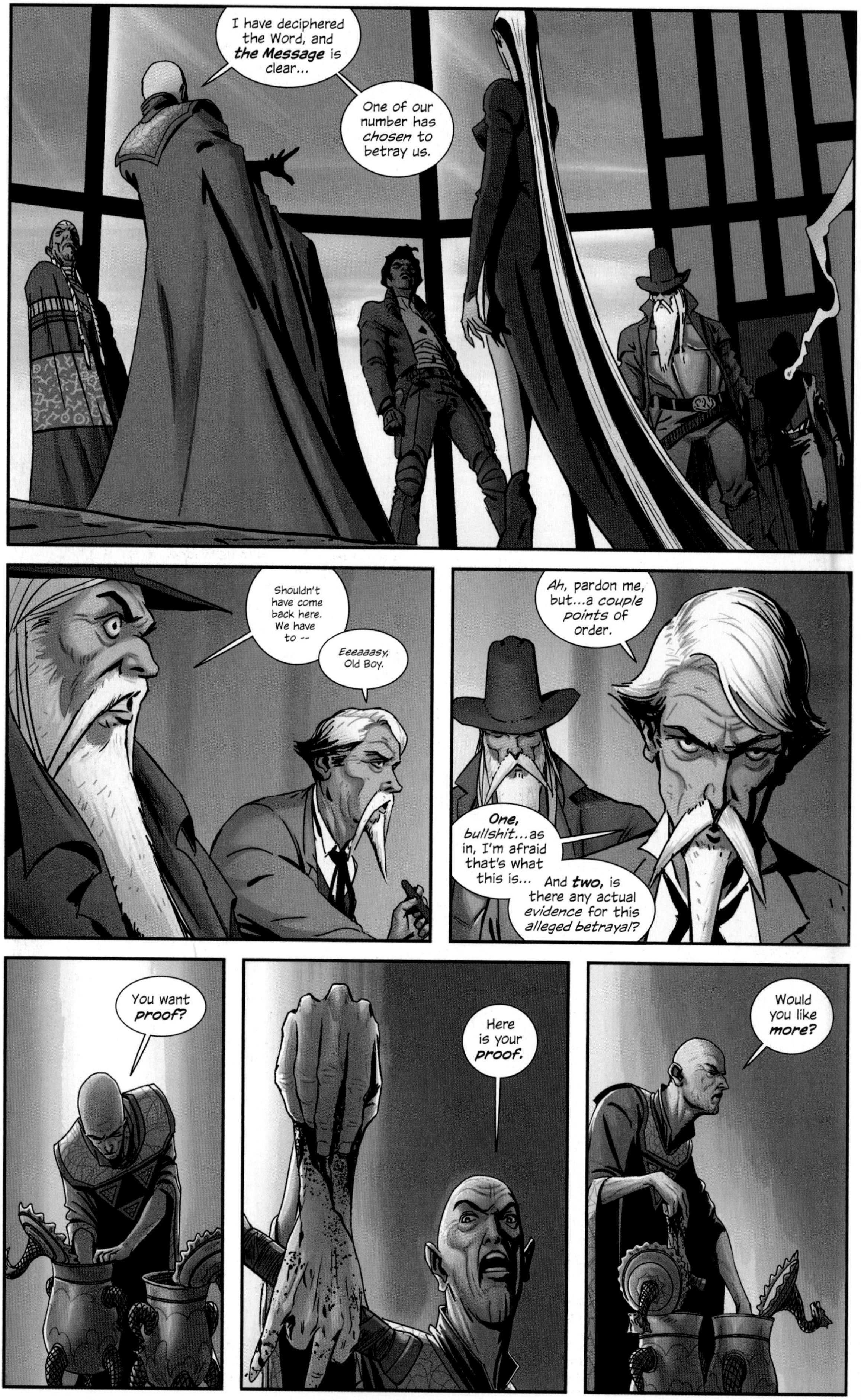
I have deciphered the Word, and **the Message** is clear...
One of our number has *chosen* to betray us.
Shouldn't have come back here. We have to --
Eeeaaasy, Old Boy.
Ah, pardon me, but...a *couple points* of order.
One, *bullshit*...as in, I'm afraid that's what this is...
And **two,** is there any actual *evidence* for this *alleged betrayal?*
You want **proof?**
Here is your **proof.**
Would you like **more?**

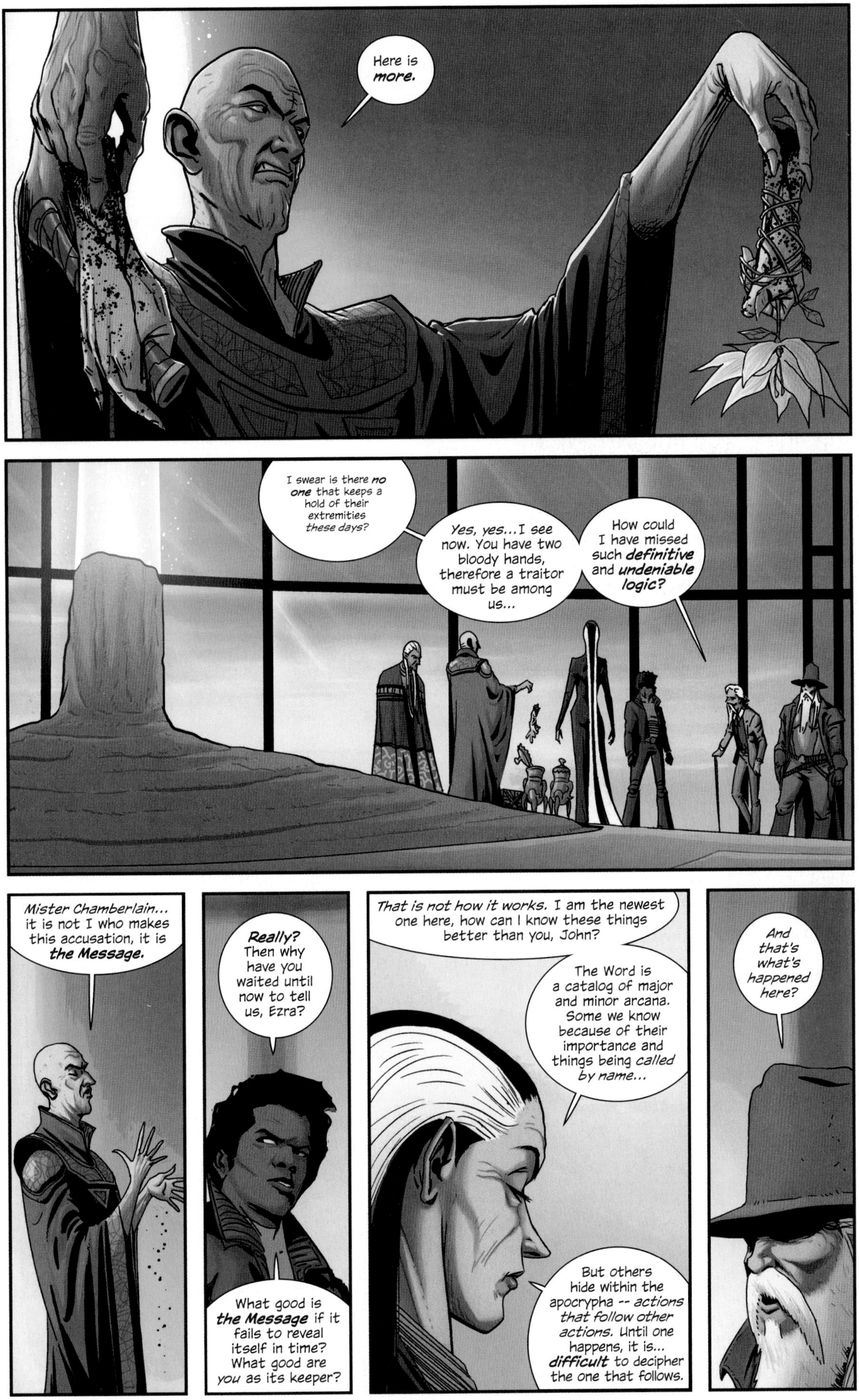
Here is *more.*
I swear is there ***no one*** that keeps a hold of their extremities *these days?*
Yes, yes... I see now. You have two bloody hands, therefore a traitor must be among us...
How could I have missed such ***definitive*** and ***undeniable logic?***
Mister Chamberlain... it is not I who makes this accusation, it is ***the Message.***
Really? Then why have you waited until now to tell us, Ezra?
What good is ***the Message*** if it fails to reveal itself in time? What good are *you* as its keeper?
That is not how it works. I am the newest one here, how can I know these things better than you, John?
The Word is a catalog of major and minor arcana. Some we know because of their importance and things being *called by name...*
But others hide within the apocrypha -- *actions that follow other actions.* Until one happens, it is... ***difficult*** to decipher the one that follows.
And that's what's happened here?

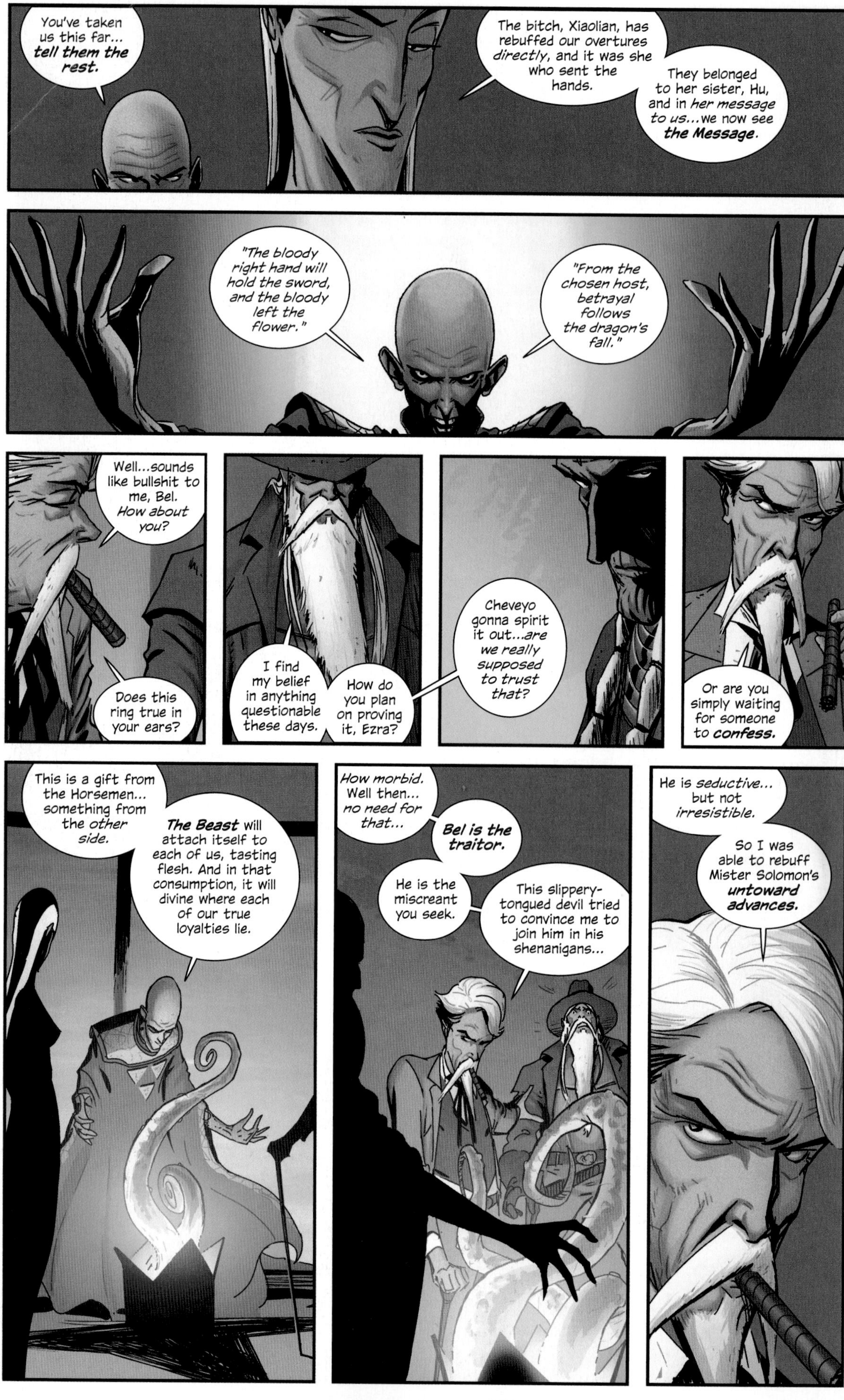
You've taken us this far... tell them the rest.
The bitch, Xiaolian, has rebuffed our overtures directly, and it was she who sent the hands.
They belonged to her sister, Hu, and in her message to us...we now see the Message.
"The bloody right hand will hold the sword, and the bloody left the flower."
"From the chosen host, betrayal follows the dragon's fall."
Well...sounds like bullshit to me, Bel. How about you?
Does this ring true in your ears?
I find my belief in anything questionable these days.
How do you plan on proving it, Ezra?
Cheveyo gonna spirit it out...are we really supposed to trust that?
Or are you simply waiting for someone to confess.
This is a gift from the Horsemen... something from the other side.
The Beast will attach itself to each of us, tasting flesh. And in that consumption, it will divine where each of our true loyalties lie.
How morbid. Well then... no need for that...
Bel is the traitor.
He is the miscreant you seek.
This slippery-tongued devil tried to convince me to join him in his shenanigans...
He is seductive... but not irresistible.
So I was able to rebuff Mister Solomon's untoward advances.

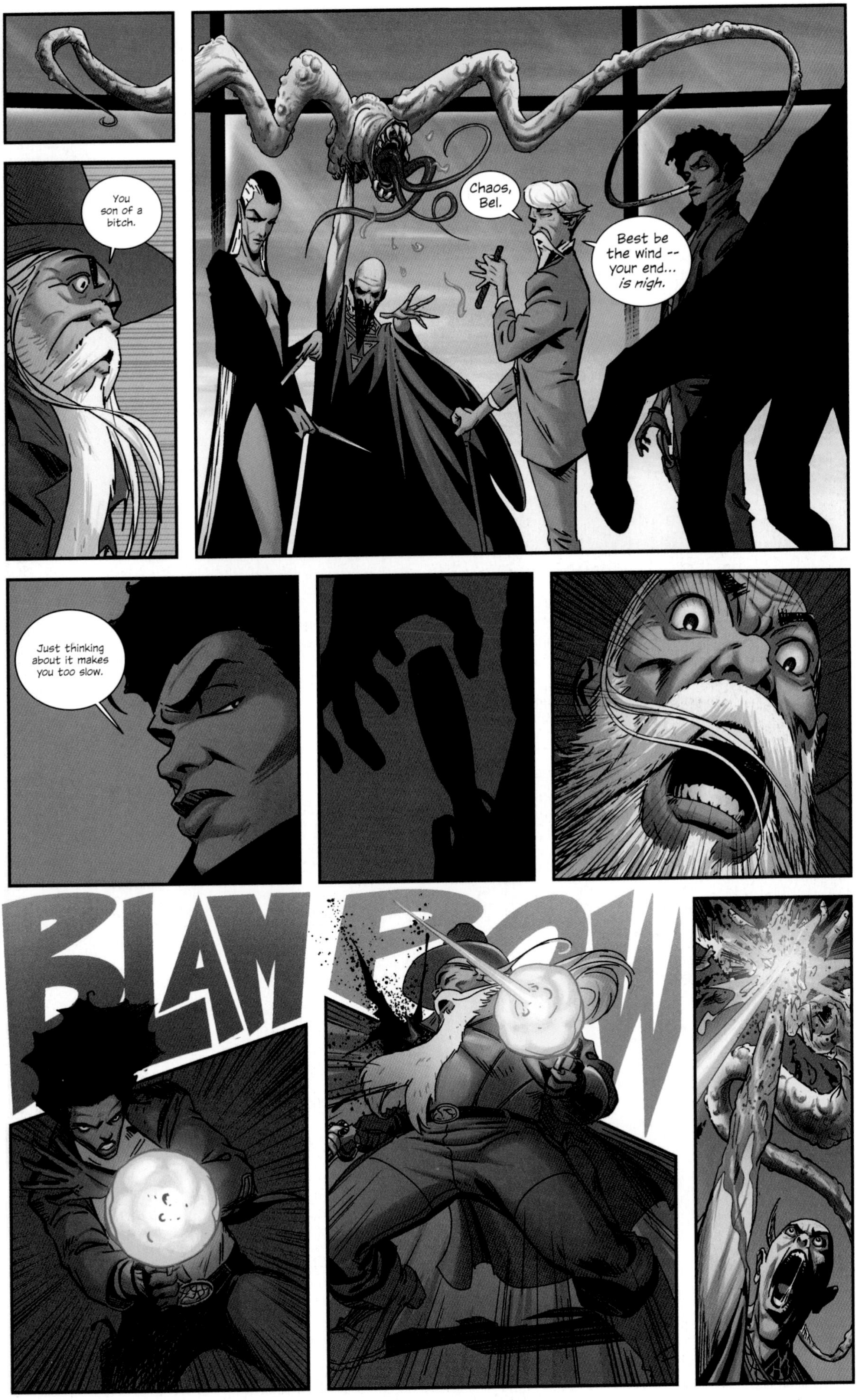
You son of a bitch.
Chaos, Bel.
Best be the wind -- your end... *is nigh.*
Just thinking about it makes you too slow.
BLAM
BOW

AAIIEEEEEE!

Well, *hot damn!*

Look at that boy *run!*

Run, Bel! *Run for your life!*

Hrmph!

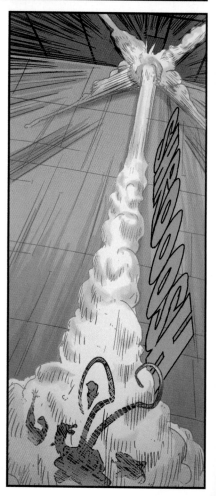

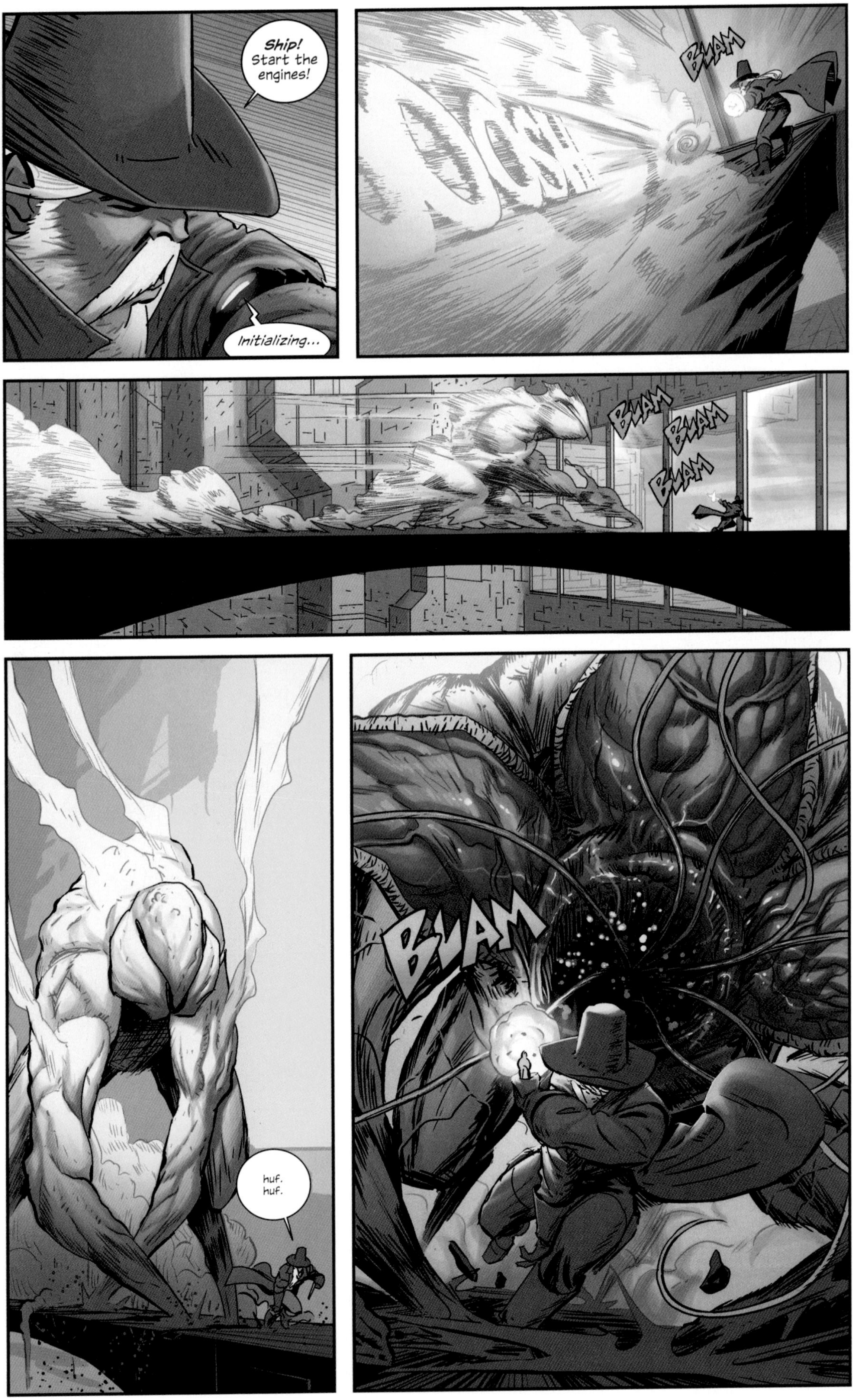
Ship! Start the engines!
Initializing...
BLAM
BLAM
BLAM
BLAM
huf. huf.
BLAM

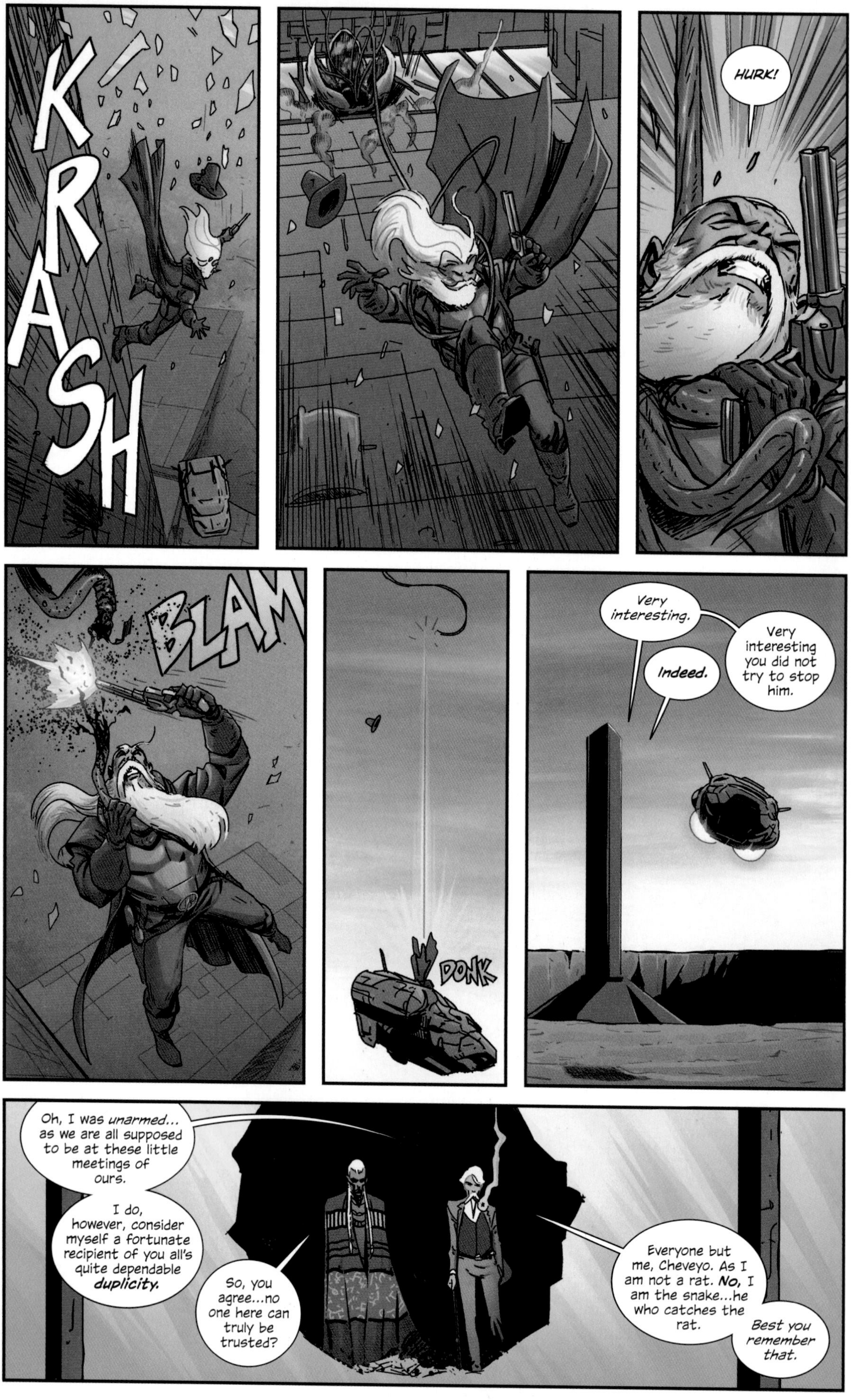
KRASH
HURK!
BLAM
DONK
Very interesting.
Indeed.
Very interesting you did not try to stop him.
Oh, I was *unarmed*... as we are all supposed to be at these little meetings of ours.
I do, however, consider myself a fortunate recipient of you all's quite dependable ***duplicity.***
So, you agree...no one here can truly be trusted?
Everyone but me, Cheveyo. As I am not a rat. ***No,*** I am the snake...he who catches the rat.
Best you remember that.

THE **OLD MAGIC** STAYS WITH
YOU **FOREVER.**

IF YOU HAVE BEEN **MARKED,**
THERE IS NO ERASING THAT
STAIN.

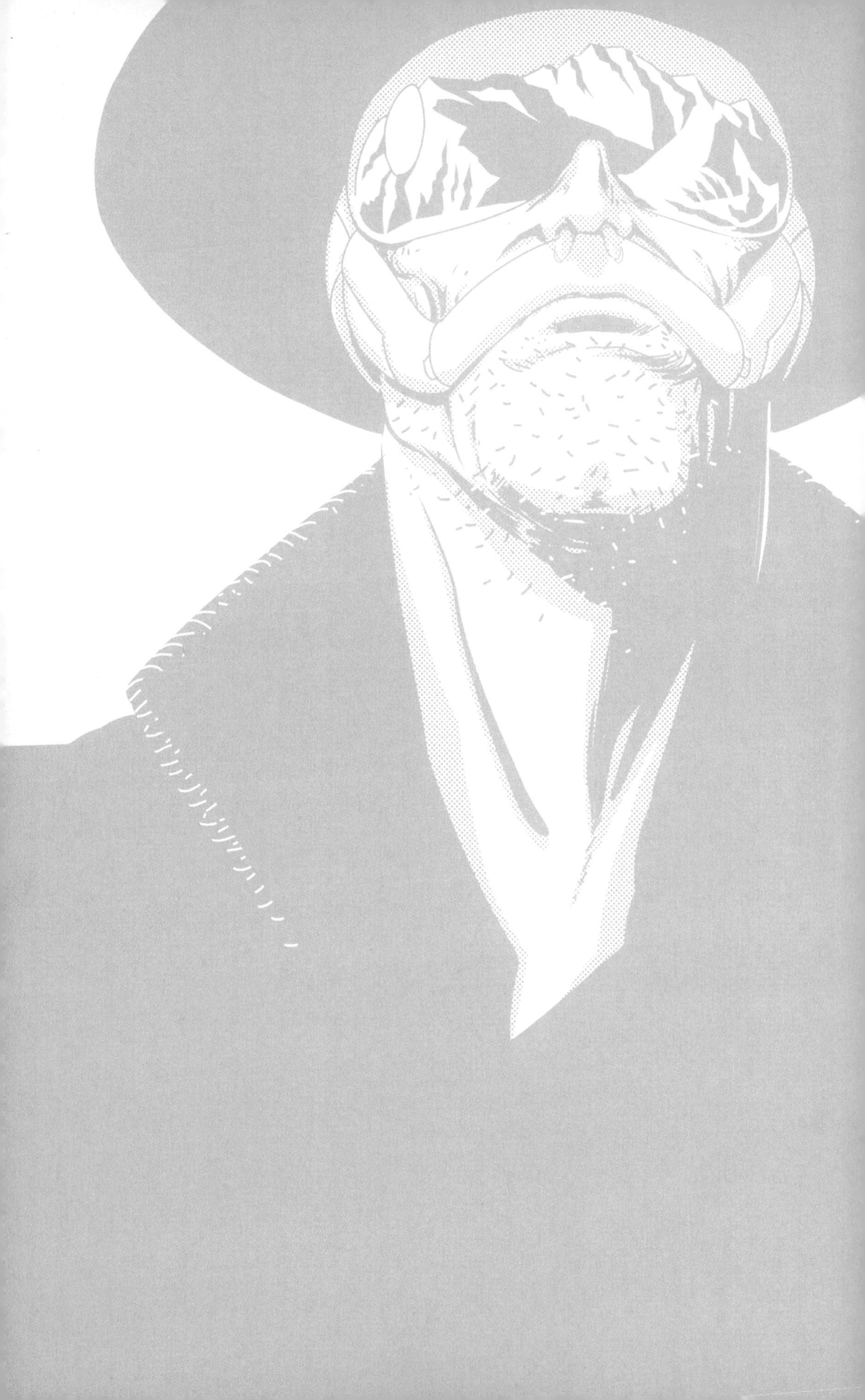

06

▲△▽ SIX: TO DO **JUSTLY,** AND TO LOVE **MERCY**

ALL LIES **DIE** IN THE DESERT.

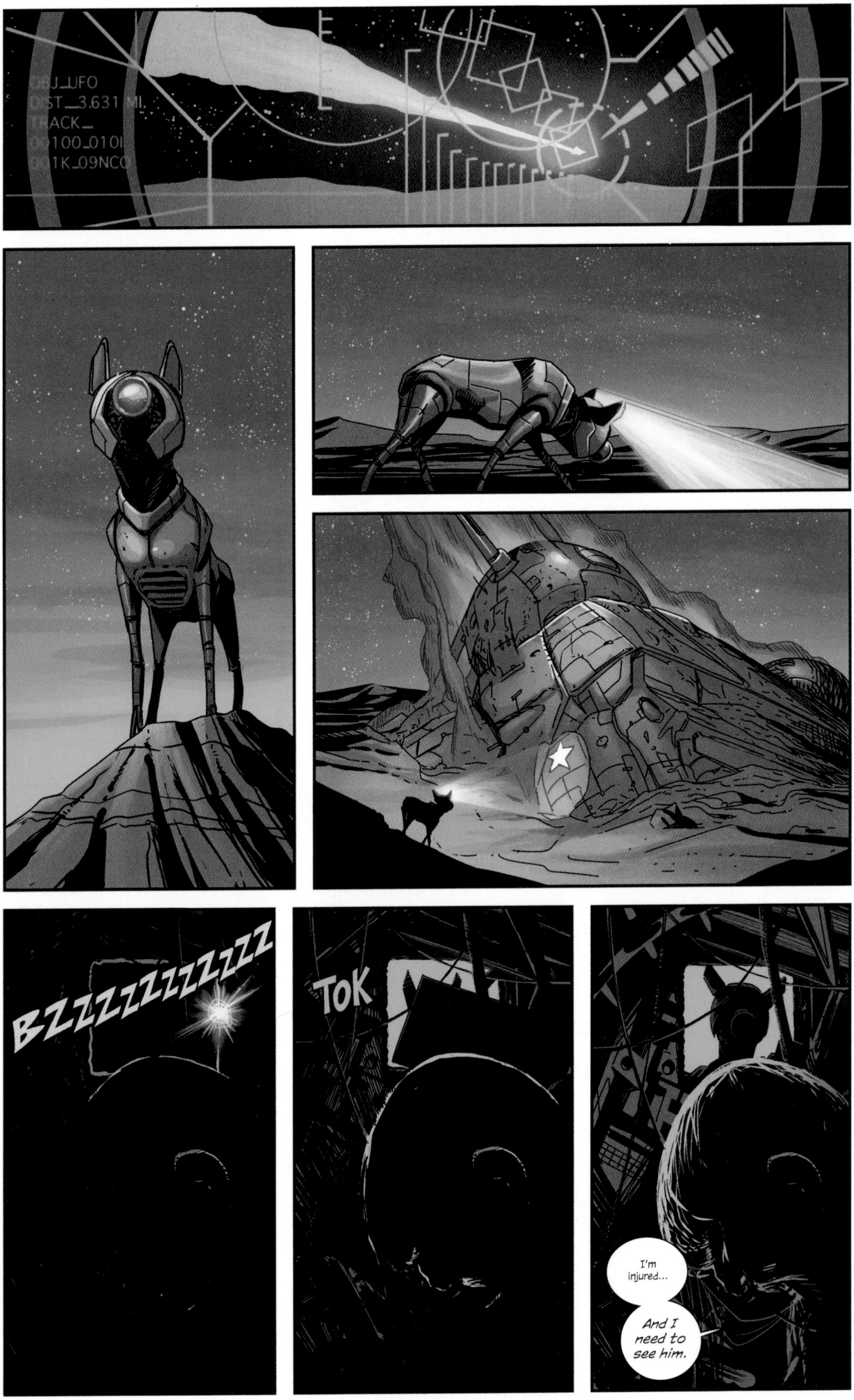
OBJ_UFO
DST_3.631 MI.
TRACK_
00100_0101
001K_09NCO
BZZZZZZZZZzzz
TOK
I'm injured...
And I need to see him.

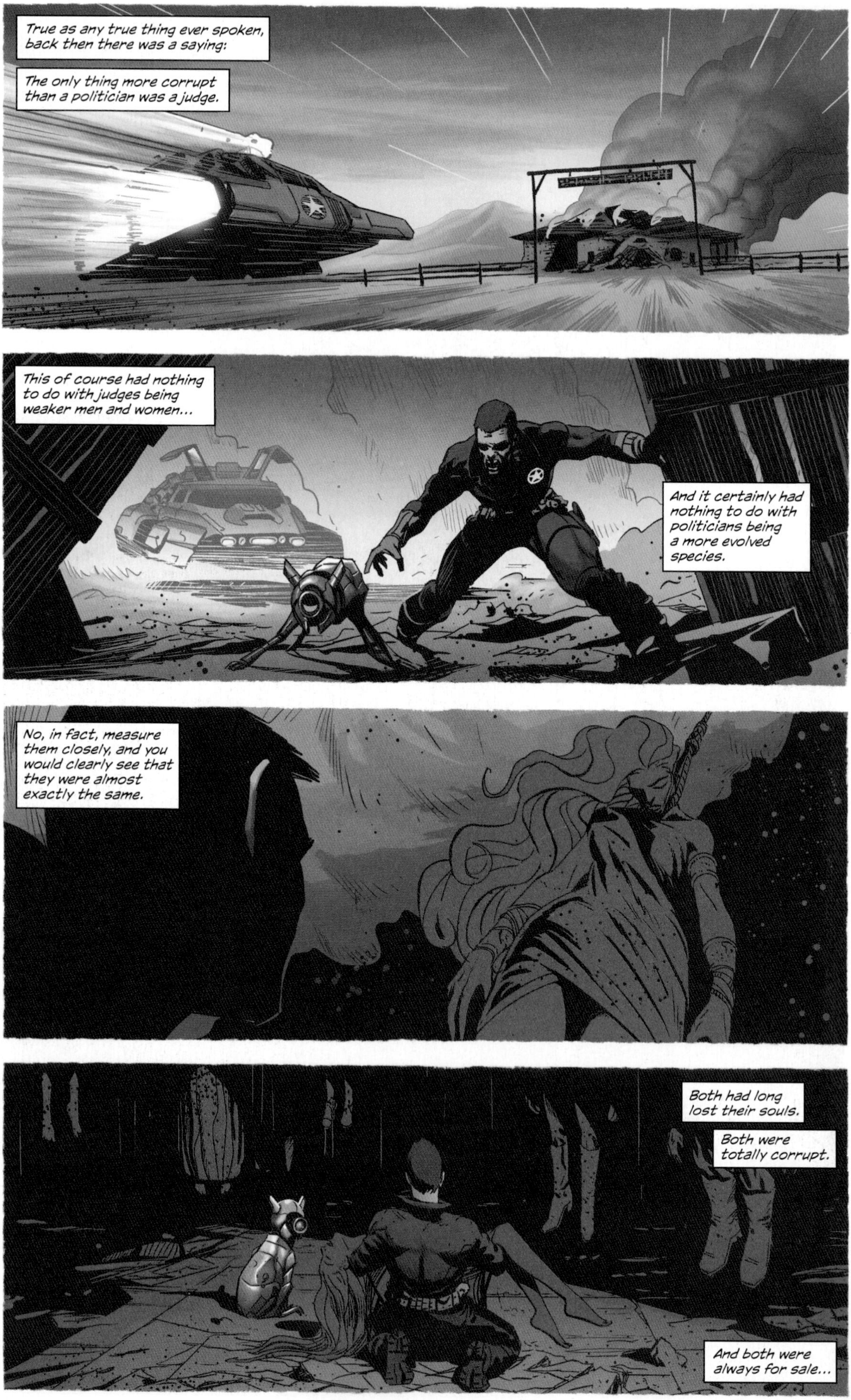
True as any true thing ever spoken, back then there was a saying:
The only thing more corrupt than a politician was a judge.
This of course had nothing to do with judges being weaker men and women...
And it certainly had nothing to do with politicians being a more evolved species.
No, in fact, measure them closely, and you would clearly see that they were almost exactly the same.
Both had long lost their souls.
Both were totally corrupt.
And both were always for sale...

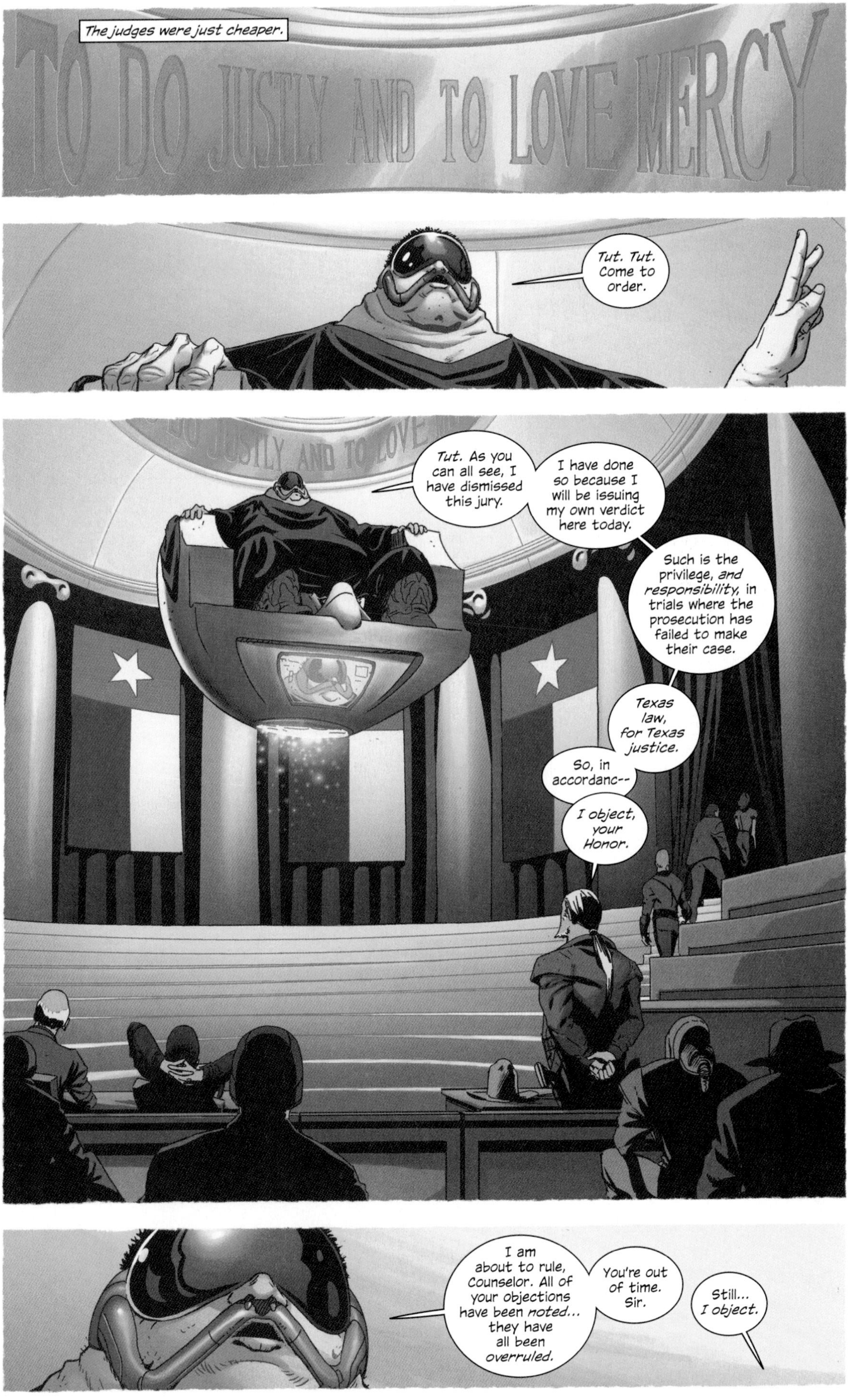
The judges were just cheaper.
TO DO JUSTLY AND TO LOVE MERCY
Tut. Tut. Come to order.
Tut. As you can all see, I have dismissed this jury.
I have done so because I will be issuing my own verdict here today.
Such is the privilege, and responsibility, in trials where the prosecution has failed to make their case.
Texas law, for Texas justice.
So, in accordanc--
I object, your Honor.
I am about to rule, Counselor. All of your objections have been noted... they have all been overruled.
You're out of time. Sir.
Still... I object.

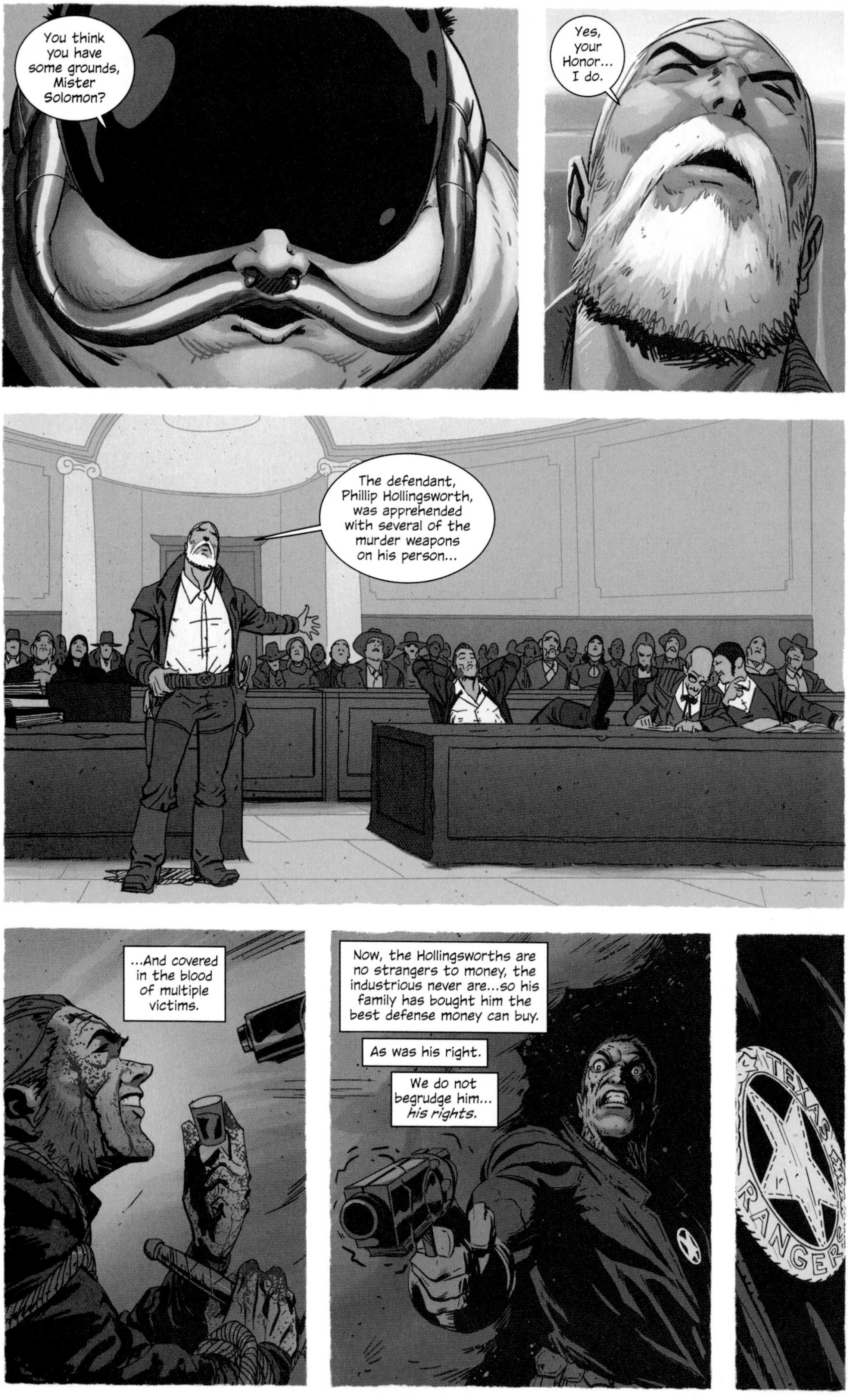
You think you have some grounds, Mister Solomon?
Yes, your Honor... I do.
The defendant, Phillip Hollingsworth, was apprehended with several of the murder weapons on his person...
...And covered in the blood of multiple victims.
Now, the Hollingsworths are no strangers to money, the industrious never are...so his family has bought him the best defense money can buy.
As was his right.
We do not begrudge him... *his rights.*
TEXAS RANGERS

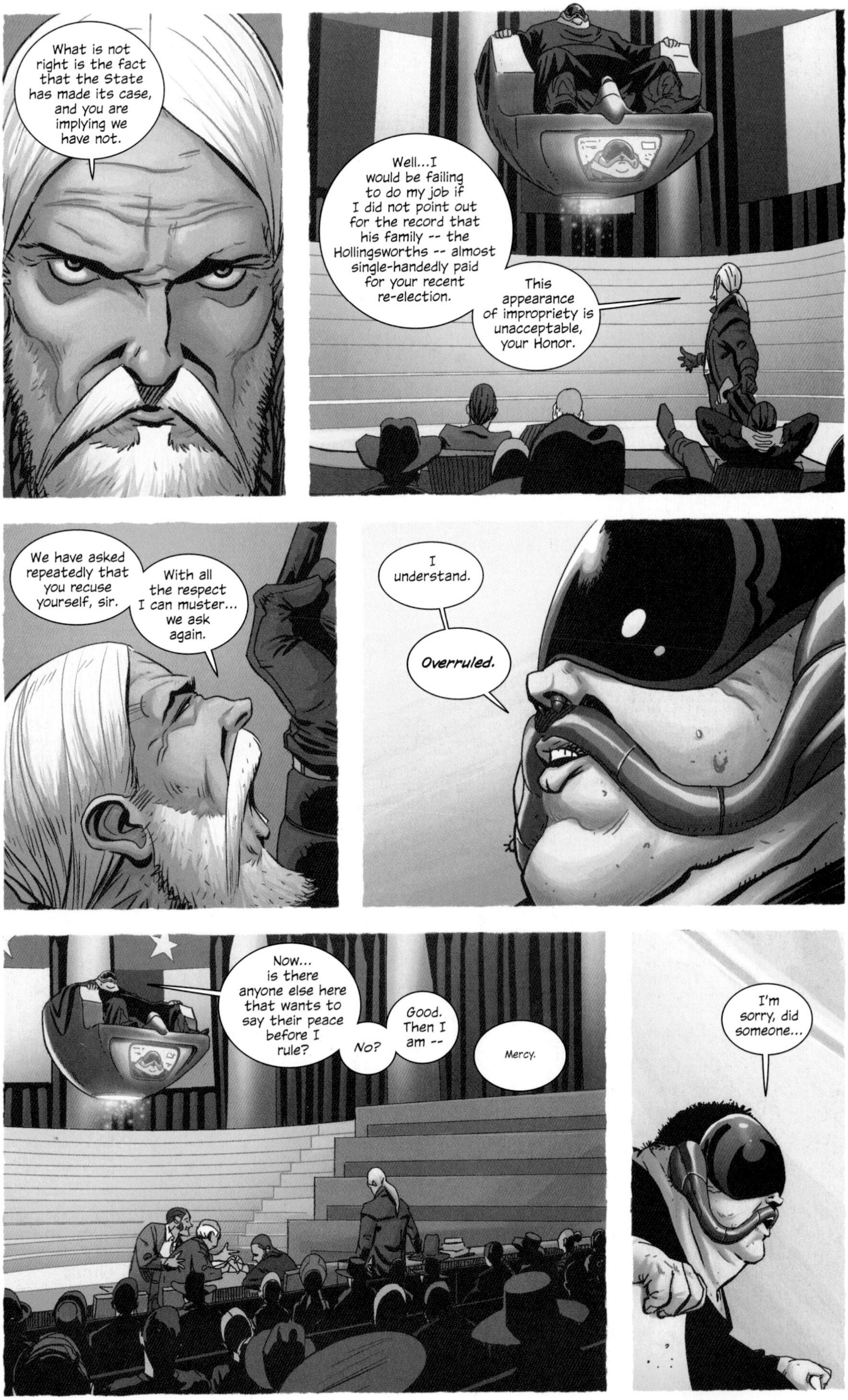

What is not right is the fact that the State has made its case, and you are implying we have not.
Well...I would be failing to do my job if I did not point out for the record that his family -- the Hollingsworths -- almost single-handedly paid for your recent re-election.
This appearance of impropriety is unacceptable, your Honor.
We have asked repeatedly that you recuse yourself, sir.
With all the respect I can muster... we ask again.
I understand.
Overruled.
Now... is there anyone else here that wants to say their peace before I rule?
No?
Good. Then I am --
Mercy.
I'm sorry, did someone...

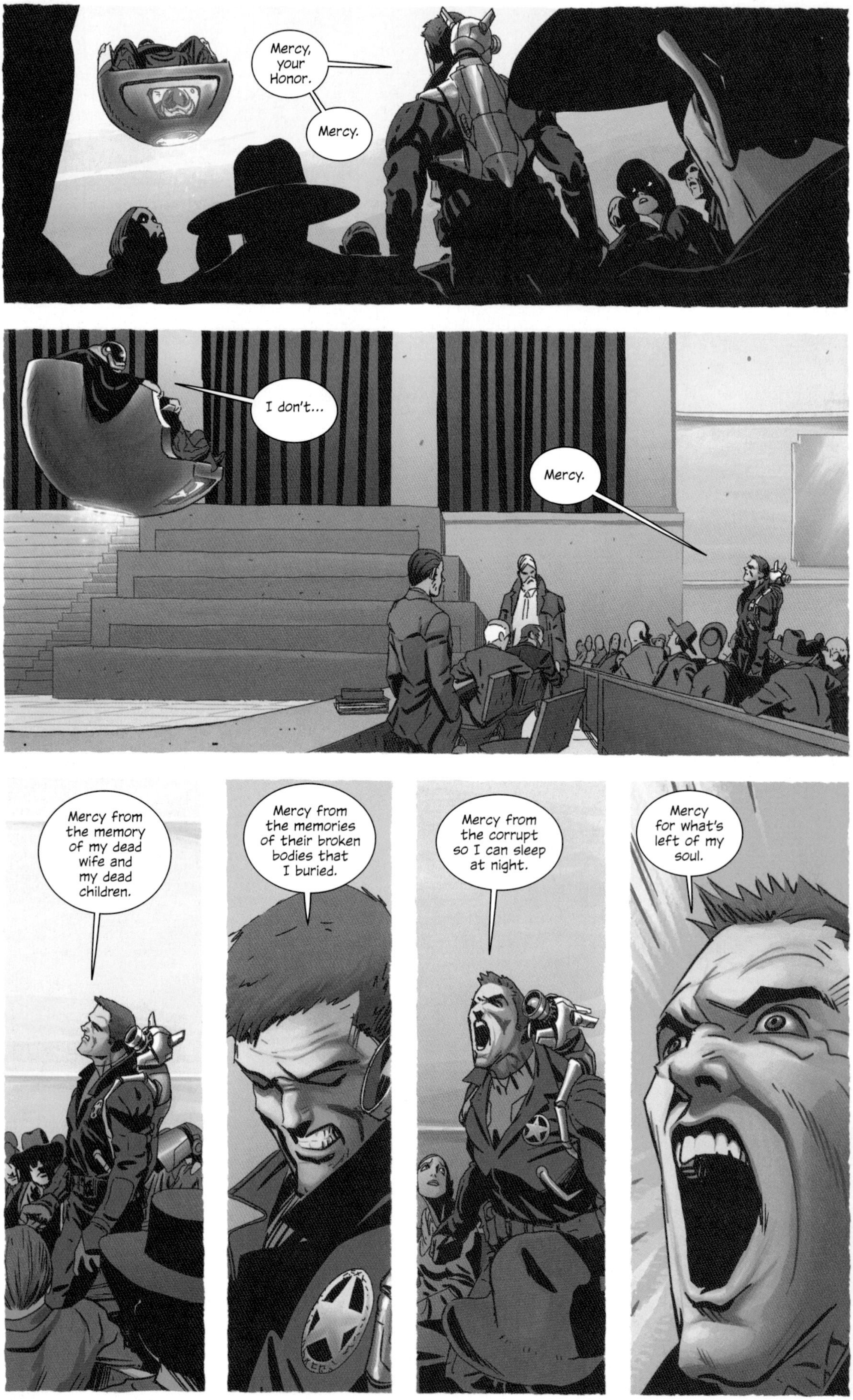
Mercy, your Honor.
Mercy.
I don't...
Mercy.
Mercy from the memory of my dead wife and my dead children.
Mercy from the memories of their broken bodies that I buried.
Mercy from the corrupt so I can sleep at night.
Mercy for what's left of my soul.

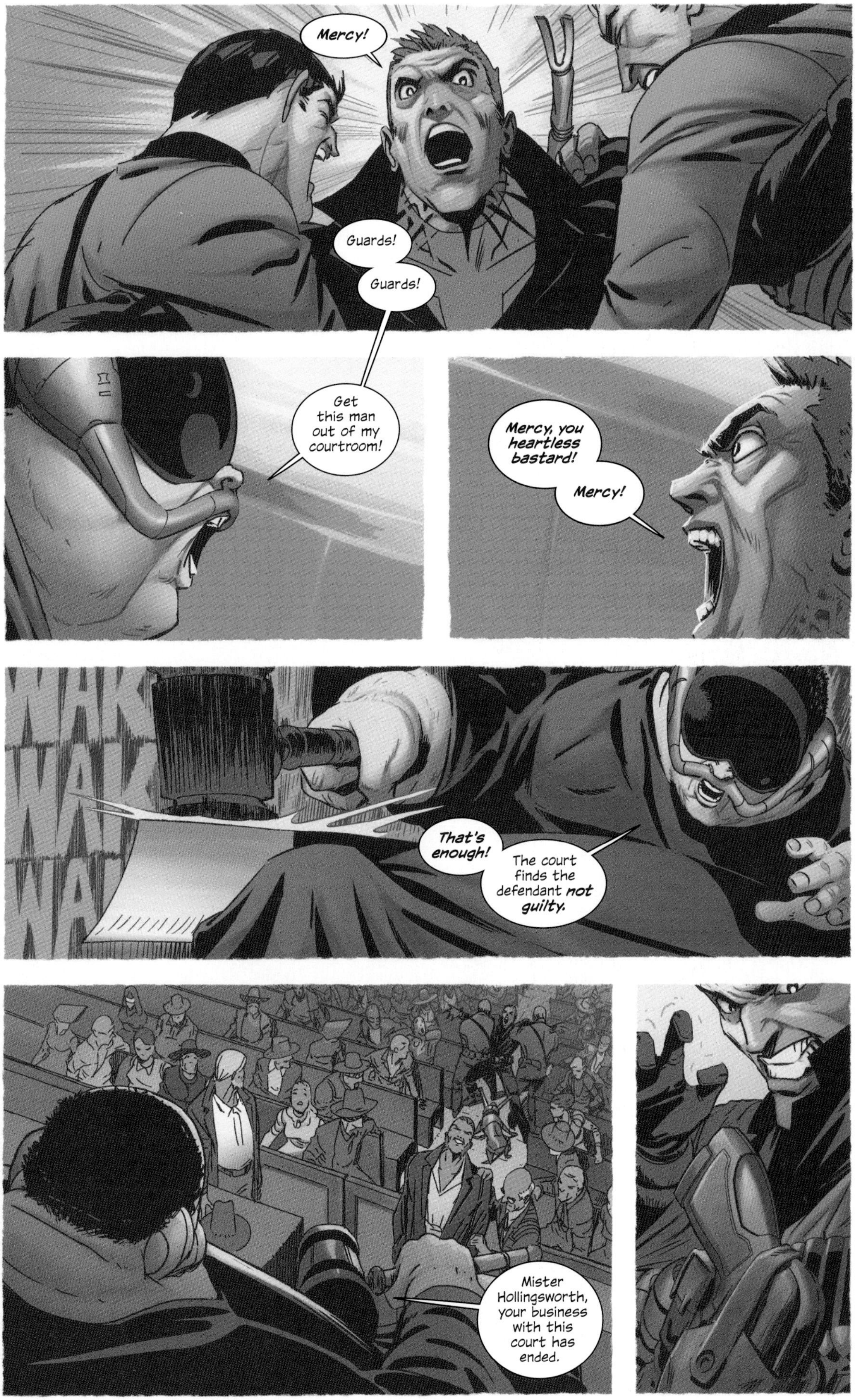
Mercy!
Guards!
Guards!
Get this man out of my courtroom!
Mercy, you heartless bastard!
Mercy!
WAK
WAK
That's enough!
The court finds the defendant *not guilty.*
Mister Hollingsworth, your business with this court has ended.

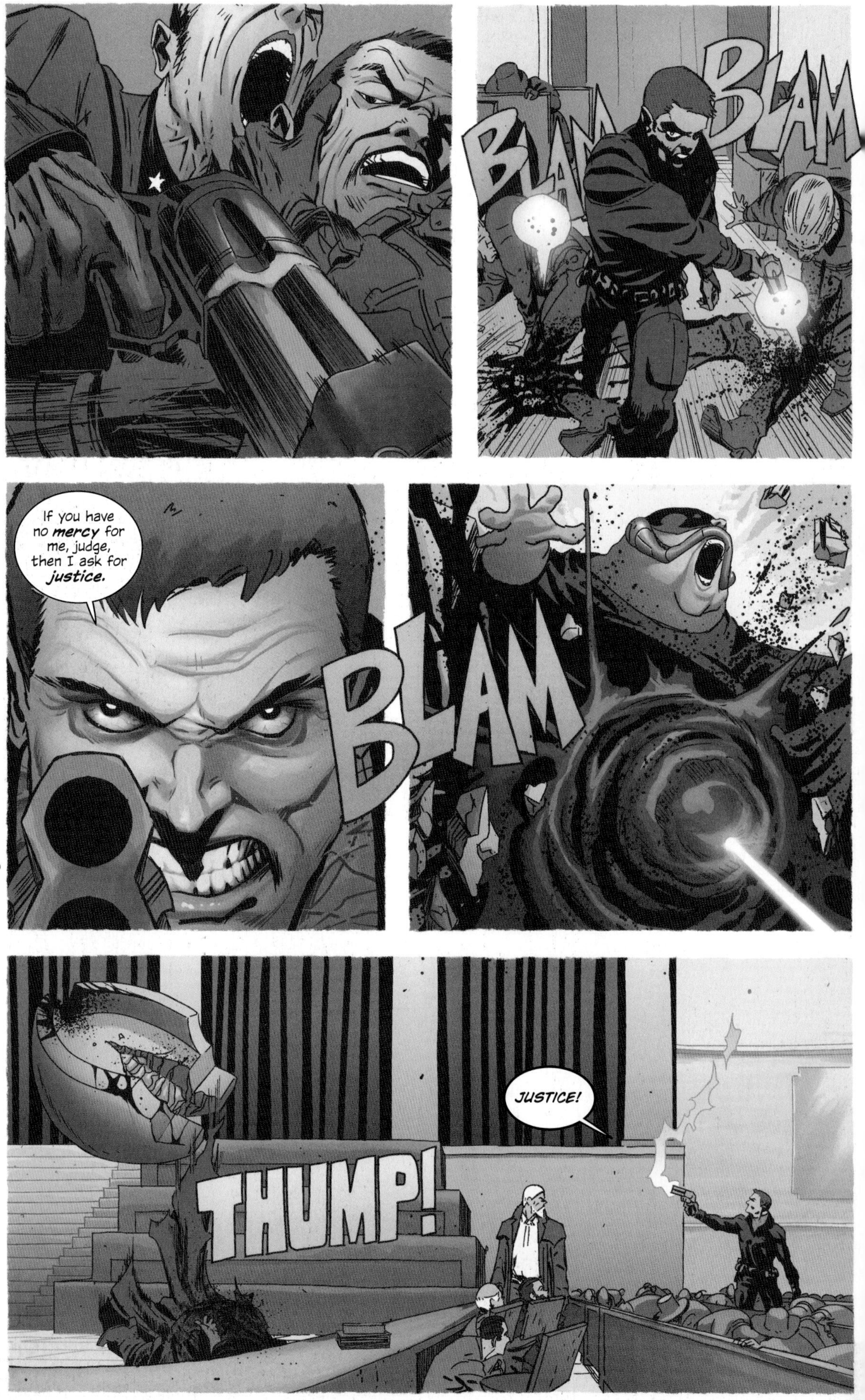
BLAM
BLAM
BLAM
If you have no *mercy* for me, judge, then I ask for *justice.*
BLAM
JUSTICE!
THUMP!

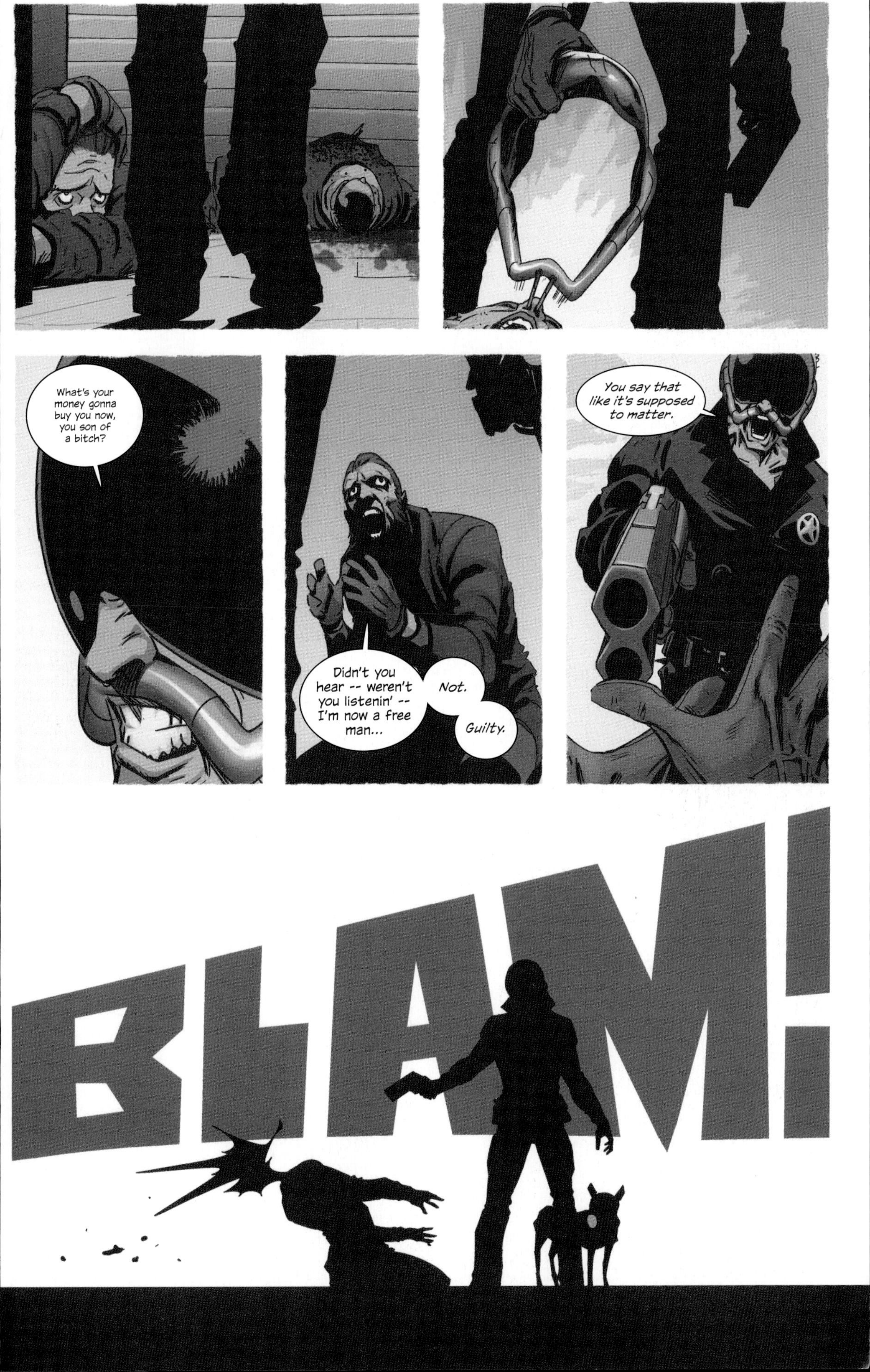
What's your money gonna buy you now, you son of a bitch?
Didn't you hear -- weren't you listenin' -- I'm now a free man...
Not.
Guilty.
You say that like it's supposed to matter.
BLAM!

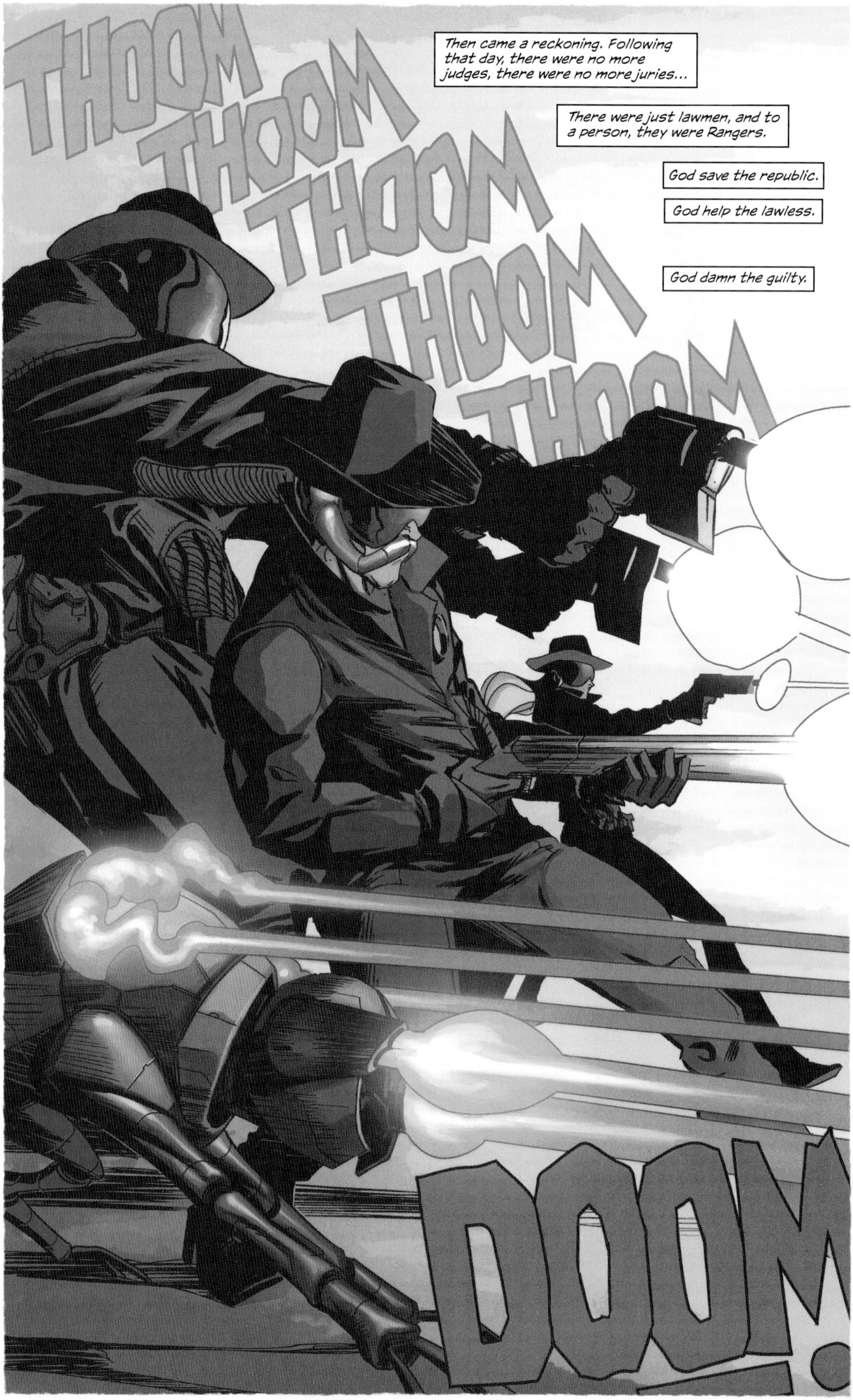
THOOM THOOM THOOM THOOM THOOM
Then came a reckoning. Following that day, there were no more judges, there were no more juries...
There were just lawmen, and to a person, they were Rangers.
God save the republic.
God help the lawless.
God damn the guilty.
DOOM!

WHEN THE **RANGERS** HAD
FINISHED WITH THE
JUDGES, THEY TURNED ON
THE **POLITICIANS.**

NO **THIEVES,** NO **LIARS,**
AND NO **WHORES** WERE
LEFT ALIVE.

AMEN.

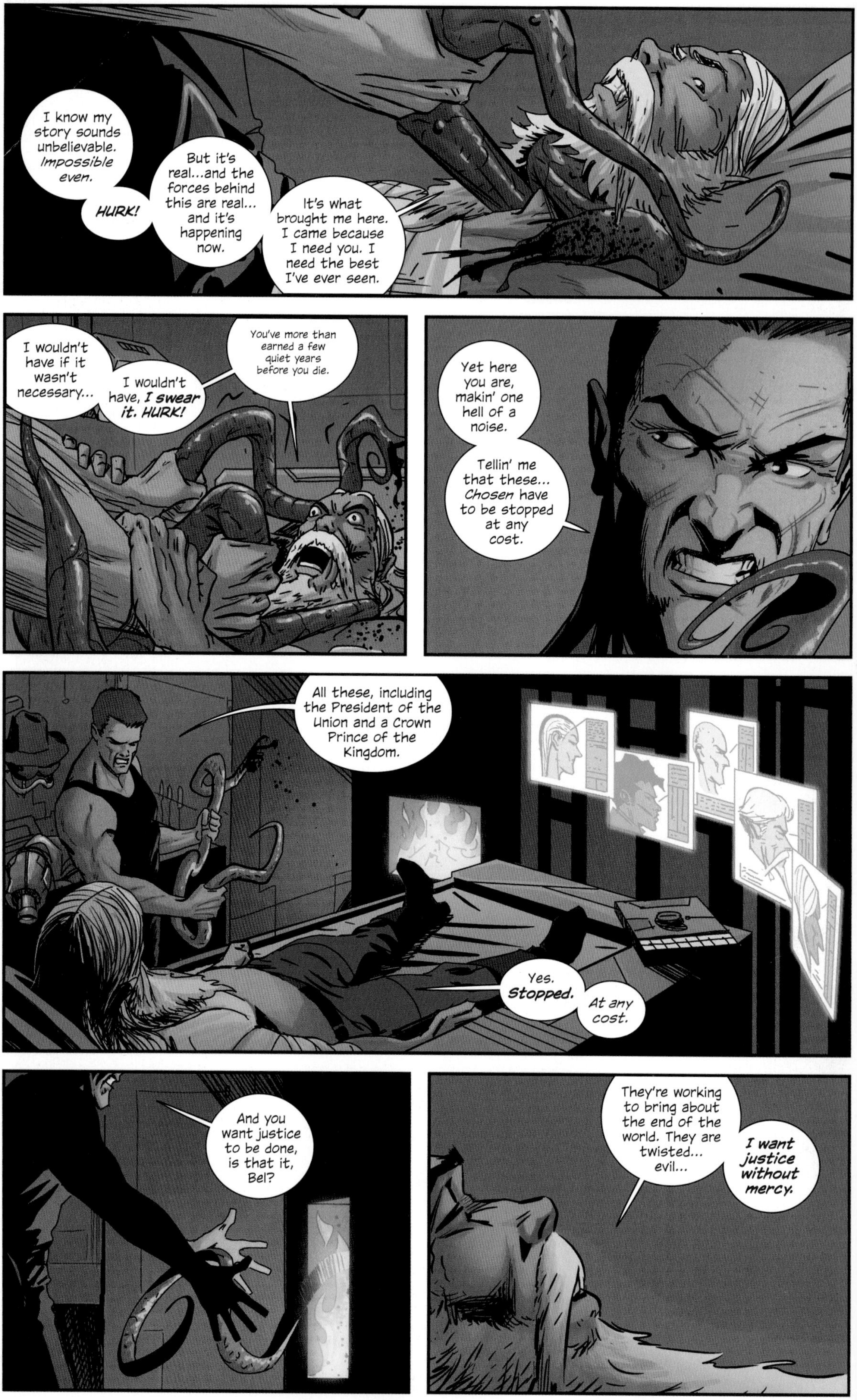
I know my story sounds unbelievable. *Impossible even.*
HURK!
But it's real...and the forces behind this are real... and it's happening now.
It's what brought me here. I came because I need you. I need the best I've ever seen.
I wouldn't have if it wasn't necessary...
I wouldn't have, ***I swear it. HURK!***
You've more than earned a few quiet years before you die.
Yet here you are, makin' one hell of a noise.
Tellin' me that these... *Chosen* have to be stopped at any cost.
All these, including the President of the Union and a Crown Prince of the Kingdom.
Yes. ***Stopped.***
At any cost.
And you want justice to be done, is that it, Bel?
They're working to bring about the end of the world. They are twisted... evil...
I want justice without mercy.

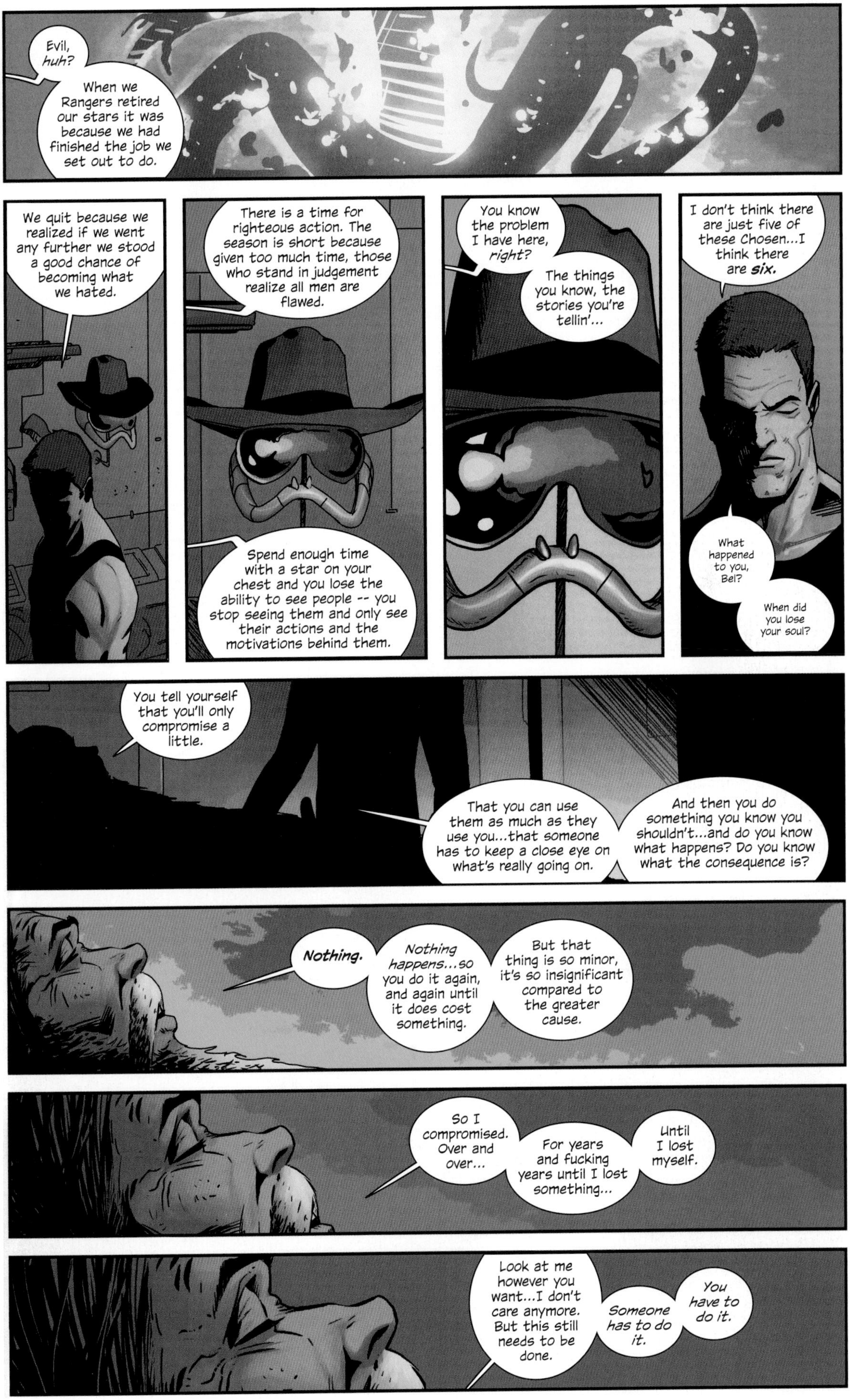
Evil, *huh?*
When we Rangers retired our stars it was because we had finished the job we set out to do.
We quit because we realized if we went any further we stood a good chance of becoming what we hated.
There is a time for righteous action. The season is short because given too much time, those who stand in judgement realize all men are flawed.
Spend enough time with a star on your chest and you lose the ability to see people -- you stop seeing them and only see their actions and the motivations behind them.
You know the problem I have here, *right?*
The things you know, the stories you're tellin'...
I don't think there are just five of these Chosen...I think there are ***six.***
What happened to you, Bel?
When did you lose your soul?
You tell yourself that you'll only compromise a little.
That you can use them as much as they use you...that someone has to keep a close eye on what's really going on.
And then you do something you know you shouldn't...and do you know what happens? Do you know what the consequence is?
Nothing.
Nothing happens...so you do it again, and again until it does cost something.
But that thing is so minor, it's so insignificant compared to the greater cause.
So I compromised. Over and over...
For years and fucking years until I lost something...
Until I lost myself.
Look at me however you want...I don't care anymore. But this still needs to be done.
Someone has to do it.
You have to do it.

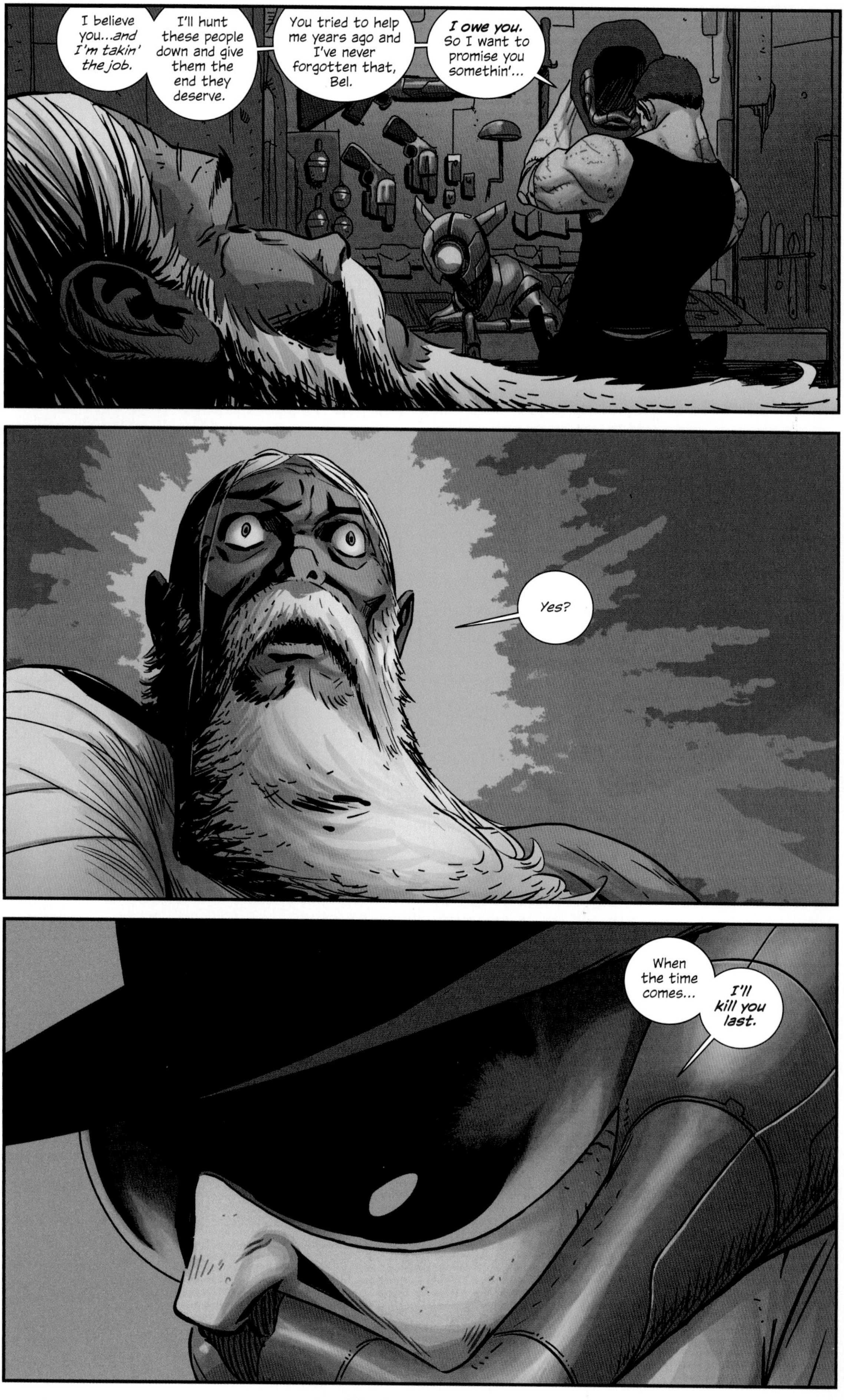
I believe you...*and I'm takin' the job.*
I'll hunt these people down and give them the end they deserve.
You tried to help me years ago and I've never forgotten that, Bel.
I owe you. So I want to promise you somethin'...
Yes?
When the time comes...
I'll kill you last.

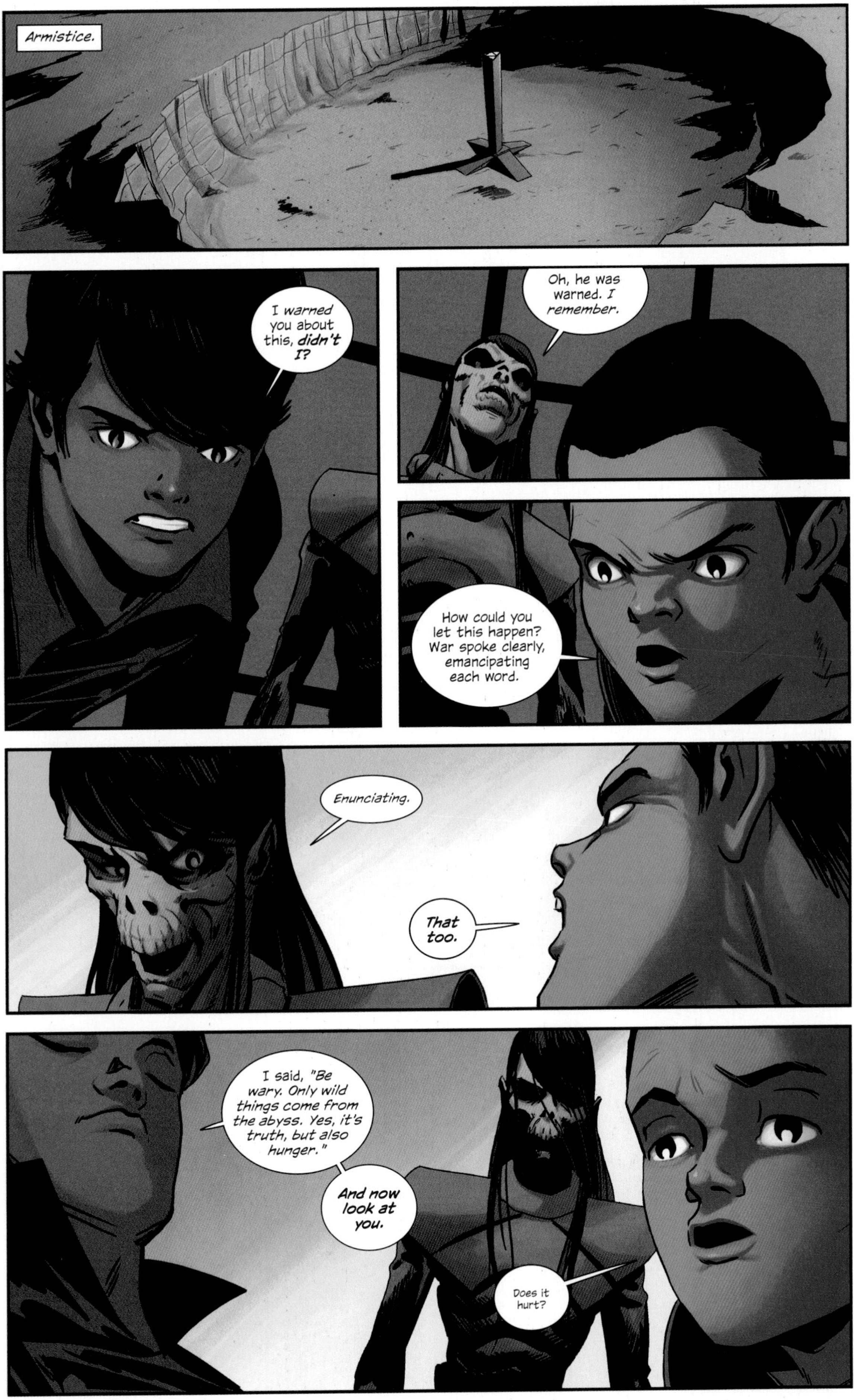
Armistice.
I *warned* you about this, ***didn't I?***
Oh, he was warned. *I remember.*
How could you let this happen? War spoke clearly, emancipating each word.
Enunciating.
That too.
I said, "Be wary. Only wild things come from the abyss. Yes, it's truth, but also hunger."
And now look at you.
Does it hurt?

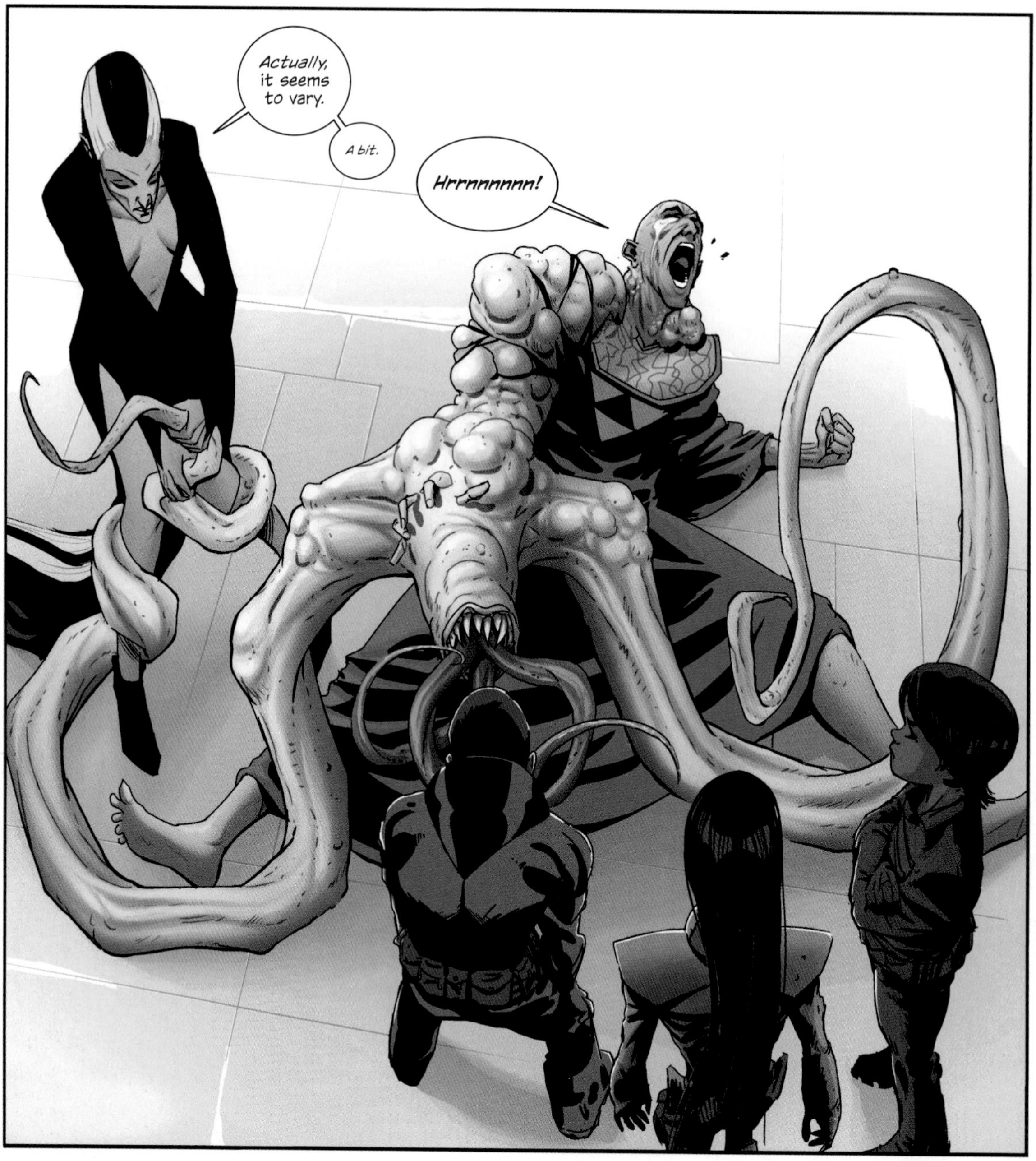
Actually, it seems to vary.
A bit.
Hrrnnnnnnn!

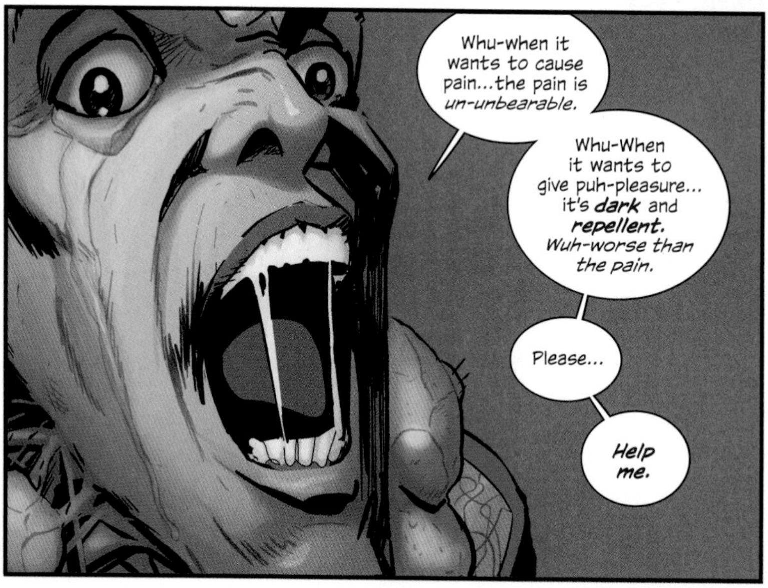
Whu-when it wants to cause pain...the pain is *un-unbearable.*
Whu-When it wants to give puh-pleasure... it's ***dark*** and ***repellent.*** *Wuh-worse than the pain.*
Please...
Help me.

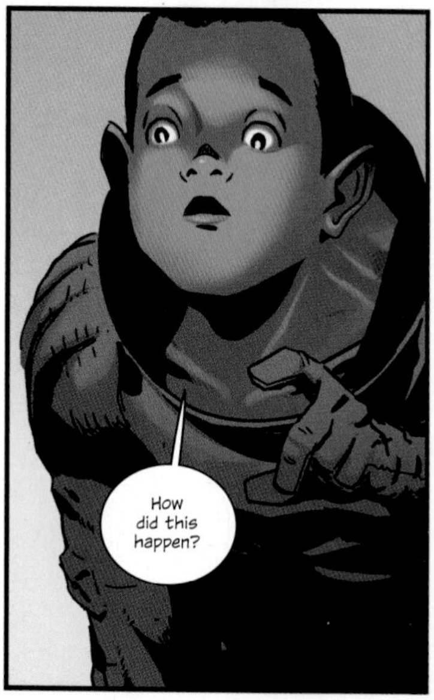
How did this happen?

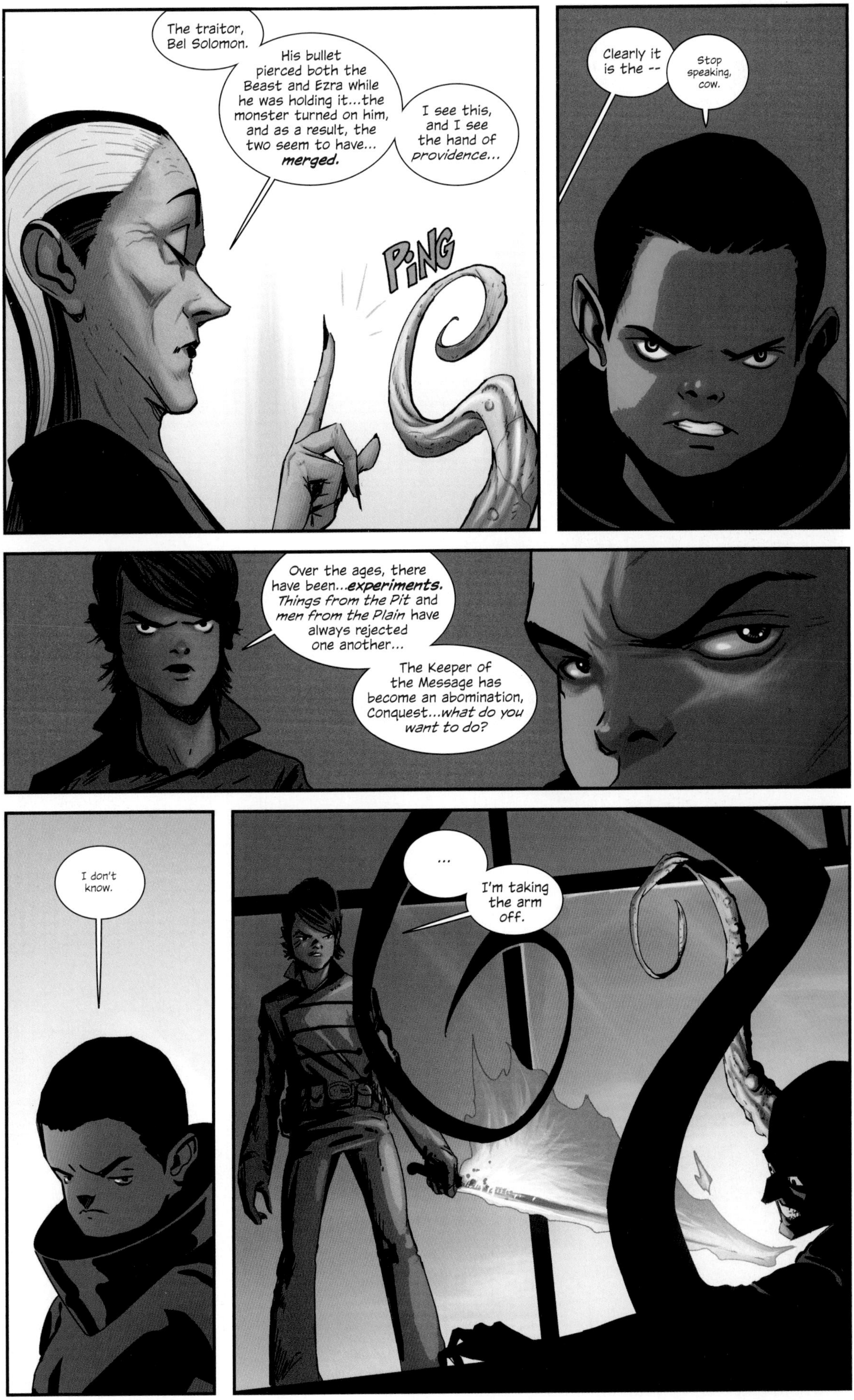
The traitor, Bel Solomon.
His bullet pierced both the Beast and Ezra while he was holding it...the monster turned on him, and as a result, the two seem to have... merged.
I see this, and I see the hand of providence...
PING
Clearly it is the --
Stop speaking, cow.
Over the ages, there have been...experiments. Things from the Pit and men from the Plain have always rejected one another...
The Keeper of the Message has become an abomination, Conquest...what do you want to do?
I don't know.
...
I'm taking the arm off.

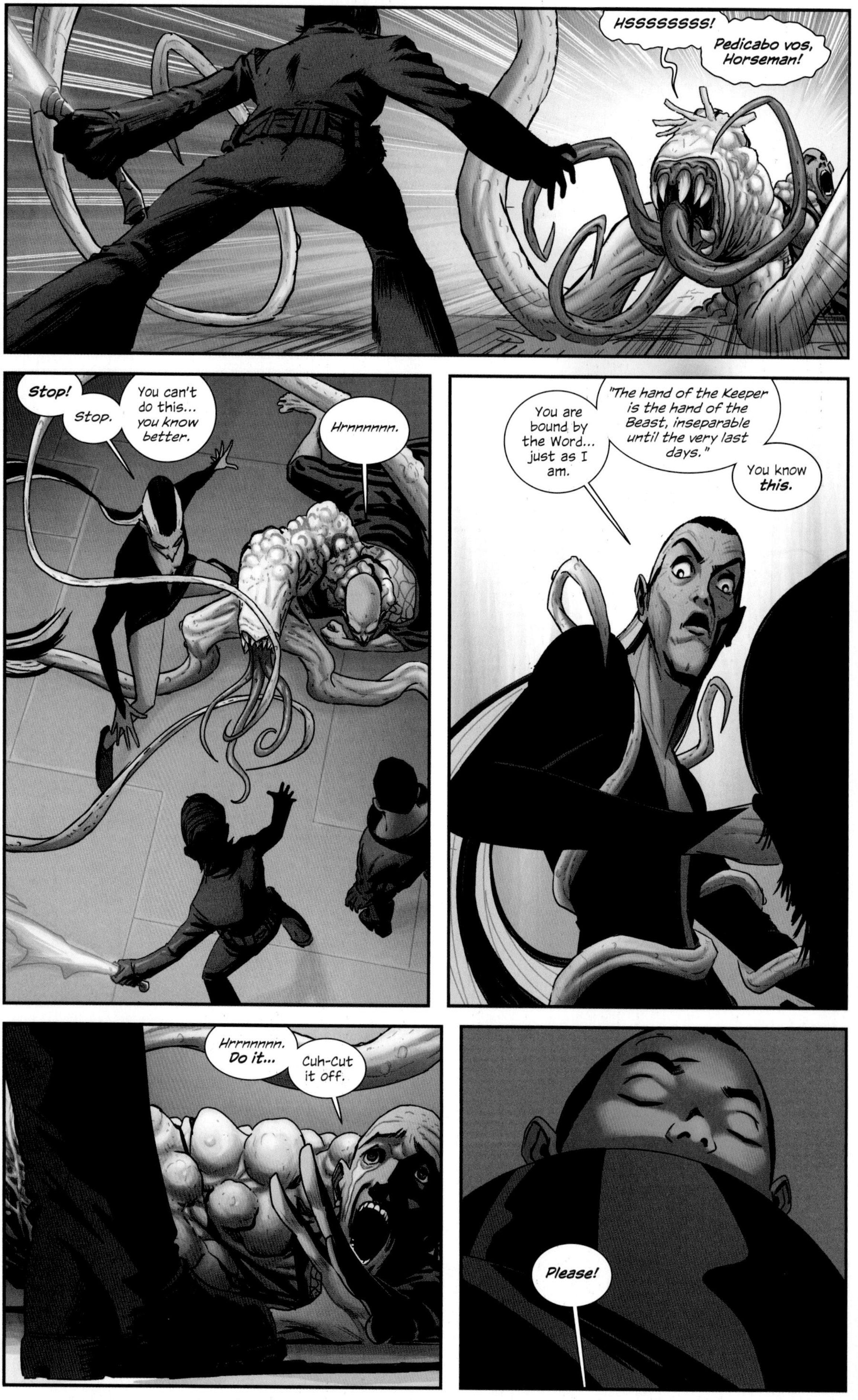
HSSSSSSSS!
Pedicabo vos, Horseman!
Stop!
Stop.
You can't do this... you know better.
Hrnnnnnn.
You are bound by the Word... just as I am.
"The hand of the Keeper is the hand of the Beast, inseparable until the very last days."
You know this.
Hrrnnnnnn. Do it...
Cuh-Cut it off.
Please!

ARE YOU **AN AGENT** OF THE
END TIMES?

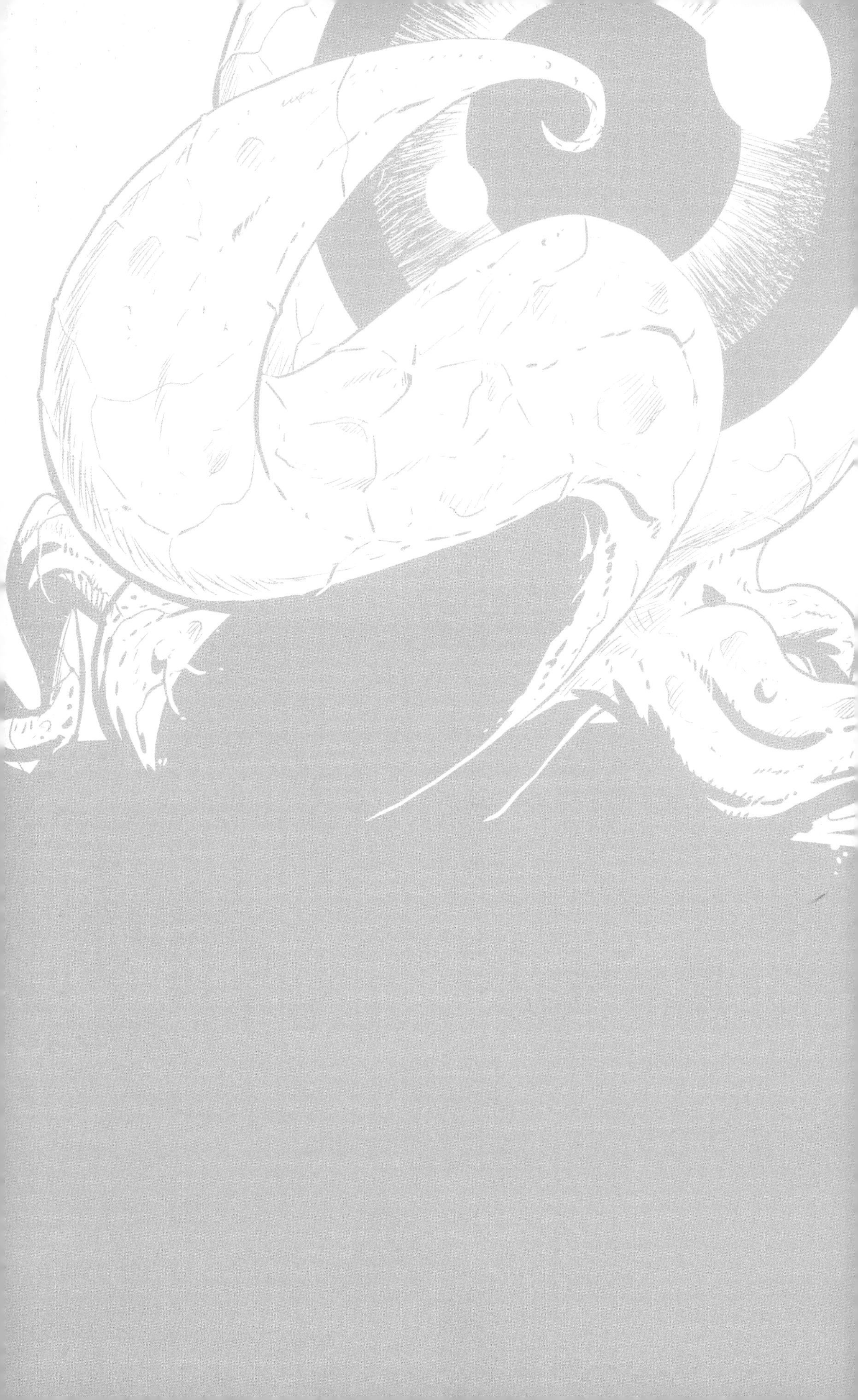

07

SEVEN: THE
PILGRIMAGE

HAVE YOU **BECOME** WHAT
THE MESSAGE DEMANDS?

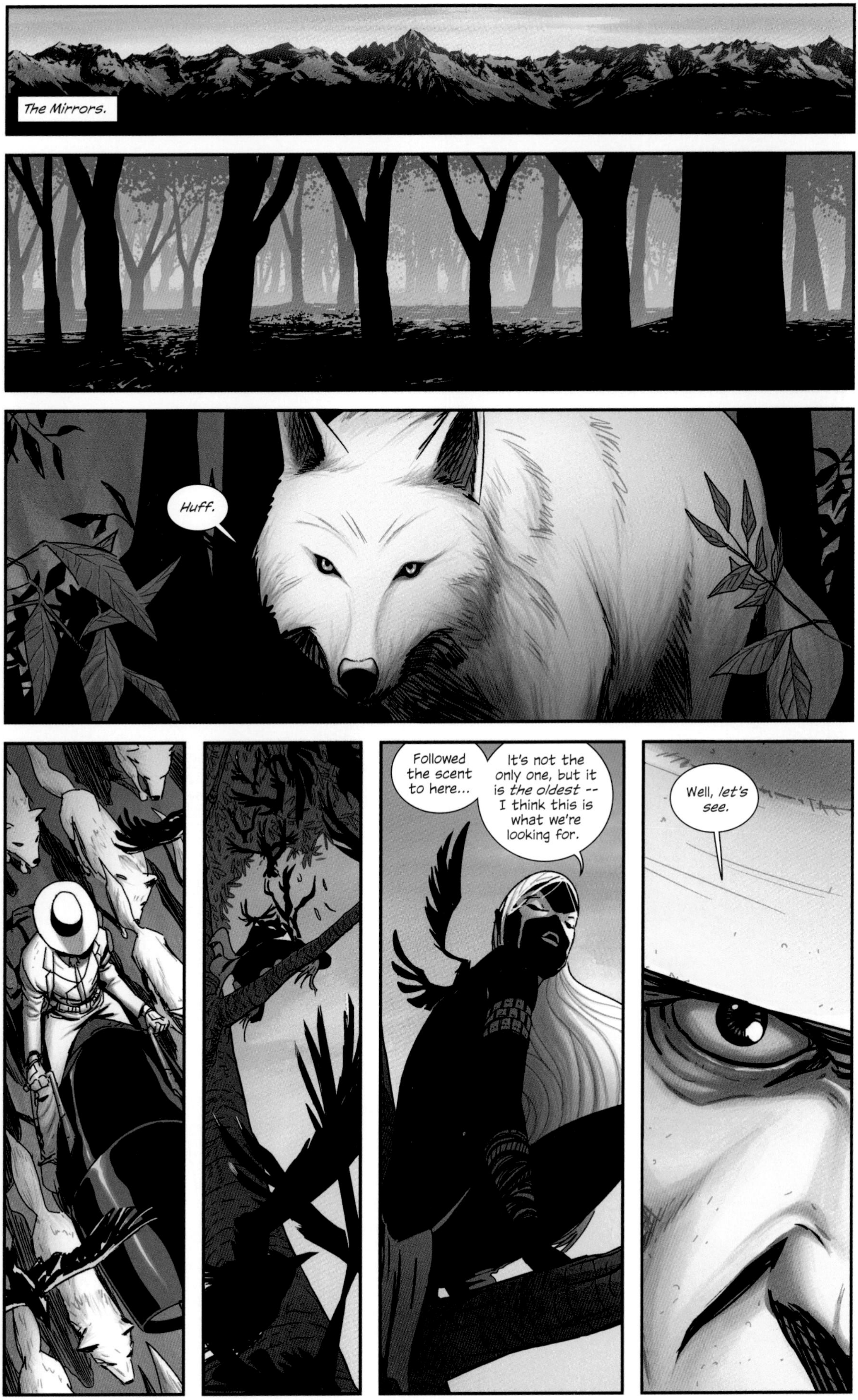
The Mirrors.
Huff.
Followed the scent to here...
It's not the only one, but it is *the oldest* -- I think this is what we're looking for.
Well, *let's* see.

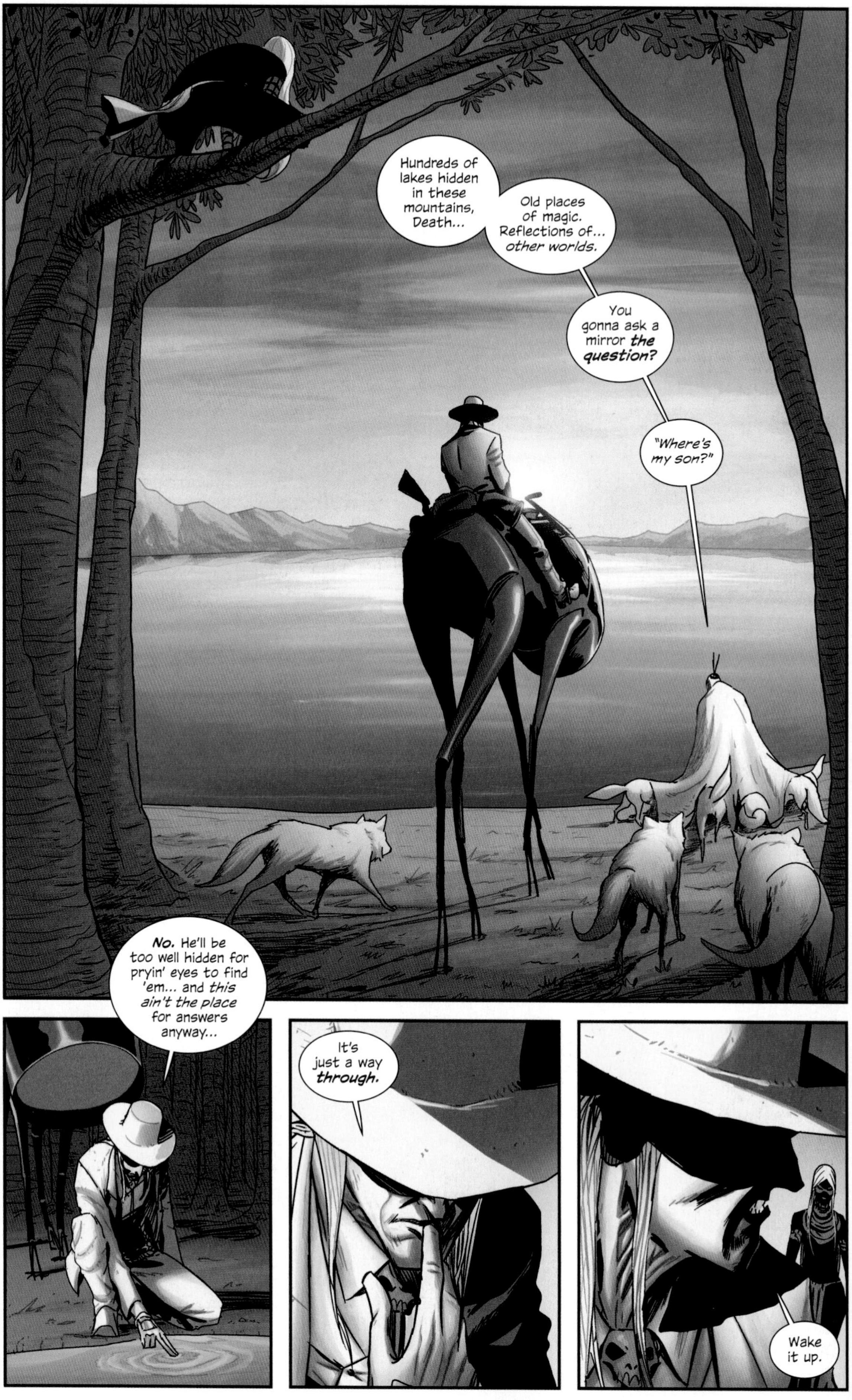
Hundreds of lakes hidden in these mountains, Death...
Old places of magic. Reflections of... *other worlds.*
You gonna ask a mirror ***the question?***
"Where's my son?"
No. He'll be too well hidden for pryin' eyes to find 'em... and *this ain't the place* for answers anyway...
It's just a way ***through.***
Wake it up.

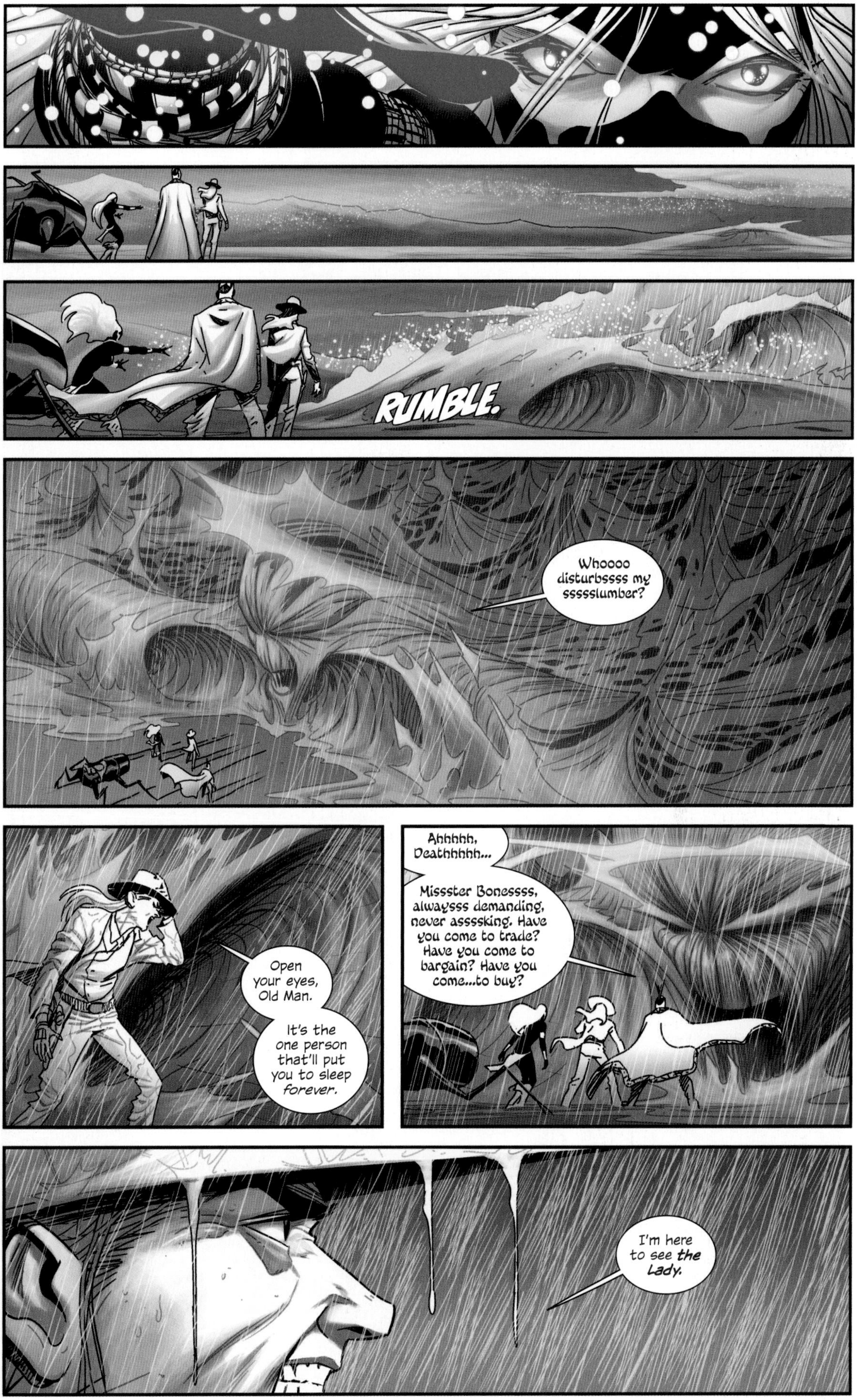
RUMBLE.
Whoooo disturbssss my sssssslumber?
Open your eyes, Old Man.
It's the one person that'll put you to sleep *forever.*
Ahhhhh, Deathhhhh...
Missster Bonessss, alwaysss demanding, never assssking. Have you come to trade? Have you come to bargain? Have you come...to buy?
I'm here to see **the Lady.**

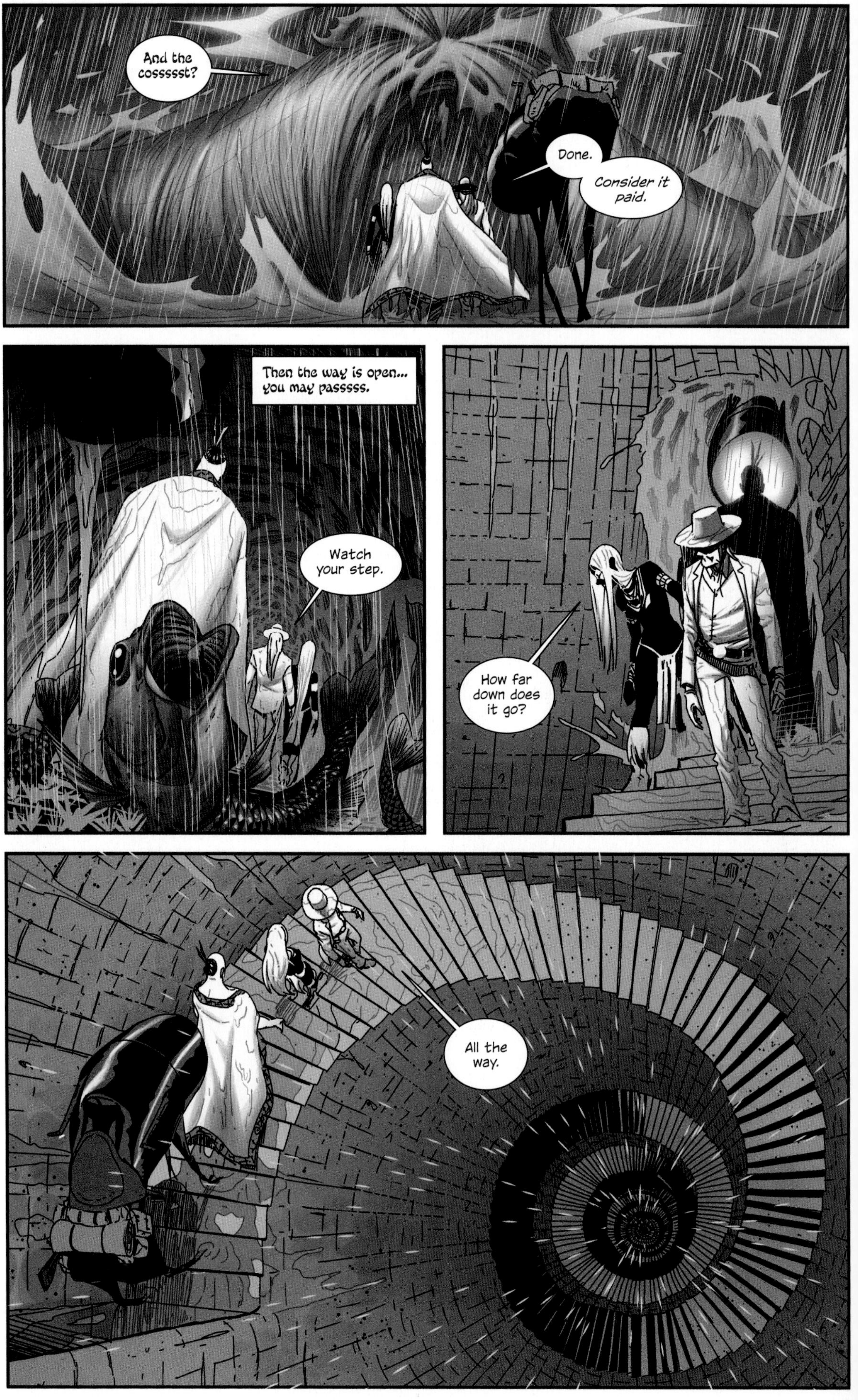
And the cossssst?
Done.
Consider it paid.
Then the way is open... you may passsss.
Watch your step.
How far down does it go?
All the way.

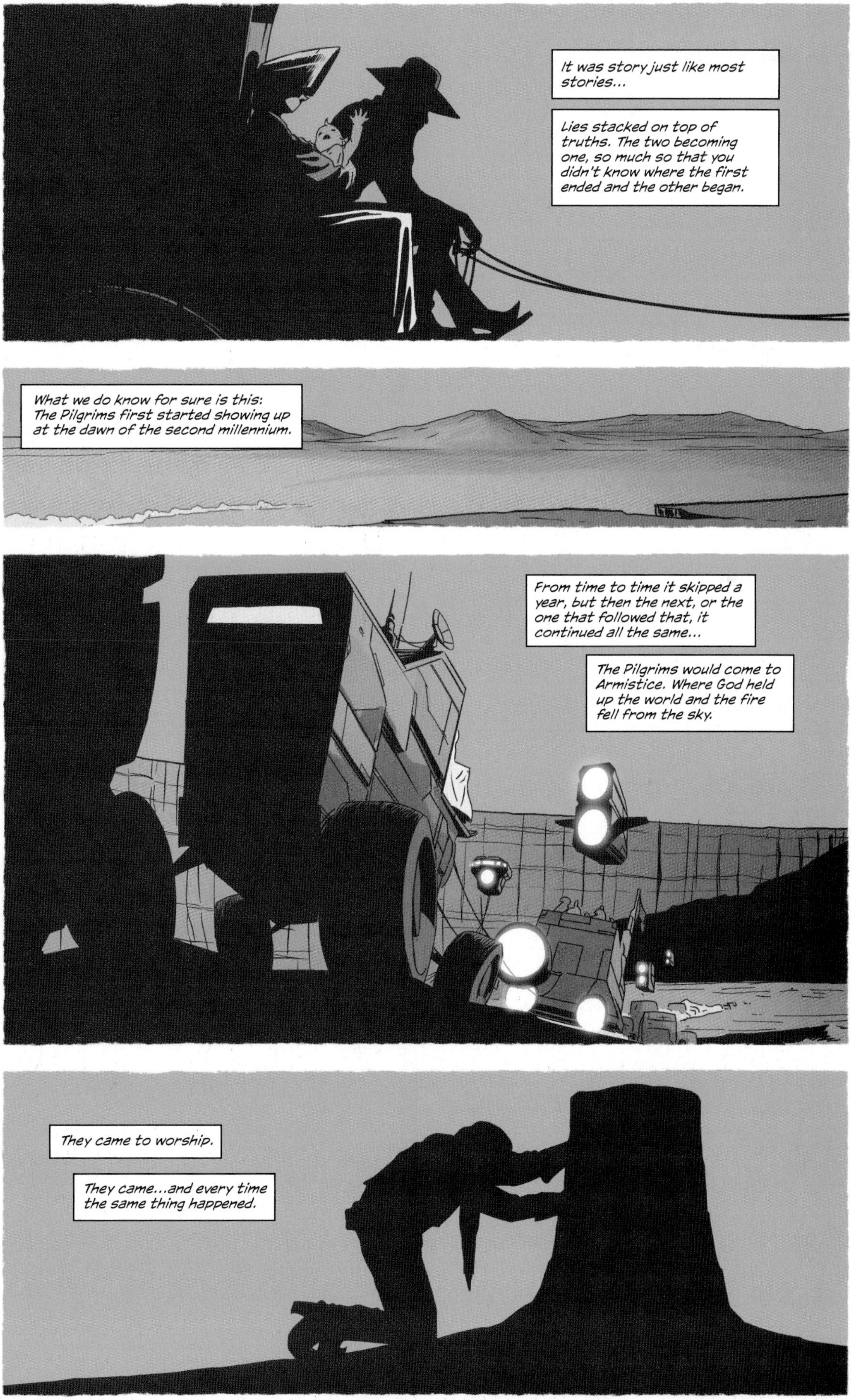
It was story just like most stories...
Lies stacked on top of truths. The two becoming one, so much so that you didn't know where the first ended and the other began.
What we do know for sure is this: The Pilgrims first started showing up at the dawn of the second millennium.
From time to time it skipped a year, but then the next, or the one that followed that, it continued all the same...
The Pilgrims would come to Armistice. Where God held up the world and the fire fell from the sky.
They came to worship.
They came...and every time the same thing happened.

They would arrive, following a prophet -- someone with some version of the Word. Someone sayin' they were an oracle of **the Message**...

A true servant of God.

So the Pilgrims would worship at the Armistice Altar, and then...

Always -- **always** -- the miraculous happened. One day they were there and then the next the Pilgrims would all suddenly just...disappear.

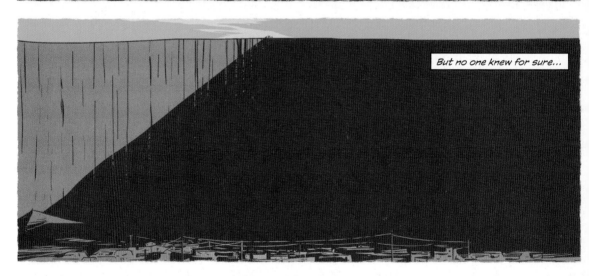

Some said it was 'cause they were taken up to the heavens -- an early rapture for the true believers.

Others said they were fools following false prophets and they paid the full price for their sins -- that the ground swallowed 'em up and they tumbled down, straight to hell.

But no one knew for sure...

As these were just stories.

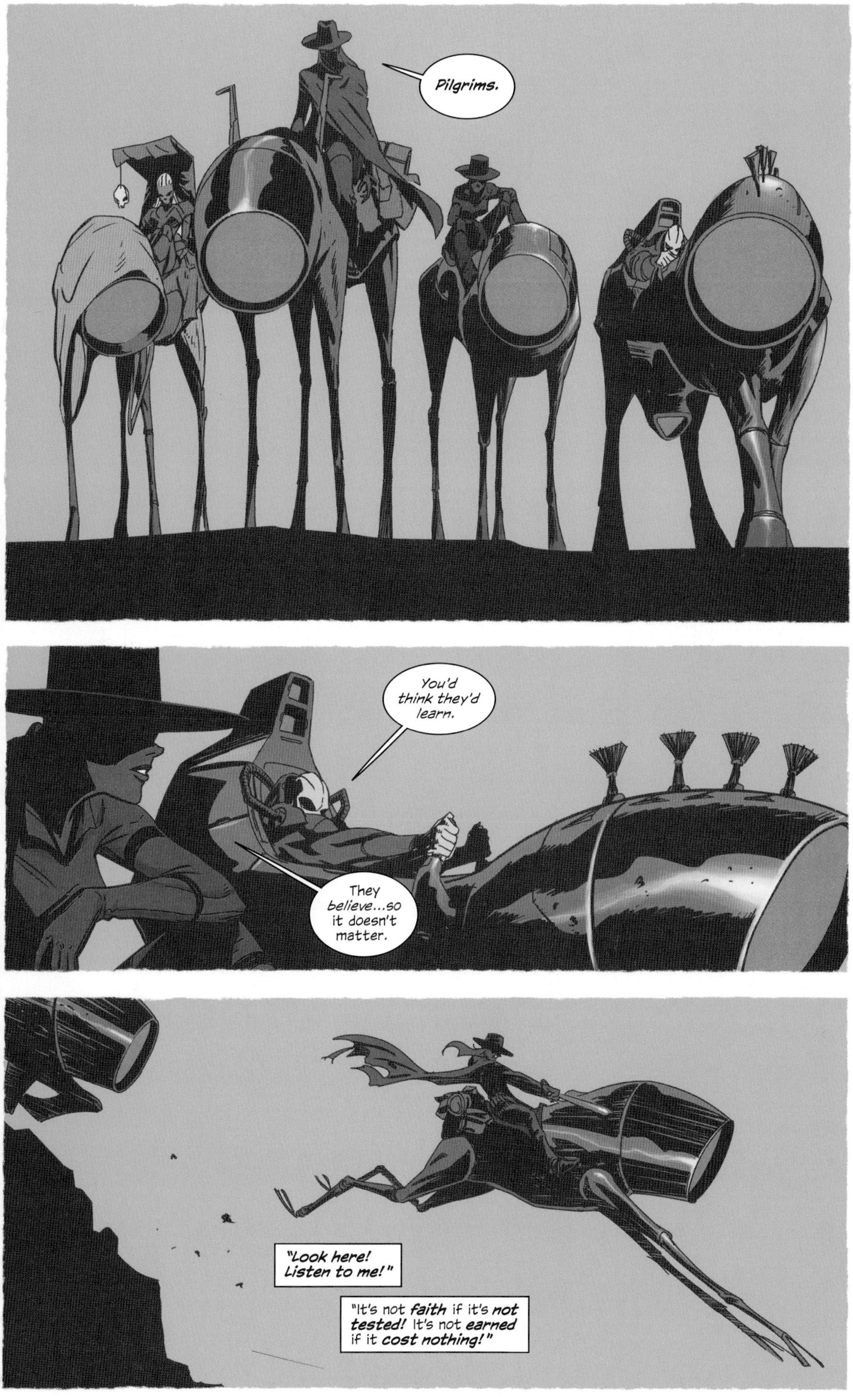
Pilgrims.
You'd think they'd learn.
They believe...so it doesn't matter.
"Look here! Listen to me!"
"It's not faith if it's not tested! It's not earned if it cost nothing!"

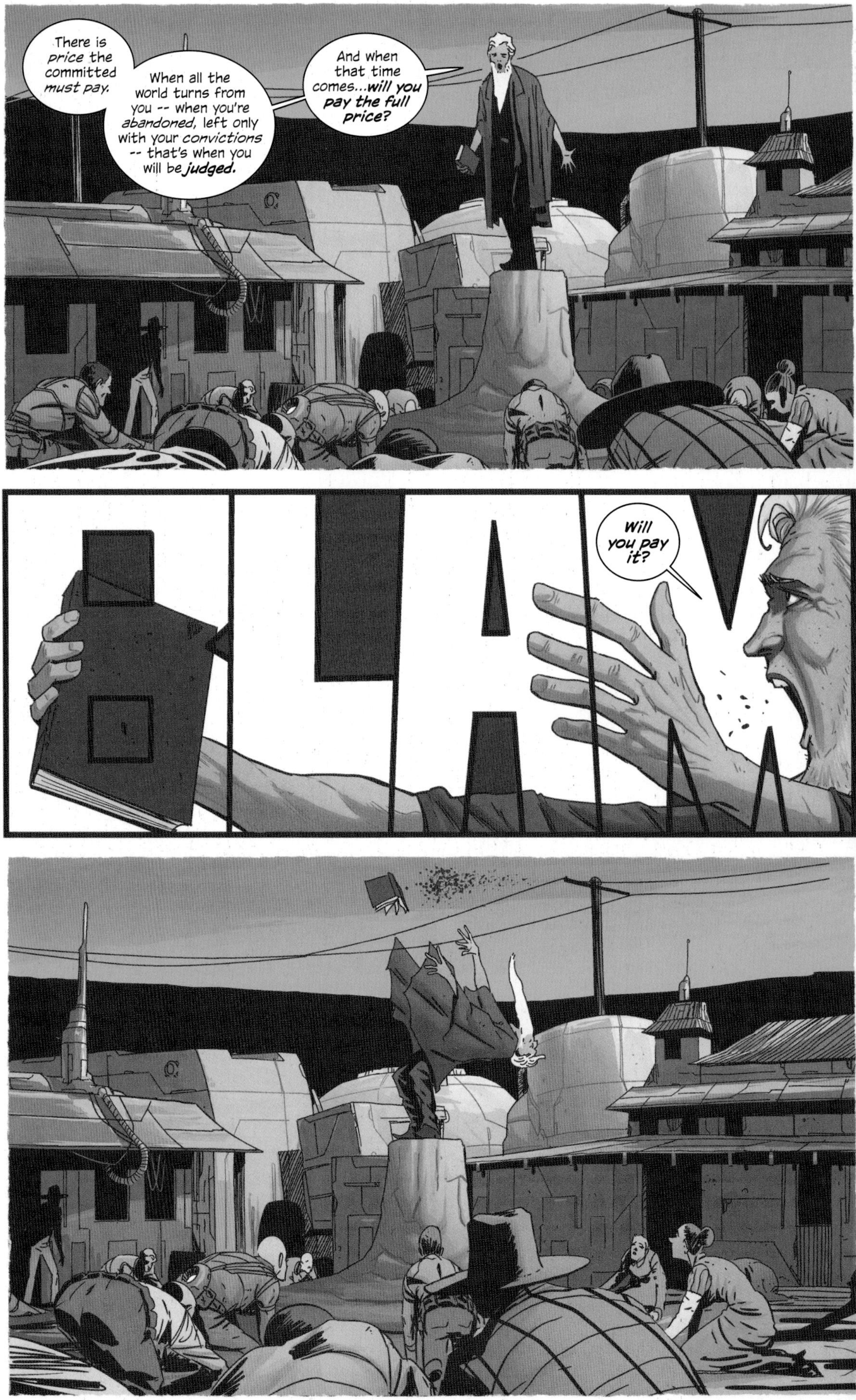
There is *price* the committed *must pay.*
When all the world turns from you -- when you're *abandoned*, left only with your *convictions* -- that's when you will be ***judged.***
And when that time comes...***will you pay the full price?***
Will you pay it?

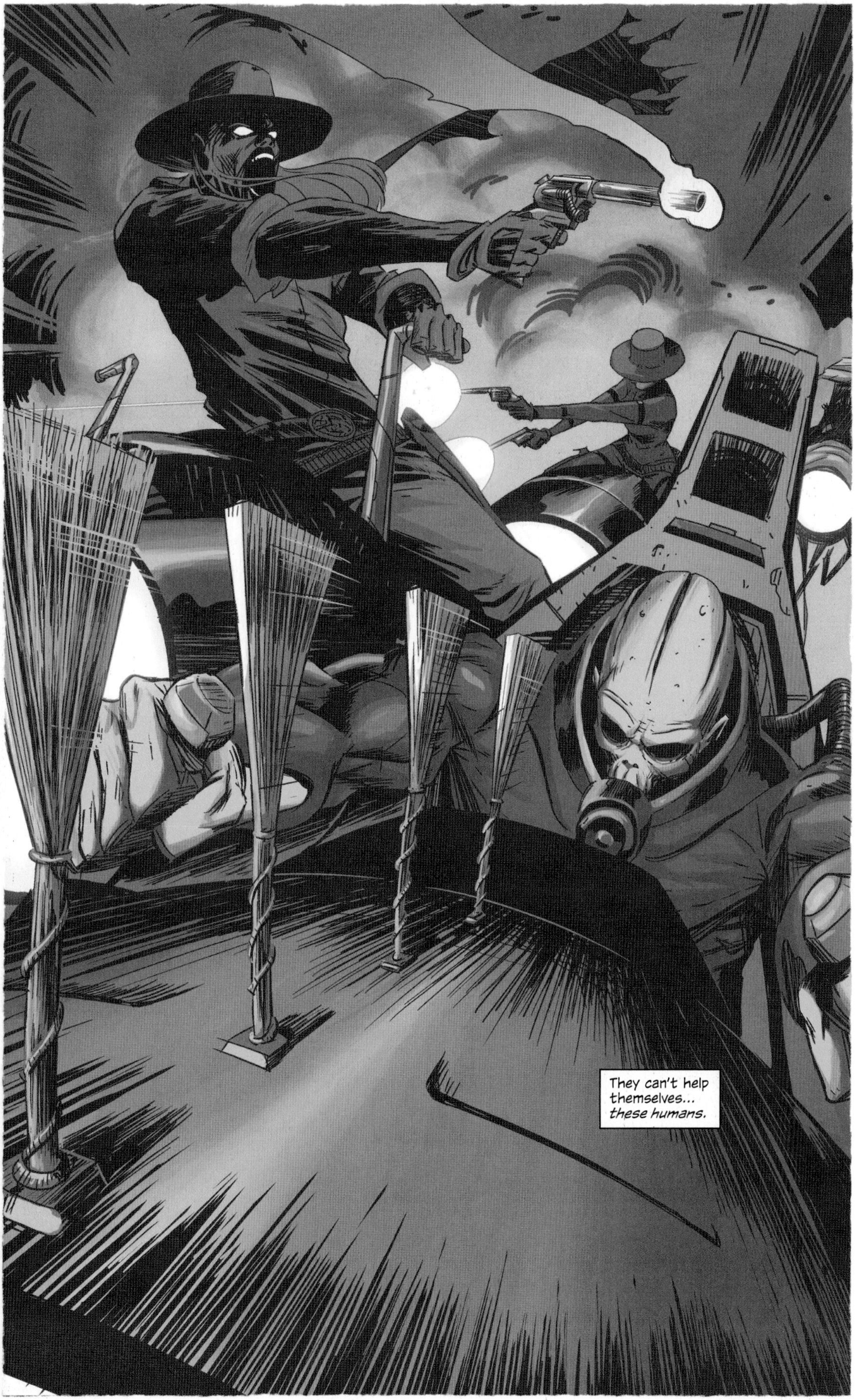
They can't help themselves... *these humans.*

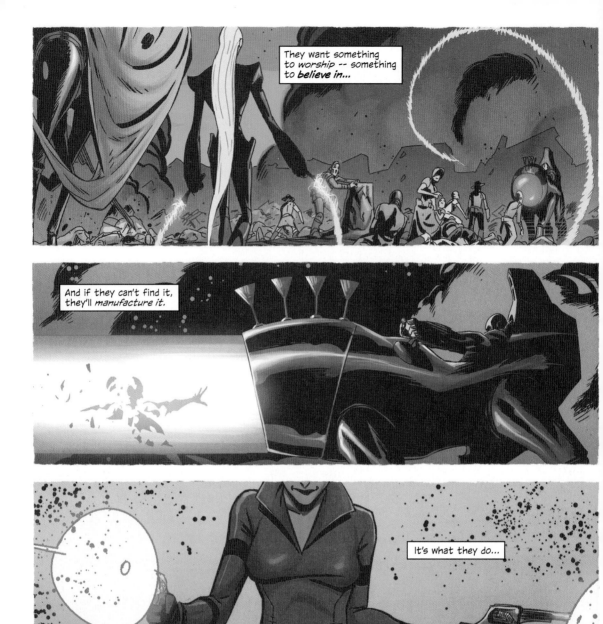

They want something to *worship* -- something to *believe in...*

And if they can't find it, they'll *manufacture it.*

It's what they do...

Grasp at things beyond their reach.

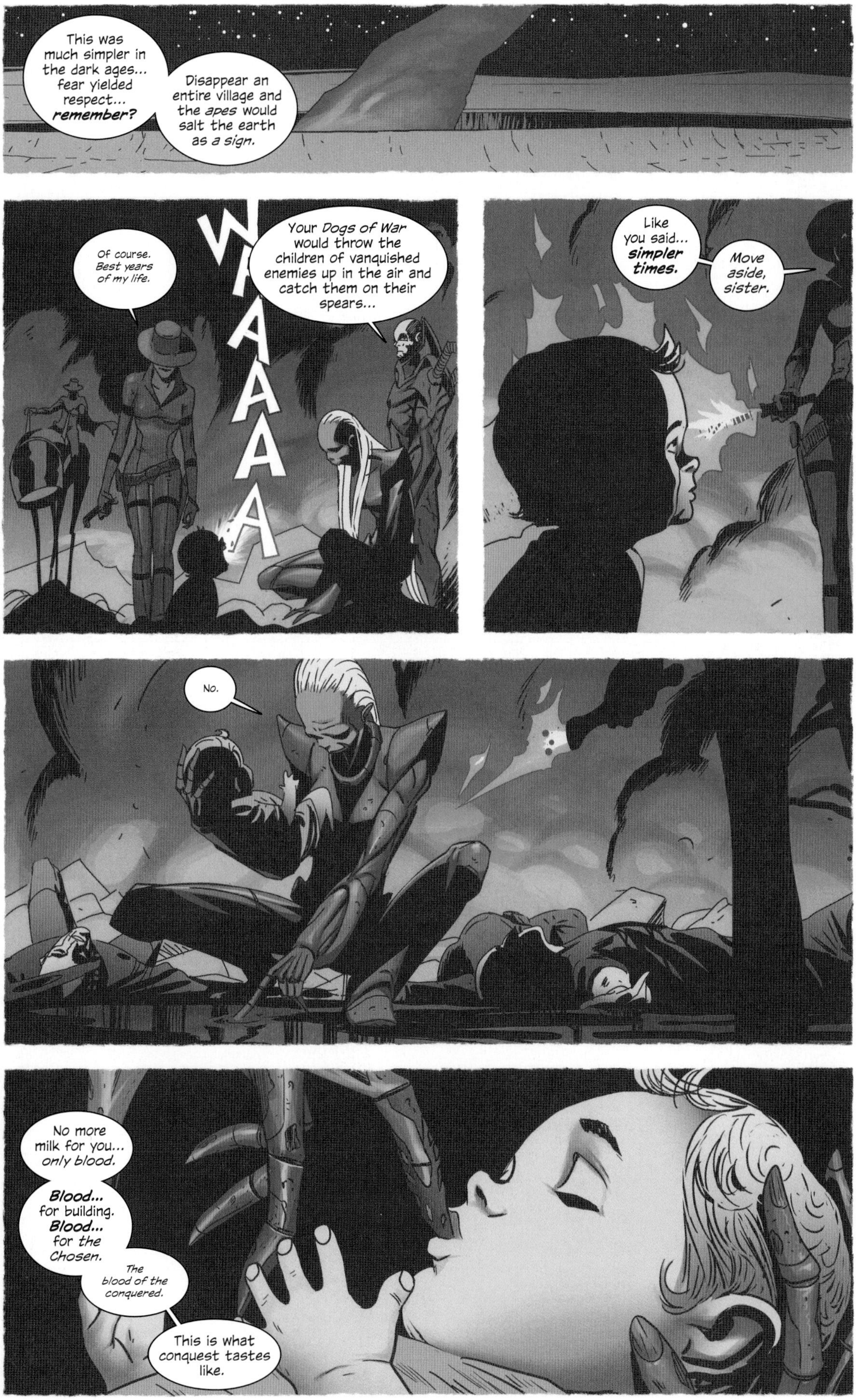
This was much simpler in the dark ages... fear yielded respect... **remember?**
Disappear an entire village and the *apes* would salt the earth as a *sign.*
Of course. Best years of my life.
WAAAAA
Your *Dogs of War* would throw the children of vanquished enemies up in the air and catch them on their spears...
Like you said... ***simpler times.***
Move aside, sister.
No.
No more milk for you... *only blood.*
Blood... for building. ***Blood...*** for *the Chosen.*
The blood of the conquered.
This is what conquest tastes like.

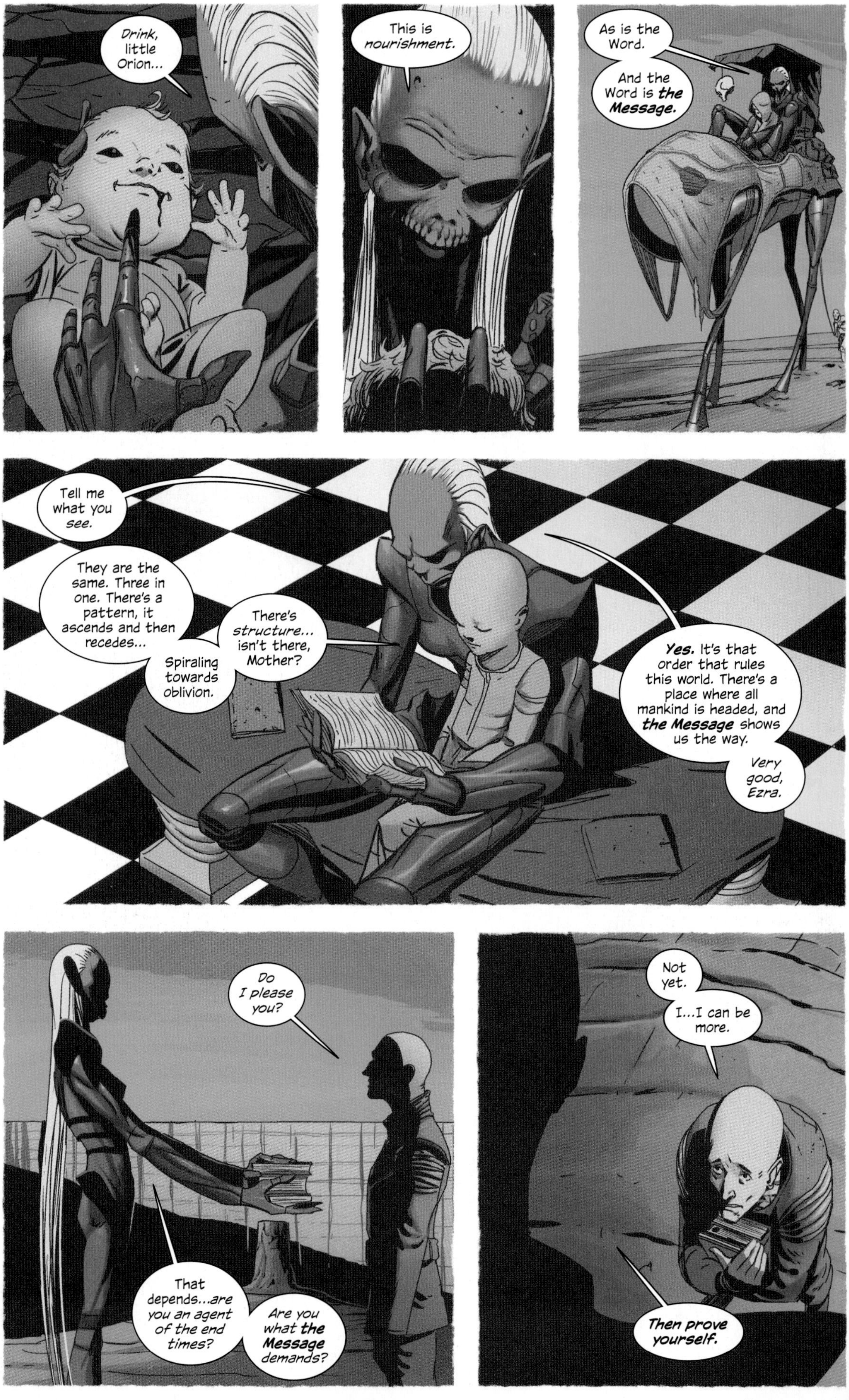

Drink, little Orion...
This is nourishment.
As is the Word.
And the Word is **the Message.**
Tell me what you see.
They are the same. Three in one. There's a pattern, it ascends and then recedes...
Spiraling towards oblivion.
There's structure... isn't there, Mother?
Yes. It's that order that rules this world. There's a place where all mankind is headed, and **the Message** shows us the way.
Very good, Ezra.
Do I please you?
That depends...are you an agent of the end times?
Are you what **the Message** demands?
Not yet.
I...I can be more.
Then prove yourself.

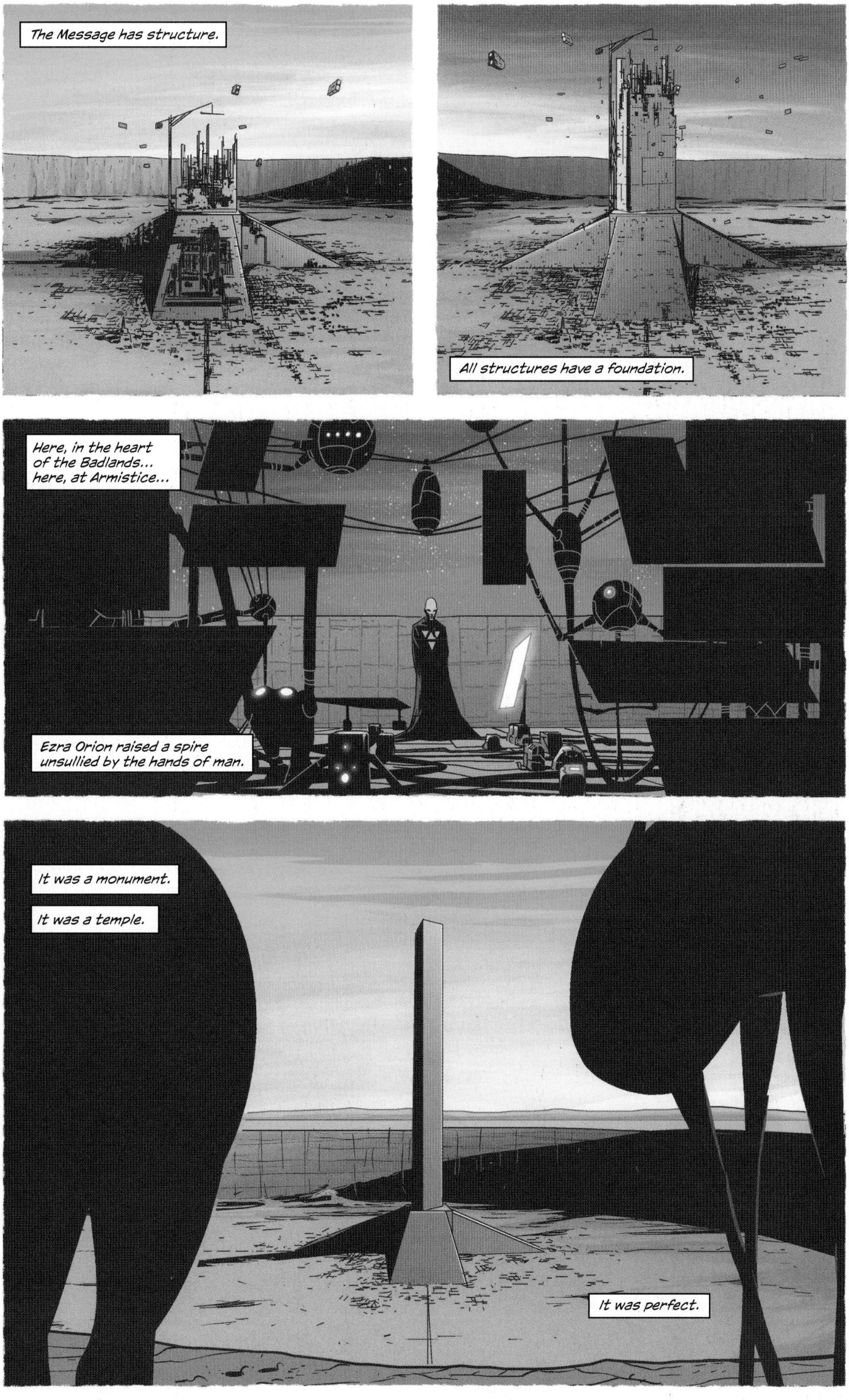
The Message has structure.
All structures have a foundation.
Here, in the heart of the Badlands... here, at Armistice...
Ezra Orion raised a spire unsullied by the hands of man.
It was a monument.
It was a temple.
It was perfect.

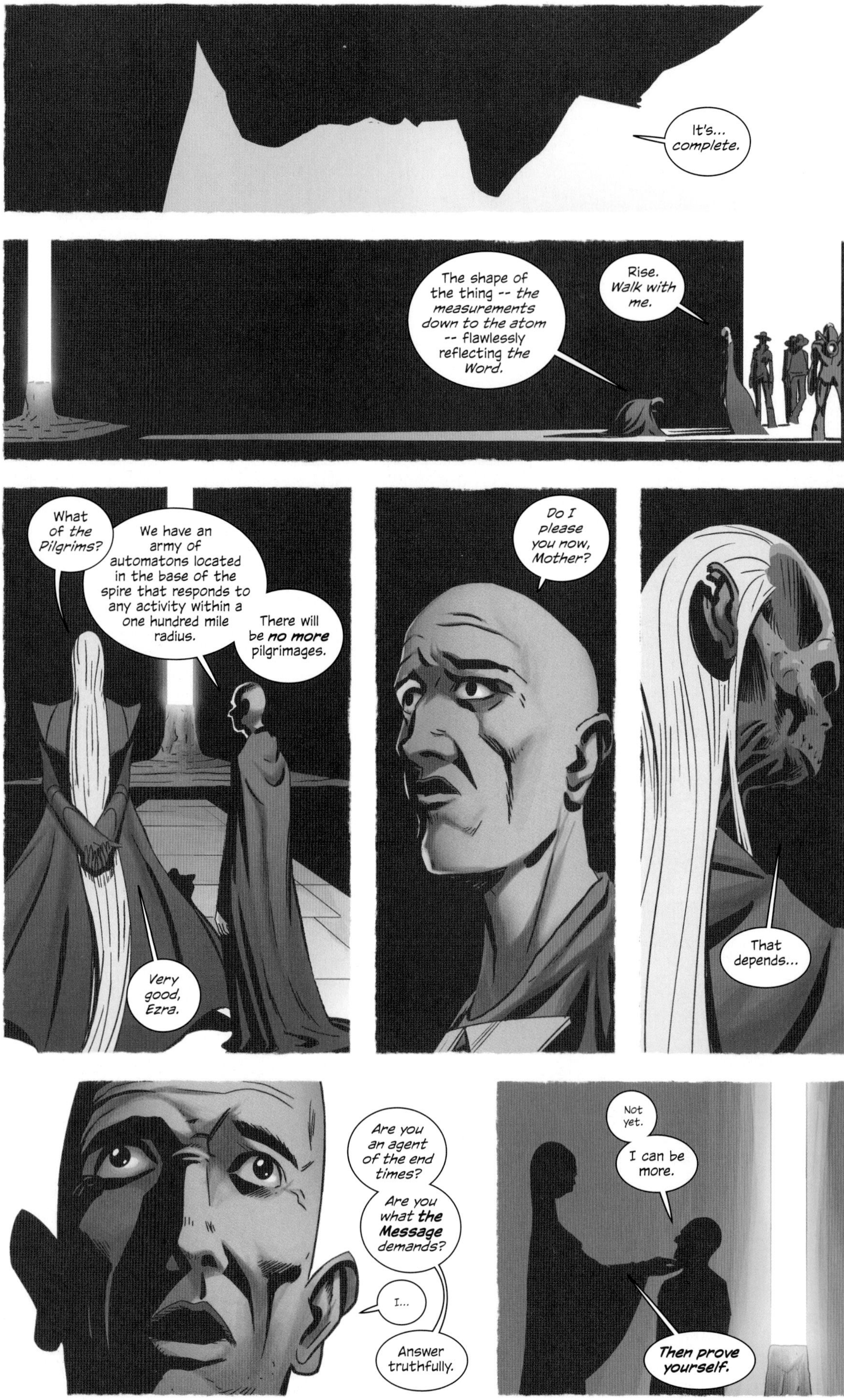
It's... complete.
The shape of the thing -- the measurements down to the atom -- flawlessly reflecting the Word.
Rise. Walk with me.
What of the Pilgrims?
We have an army of automatons located in the base of the spire that responds to any activity within a one hundred mile radius.
There will be no more pilgrimages.
Very good, Ezra.
Do I please you now, Mother?
That depends...
Are you an agent of the end times?
Are you what the Message demands?
I...
Answer truthfully.
Not yet.
I can be more.
Then prove yourself.

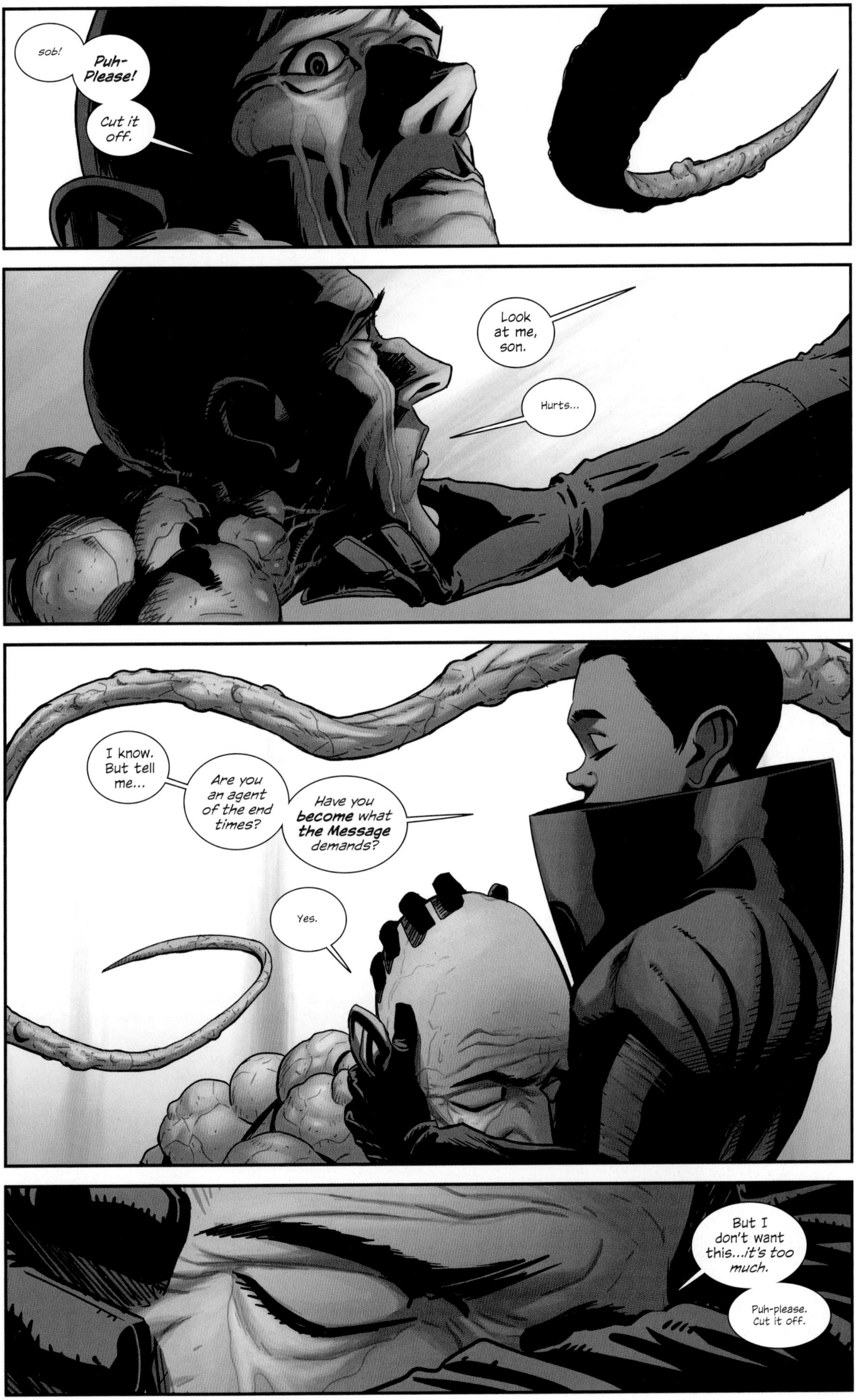
sob!
Puh-Please!
Cut it off.
Look at me, son.
Hurts...
I know. But tell me...
Are you an agent of the end times?
Have you become what the Message demands?
Yes.
But I don't want this...it's too much.
Puh-please. Cut it off.

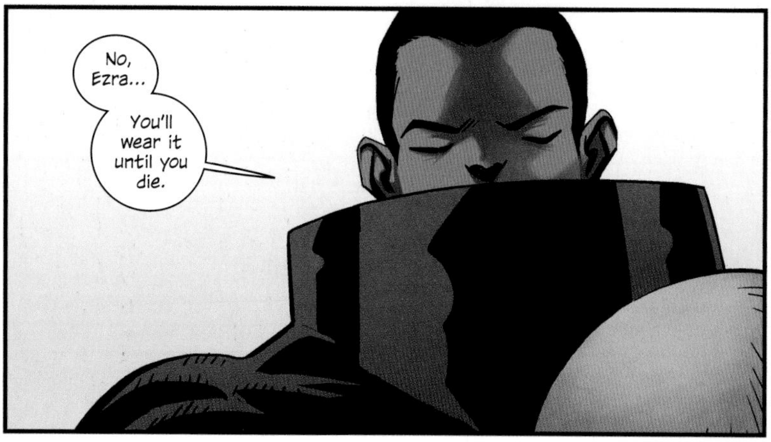
No, Ezra...
You'll wear it until you die.

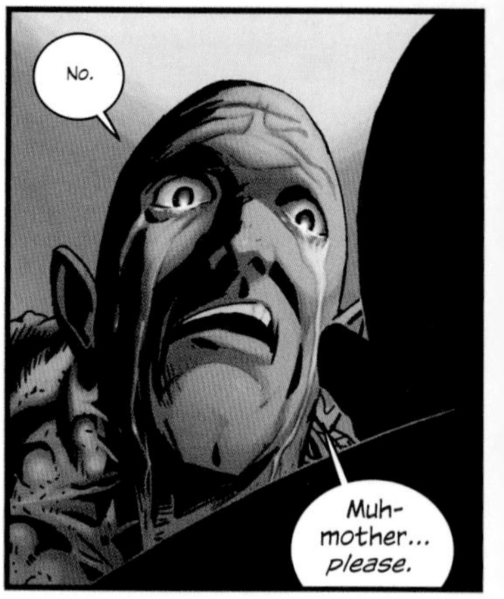
No.
Muh-mother... *please.*

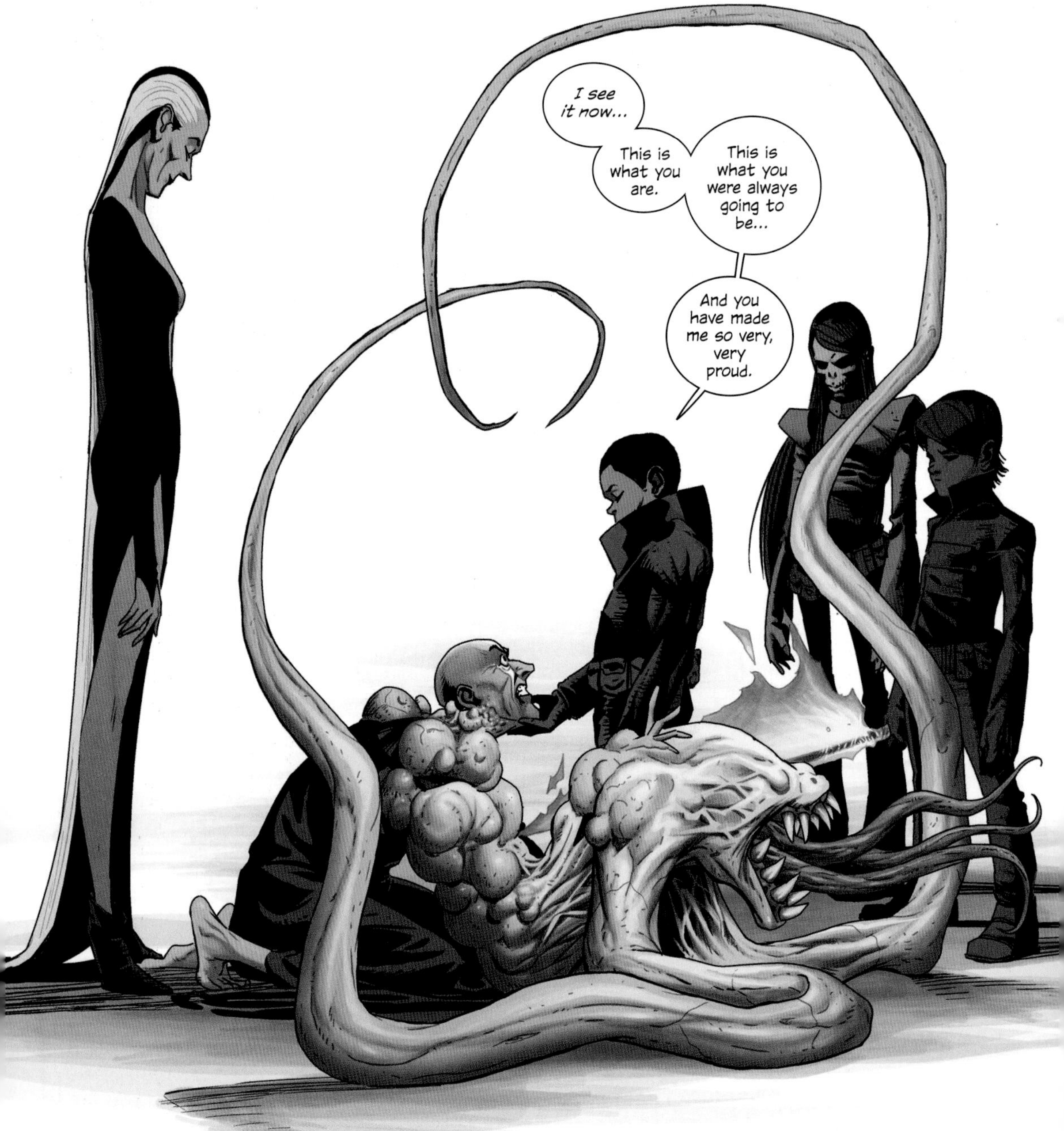
I see it now...
This is what you are.
This is what you were always going to be...
And you have made me so very, very proud.

SOON ALL OF THIS WILL COME **CRUMBLING DOWN.**

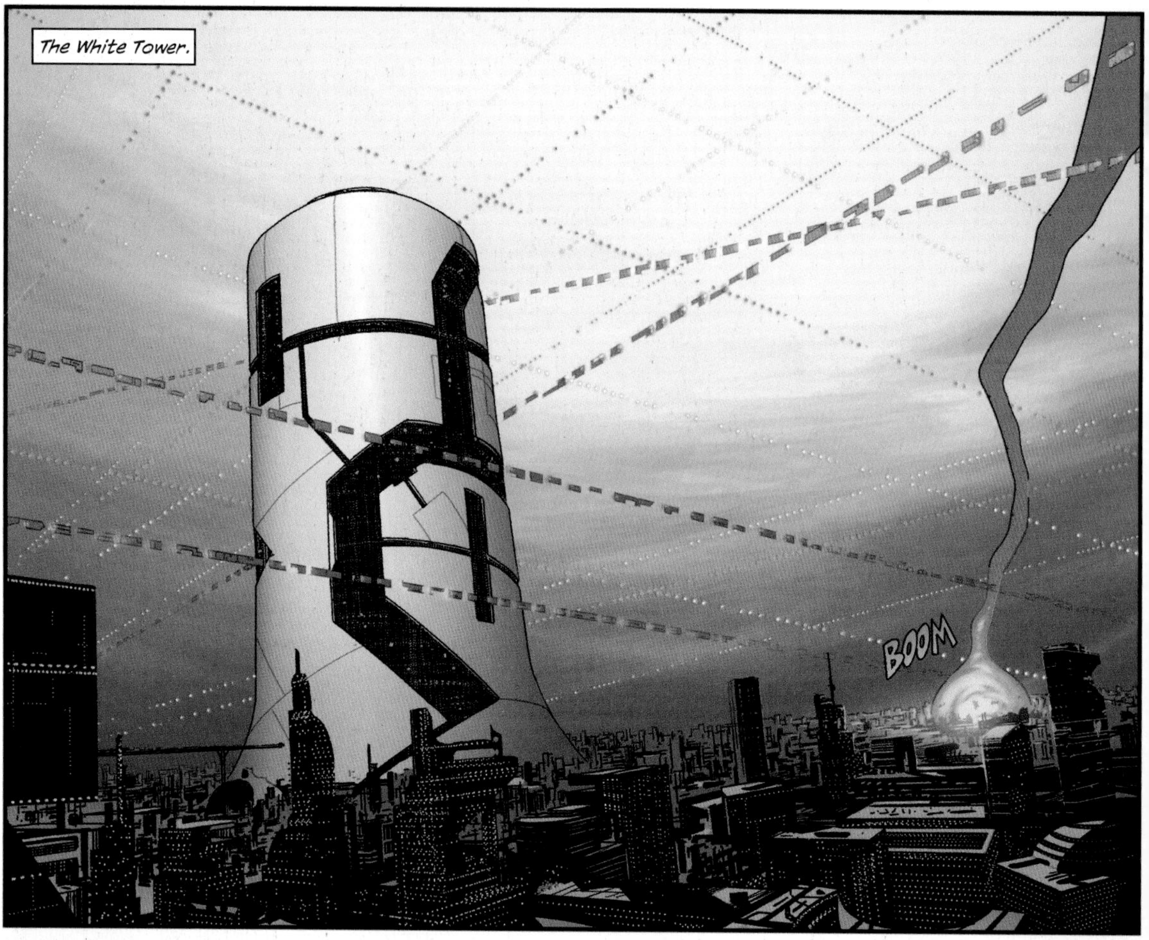
The White Tower.
BOOM

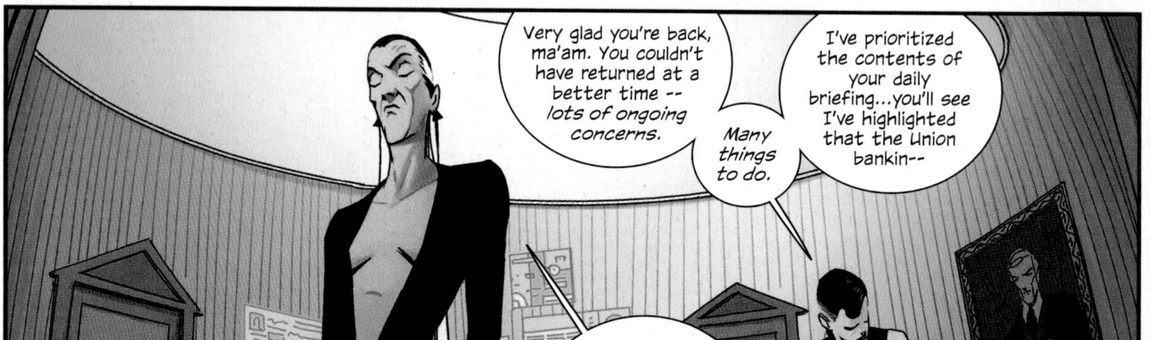
Very glad you're back, ma'am. You couldn't have returned at a better time -- *lots of ongoing concerns.*
Many things to do.
I've prioritized the contents of your daily briefing...you'll see I've highlighted that the Union bankin--
I chose you as my Chief of Staff, Ms. Lux, because you have always had a way of cutting through the ***meat*** and getting right to the ***bone.***

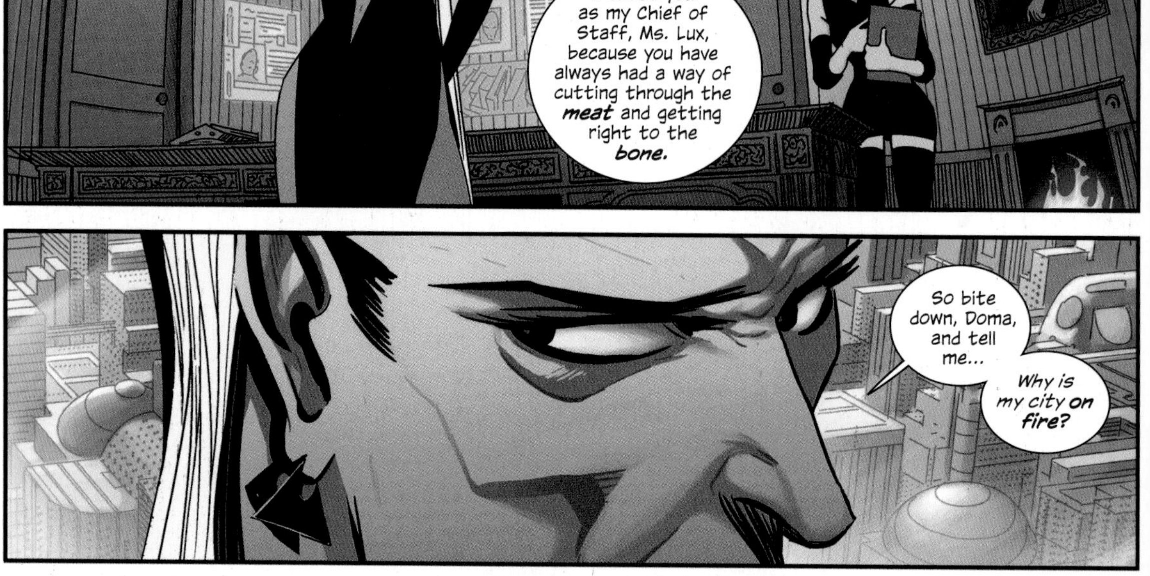
So bite down, Doma, and tell me...
*Why is my city **on fire?***

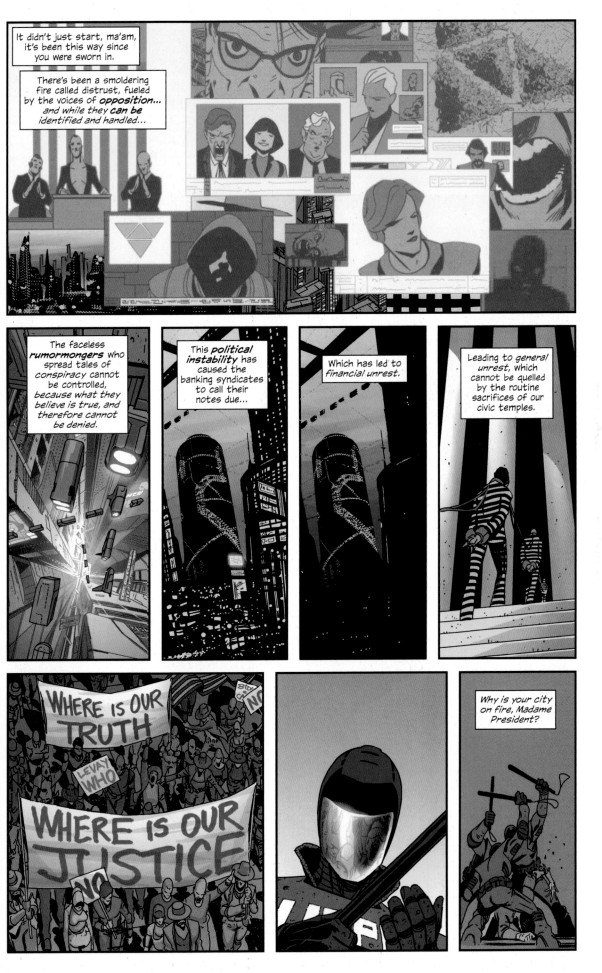

It didn't just start, ma'am, it's been this way since you were sworn in.

There's been a smoldering fire called distrust, fueled by the voices of *opposition*... and while they *can be* identified and handled...

The faceless *rumormongers* who spread tales of conspiracy cannot be controlled, because what they believe is true, and therefore cannot be denied.

This *political instability* has caused the banking syndicates to call their notes due...

Which has led to *financial unrest.*

Leading to *general unrest*, which cannot be quelled by the routine sacrifices of our civic temples.

WHERE IS OUR TRUTH

NO STOP

LEVAY WHO

WHERE IS OUR JUSTICE

NO

Why is your city on fire, Madame President?

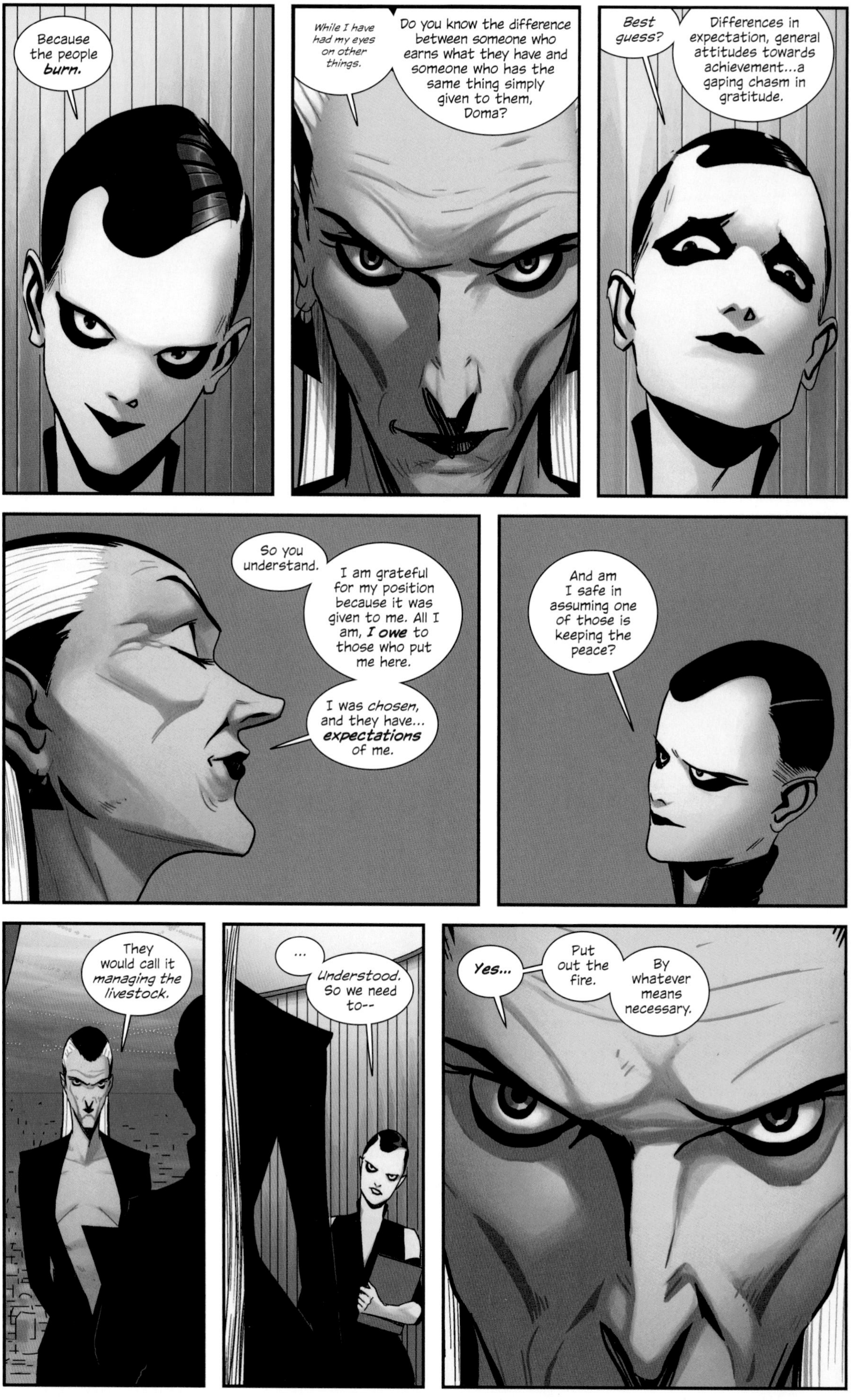
Because the people burn.
While I have had my eyes on other things.
Do you know the difference between someone who earns what they have and someone who has the same thing simply given to them, Doma?
Best guess?
Differences in expectation, general attitudes towards achievement...a gaping chasm in gratitude.
So you understand.
I am grateful for my position because it was given to me. All I am, I owe to those who put me here.
I was chosen, and they have... expectations of me.
And am I safe in assuming one of those is keeping the peace?
They would call it managing the livestock.
...
Understood. So we need to--
Yes...
Put out the fire.
By whatever means necessary.

AND WHAT WILL **RISE** FROM
THE **RUIN?**

NOTHING. JUST AS GOD
INTENDED. JUST AS WE
DESERVE.

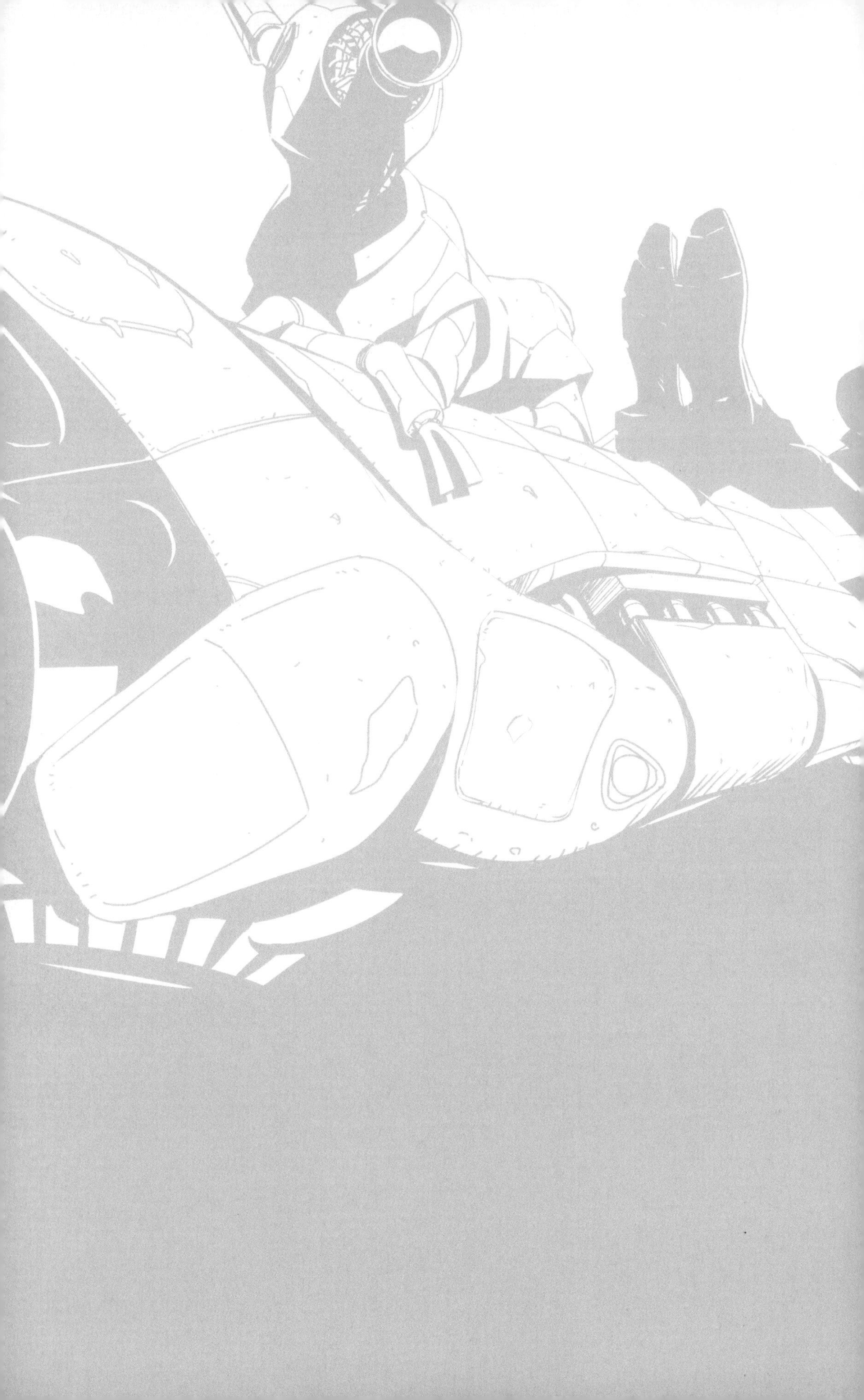

08

EIGHT: THE STREET
IS BURNING

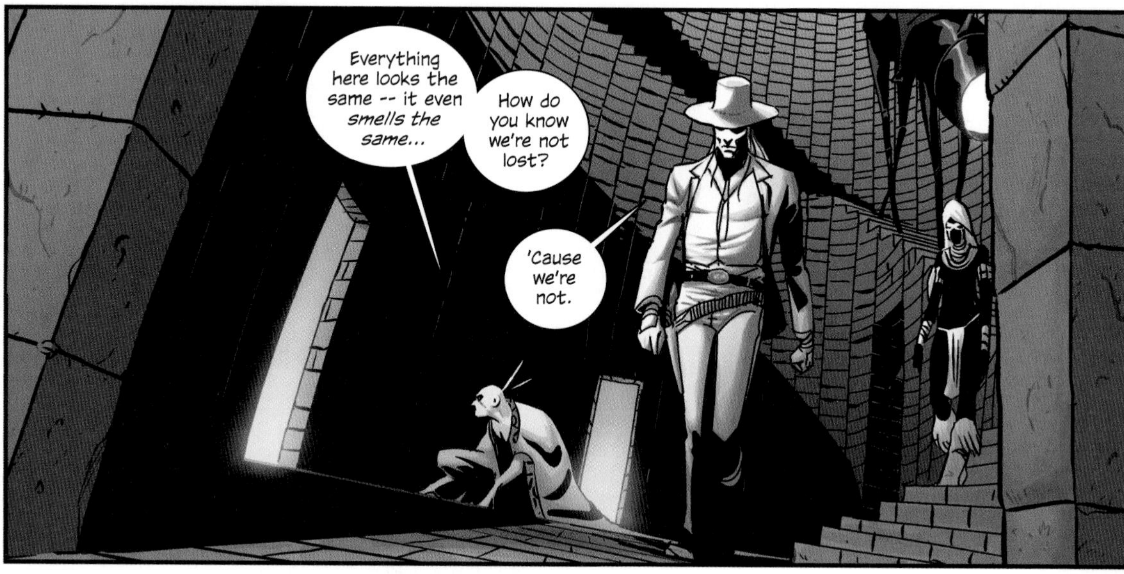
Everything here looks the same -- it even *smells the same...*
How do you know we're not lost?
'Cause we're not.

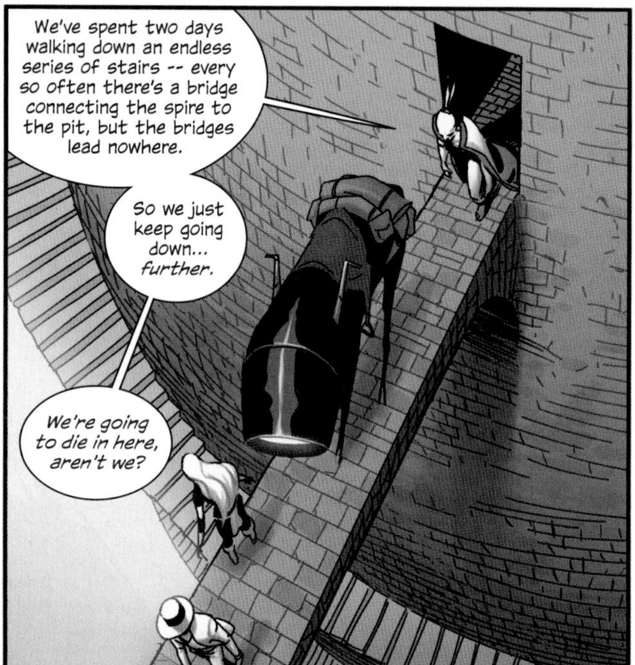
We've spent two days walking down an endless series of stairs -- every so often there's a bridge connecting the spire to the pit, but the bridges lead nowhere.
So we just keep going down... *further.*
We're going to die in here, aren't we?

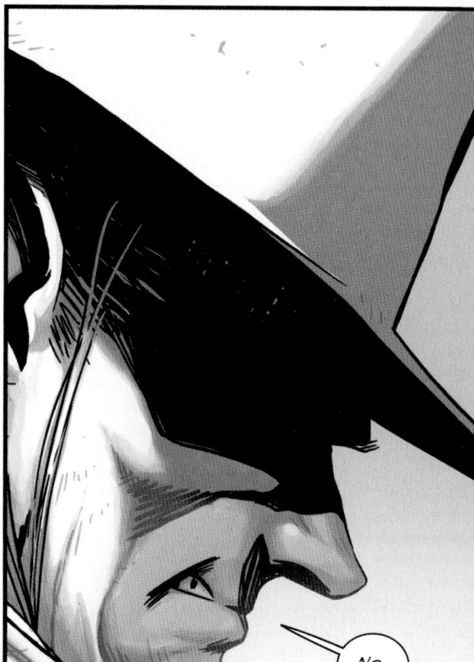
No.
There's no dying in *this place.*

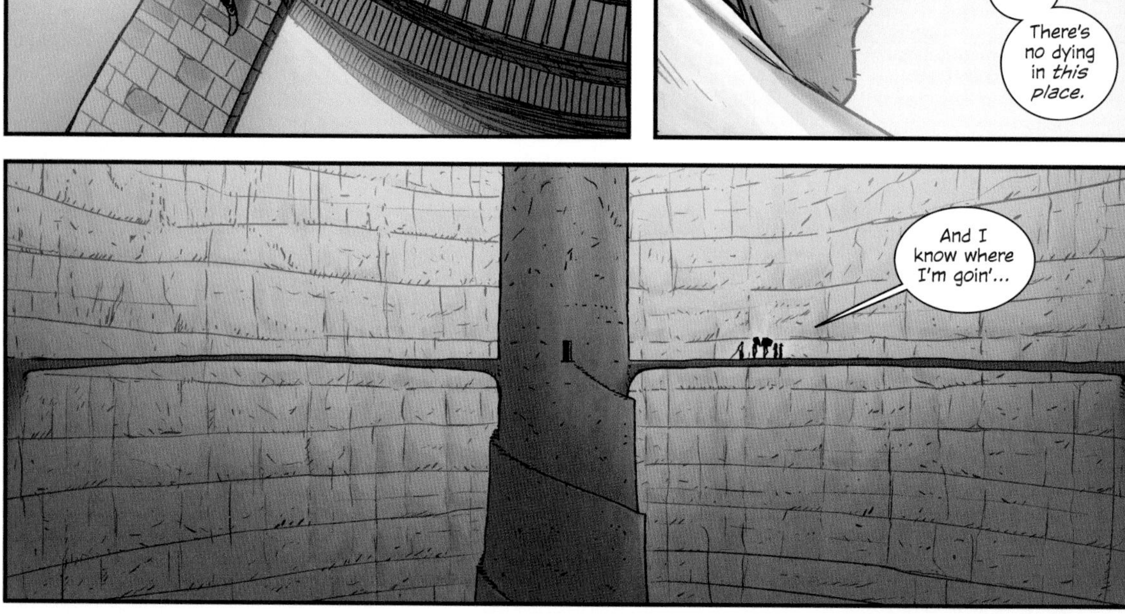
And I know where I'm goin'...

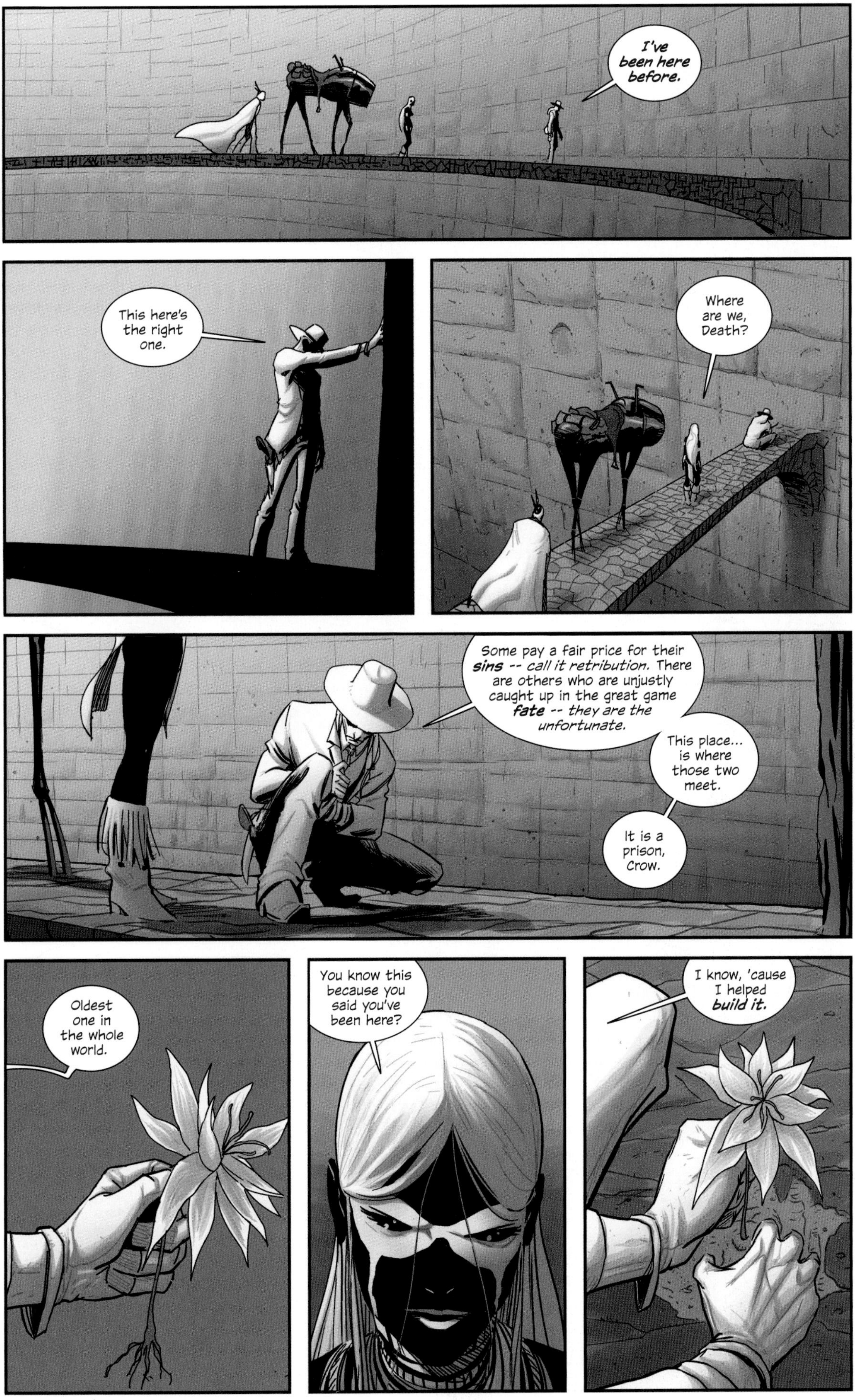
I've been here before.
This here's the right one.
Where are we, Death?
Some pay a fair price for their *sins -- call it retribution.* There are others who are unjustly caught up in the great game *fate -- they are the unfortunate.*
This place... is where those two meet.
It is a prison, Crow.
Oldest one in the whole world.
You know this because you said you've been here?
I know, 'cause I helped *build it.*

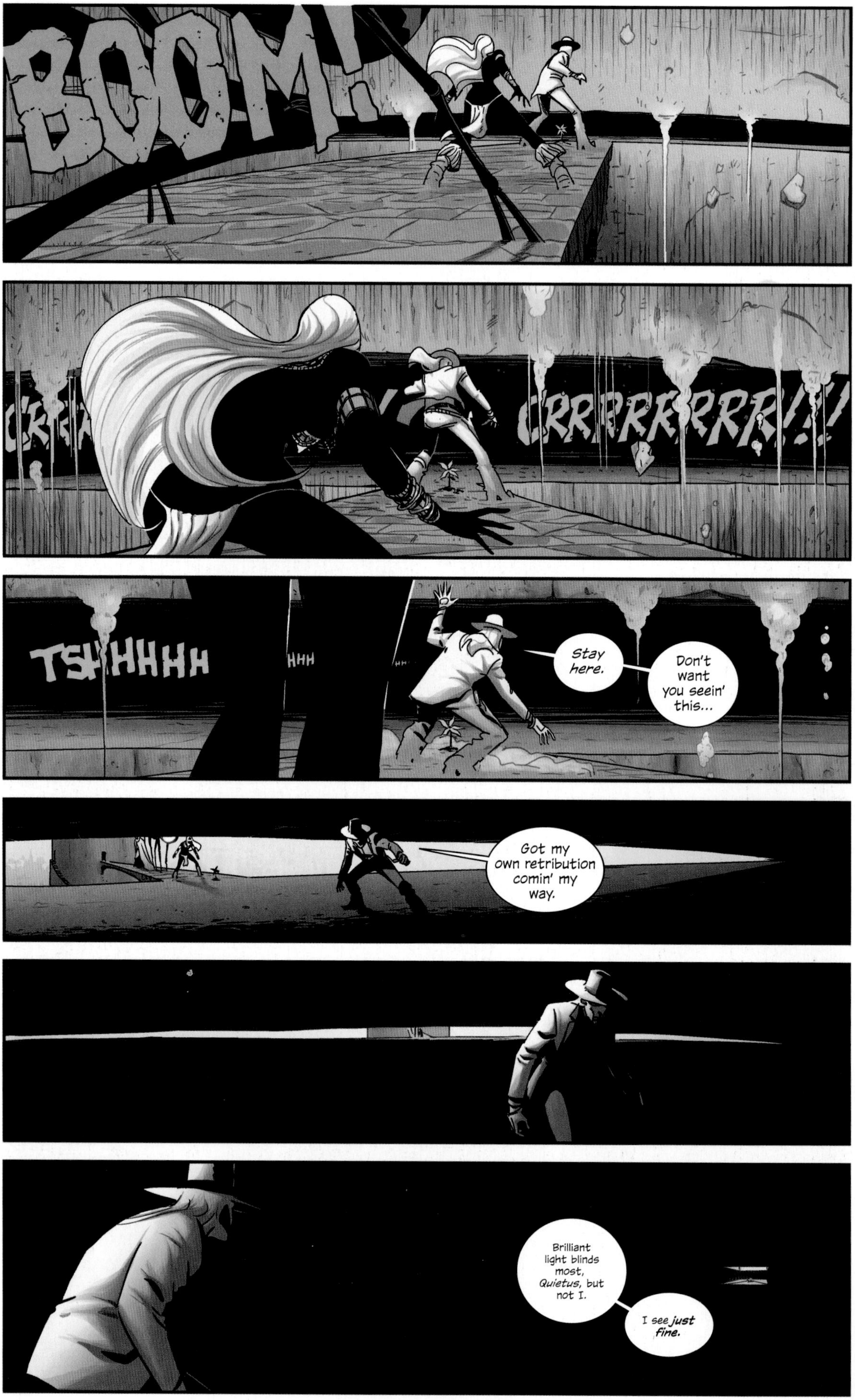
BOOM!
CRRRRRRRR!!!
TSHHHHH
Stay here.
Don't want you seein' this...
Got my own retribution comin' my way.
Brilliant light blinds most, *Quietus*, but not I.
I see ***just fine.***

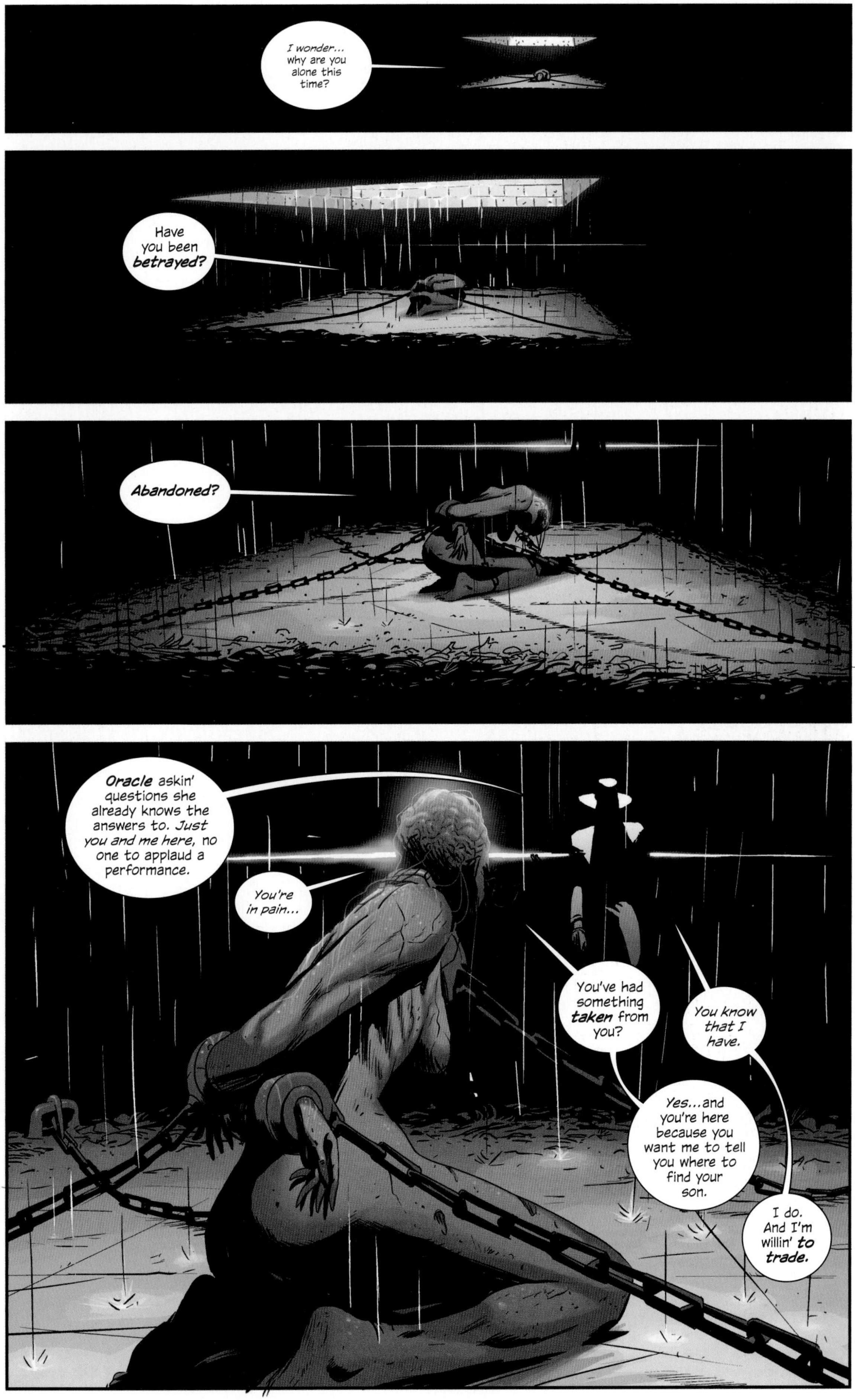
I wonder... why are you alone this time?
Have you been betrayed?
Abandoned?
Oracle askin' questions she already knows the answers to. Just you and me here, no one to applaud a performance.
You're in pain...
You've had something taken from you?
You know that I have.
Yes...and you're here because you want me to tell you where to find your son.
I do. And I'm willin' to trade.

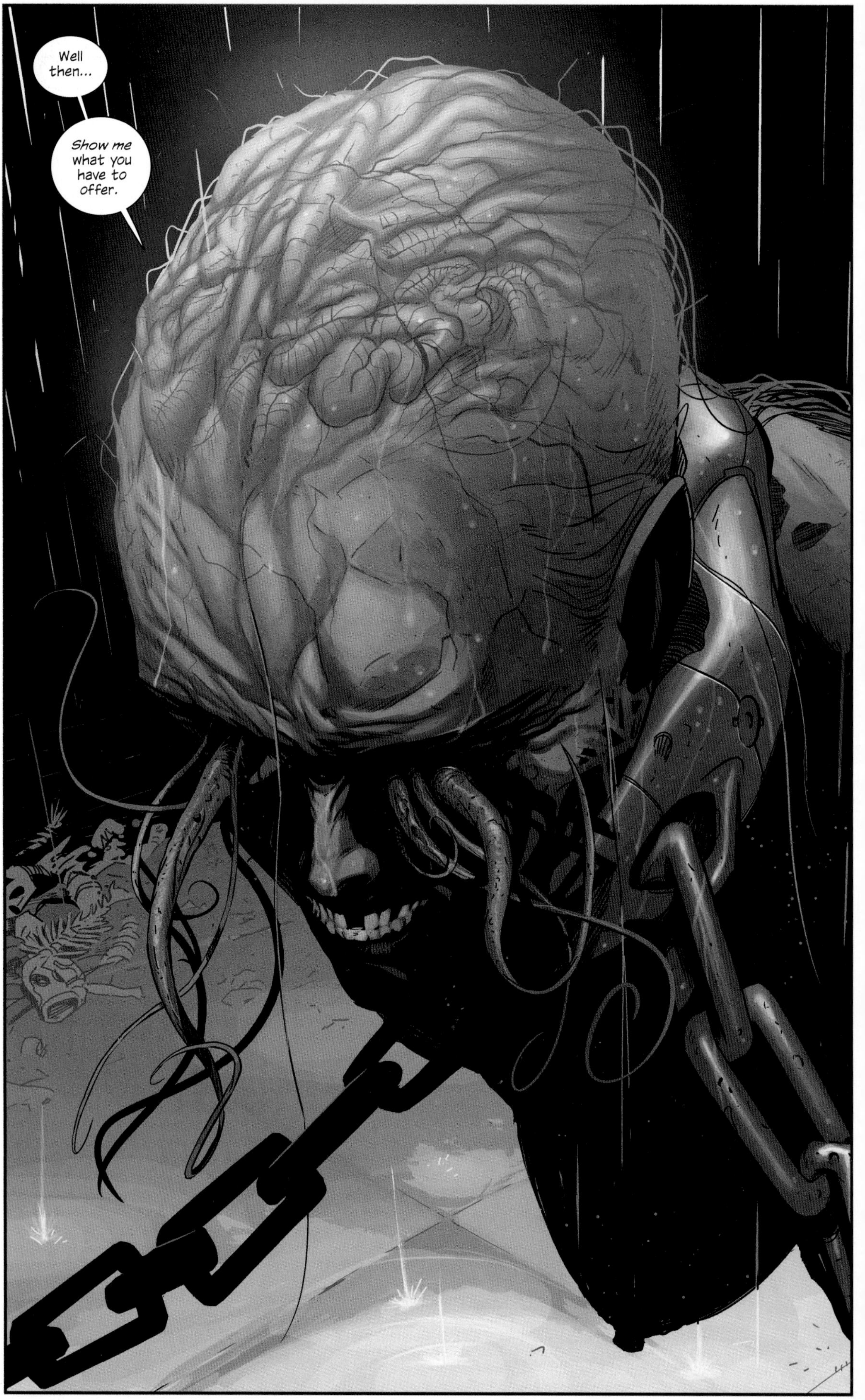
Well then...
Show me what you have to offer.

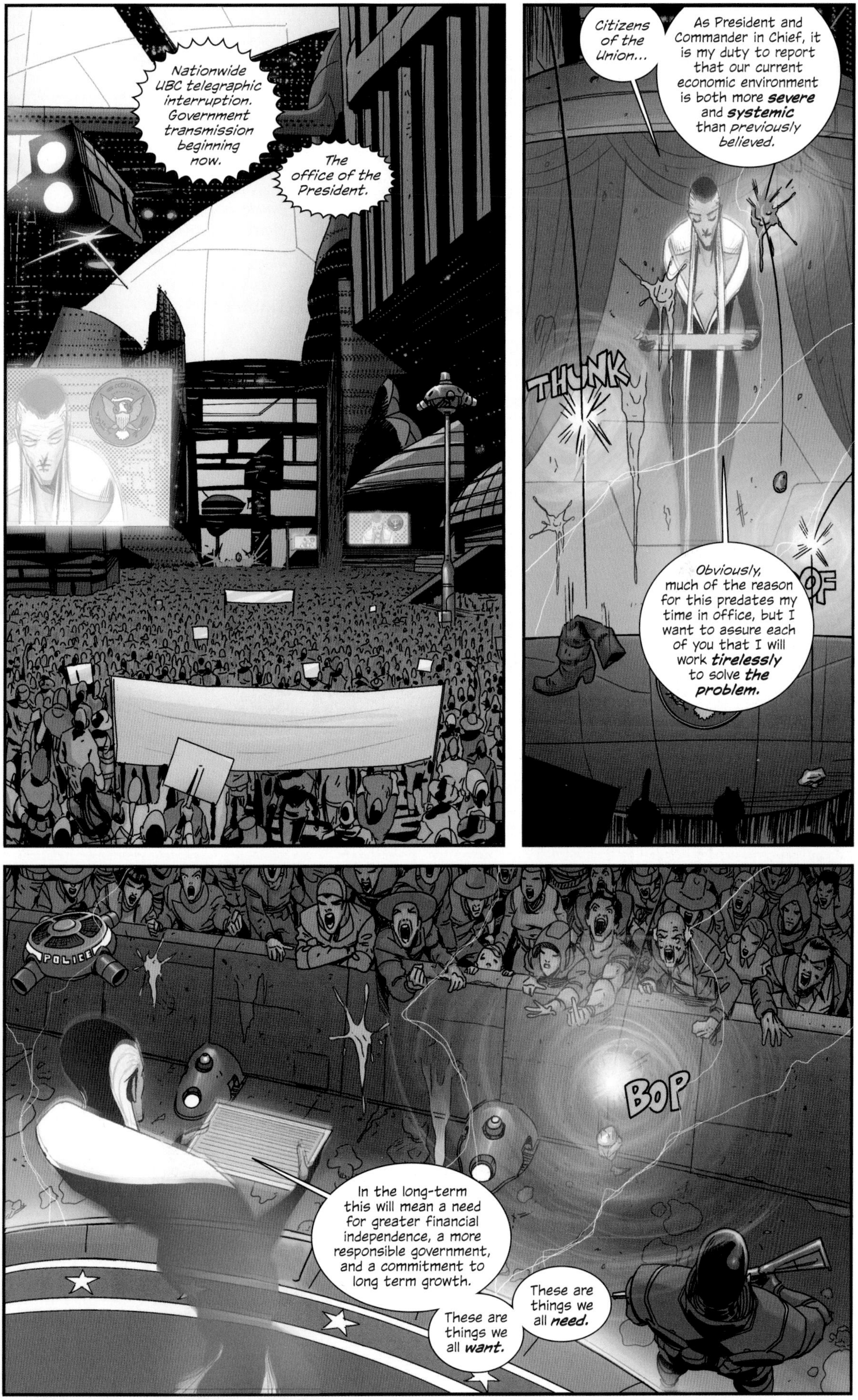

Nationwide UBC telegraphic interruption. Government transmission beginning now.
The office of the President.
Citizens of the Union...
As President and Commander in Chief, it is my duty to report that our current economic environment is both more **severe** and **systemic** than *previously* believed.
THUNK
Obviously, much of the reason for this predates my time in office, but I want to assure each of you that I will work **tirelessly** to solve **the problem.**
OF
POLICE
BOP
In the long-term this will mean a need for greater financial independence, a more responsible government, and a commitment to long term growth.
These are things we all **want.**
These are things we all **need.**

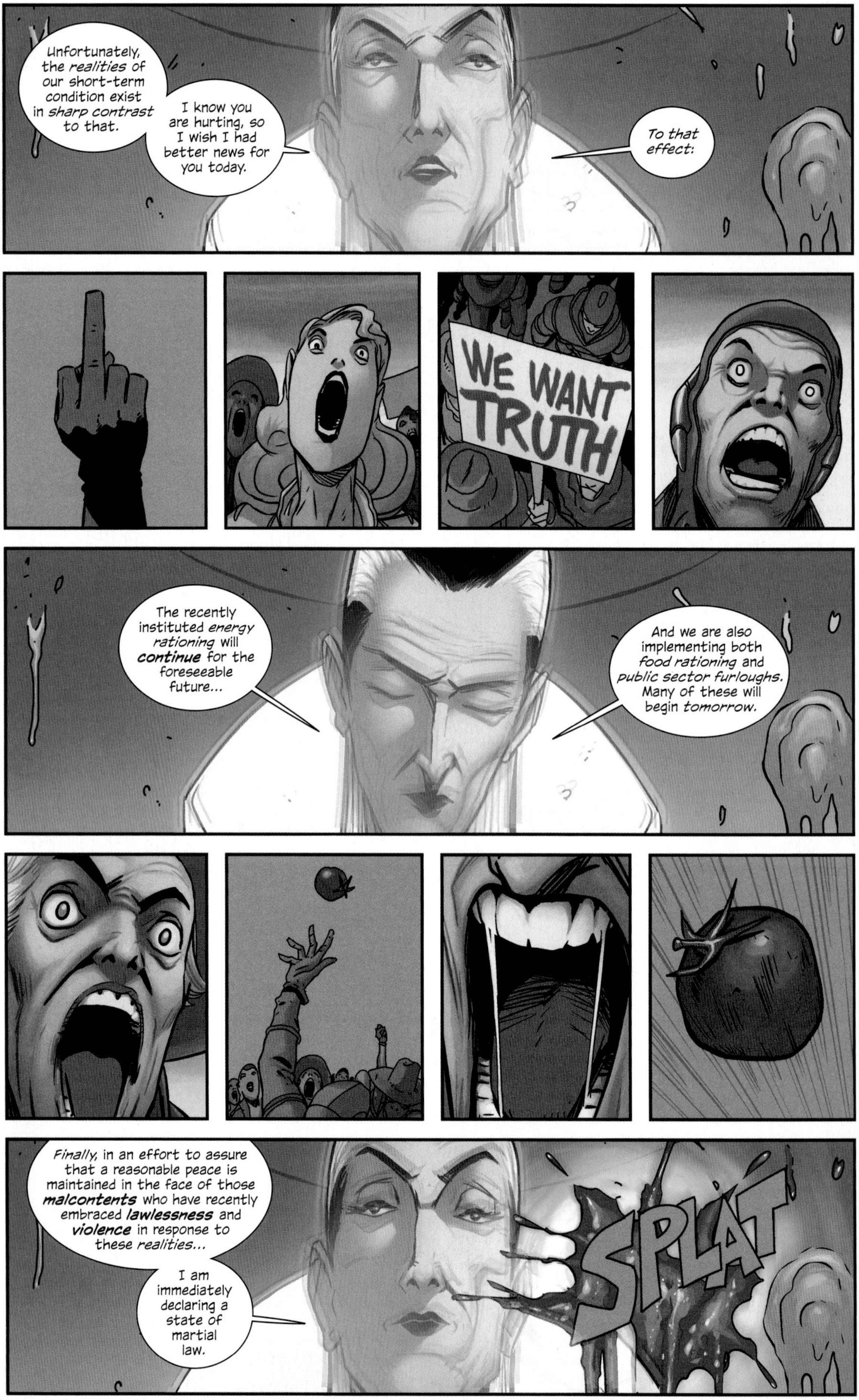

Unfortunately, the *realities* of our short-term condition exist in *sharp contrast* to that.
I know you are hurting, so I wish I had better news for you today.
To that effect:
WE WANT TRUTH
The recently instituted *energy rationing* will ***continue*** for the foreseeable future...
And we are also implementing both *food rationing* and *public sector furloughs.* Many of these will begin *tomorrow.*
Finally, in an effort to assure that a reasonable peace is maintained in the face of those ***malcontents*** who have recently embraced ***lawlessness*** and ***violence*** in response to these *realities...*
I am immediately declaring a state of martial law.
SPLAT

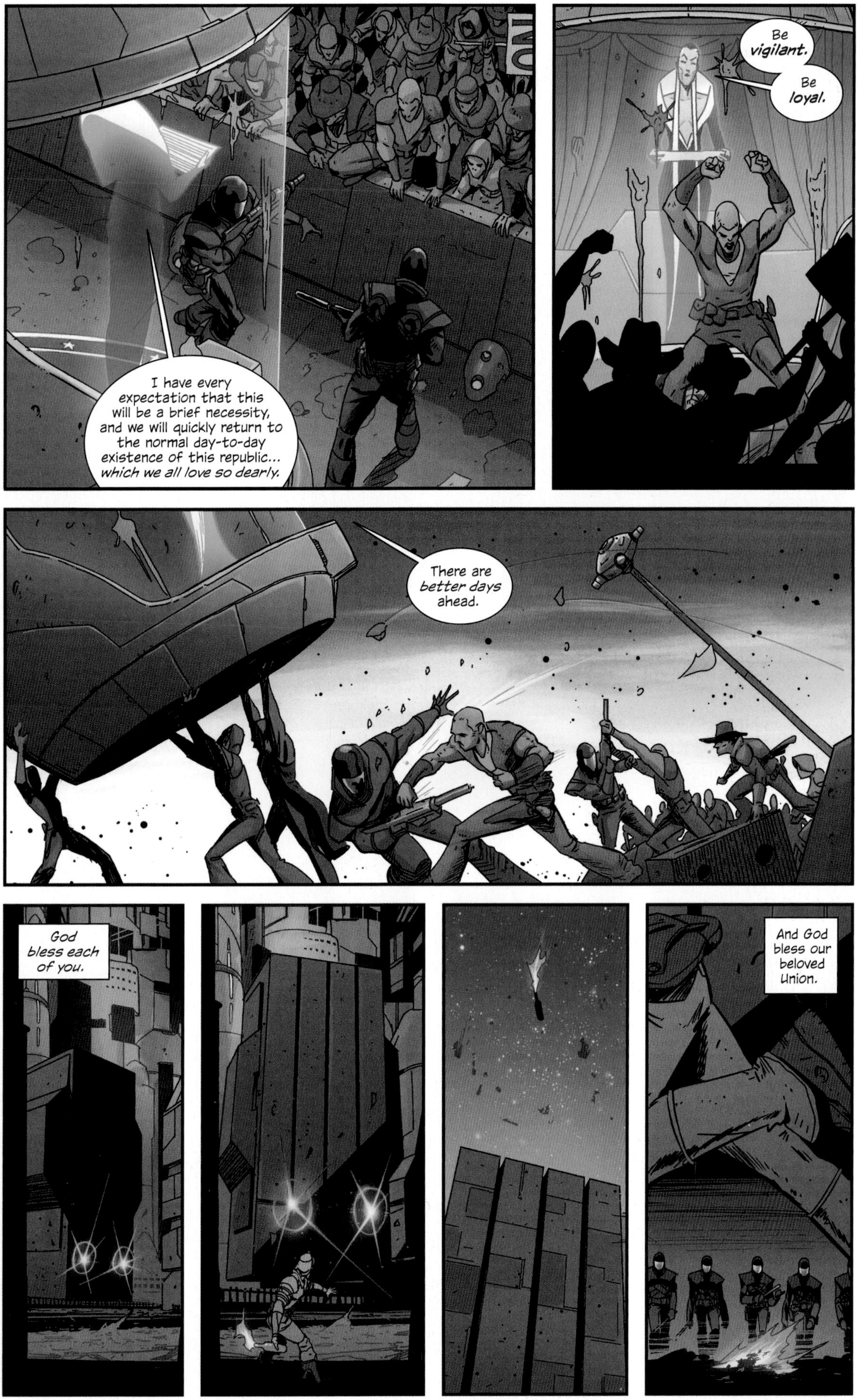
I have every expectation that this will be a brief necessity, and we will quickly return to the normal day-to-day existence of this republic... *which we all love so dearly.*
Be *vigilant.*
Be *loyal.*
There are *better days* ahead.
God bless each of you.
And God bless our beloved Union.

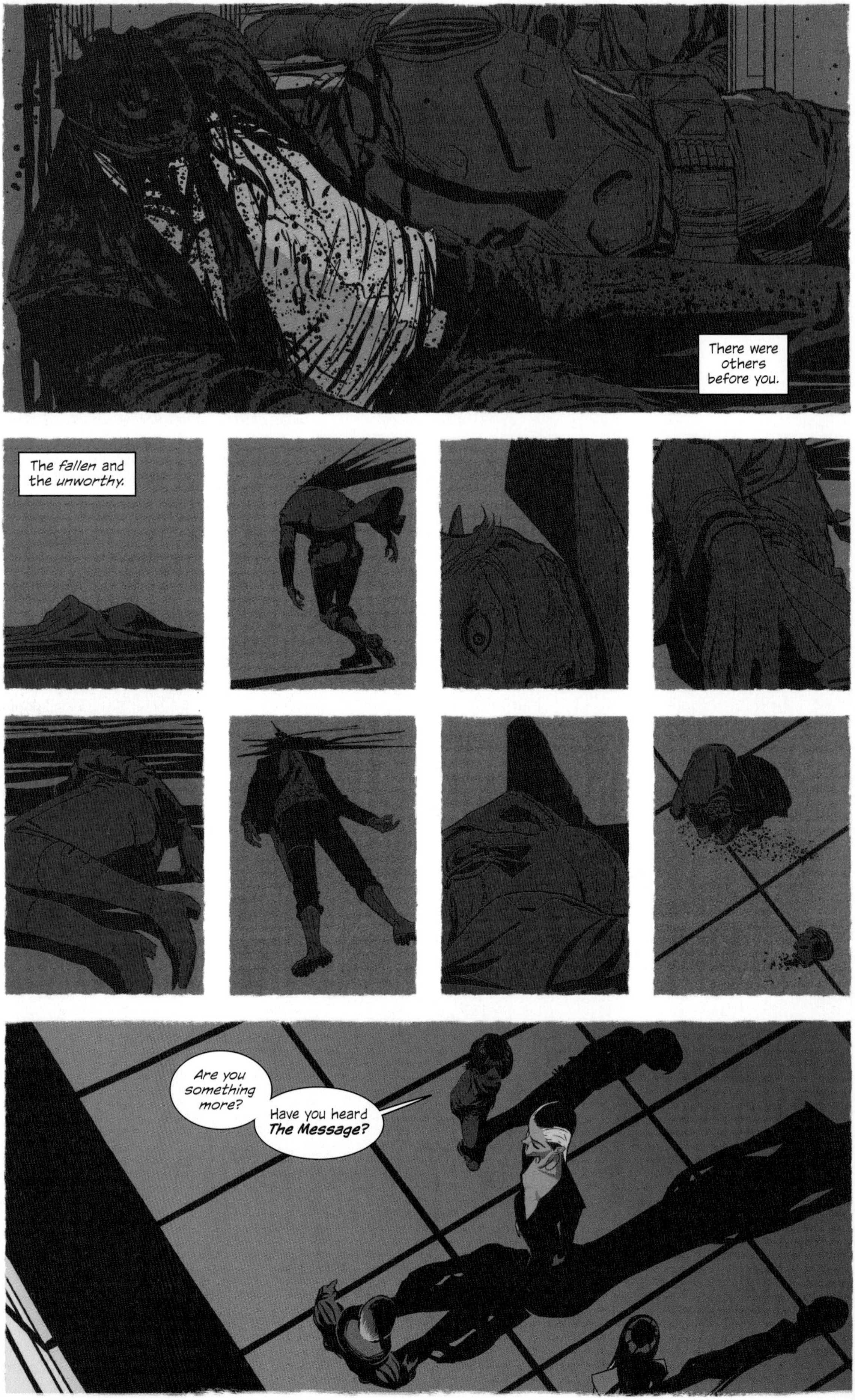
There were others before you.
The fallen and the unworthy.
Are you something more?
Have you heard The Message?

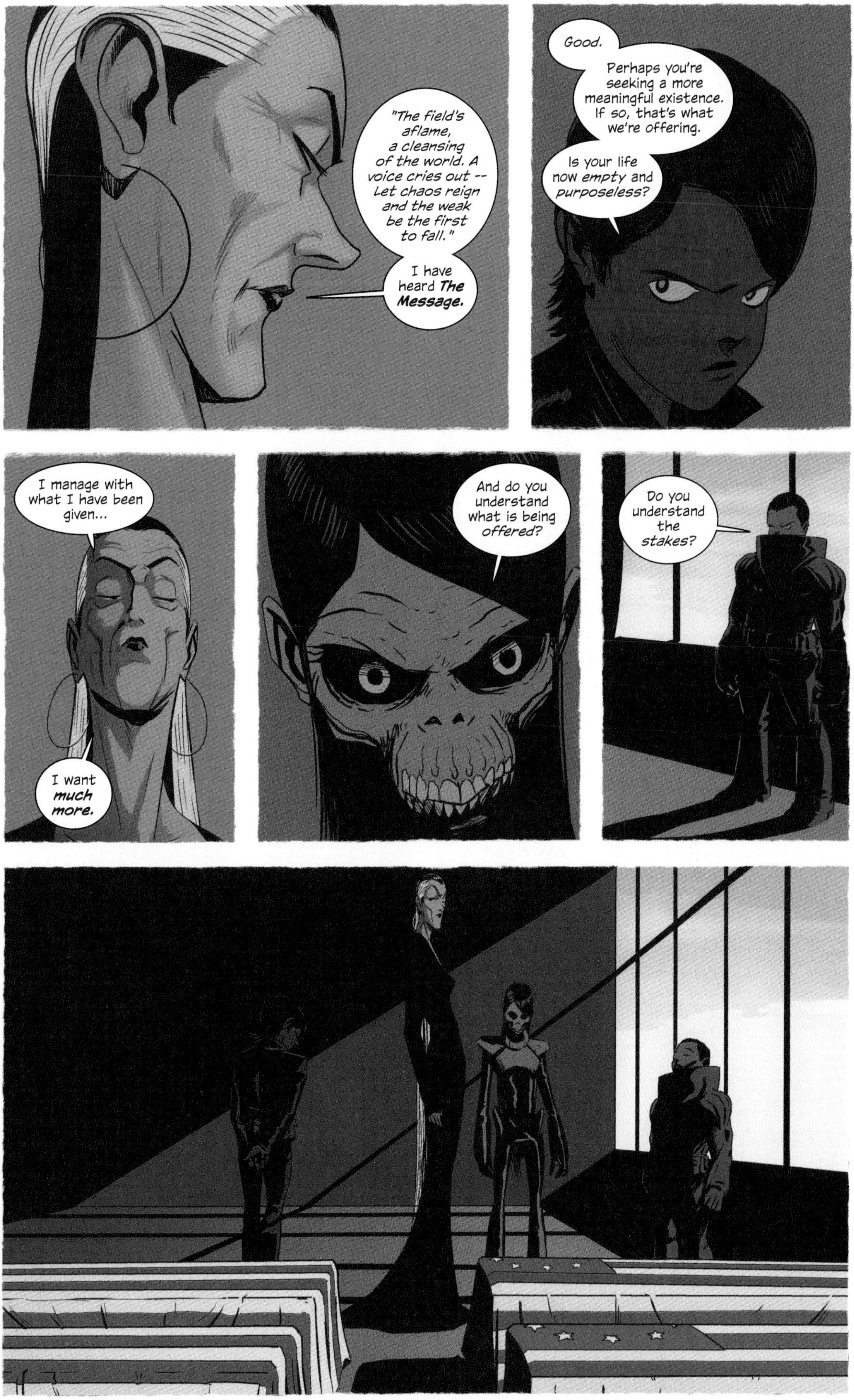
"The field's aflame, a cleansing of the world. A voice cries out -- Let chaos reign and the weak be the first to fall."
I have heard **The Message.**
Good.
Perhaps you're seeking a more meaningful existence. If so, that's what we're offering.
Is your life now *empty* and *purposeless?*
I manage with what I have been given...
I want ***much more.***
And do you understand what is being *offered?*
Do you understand the *stakes?*

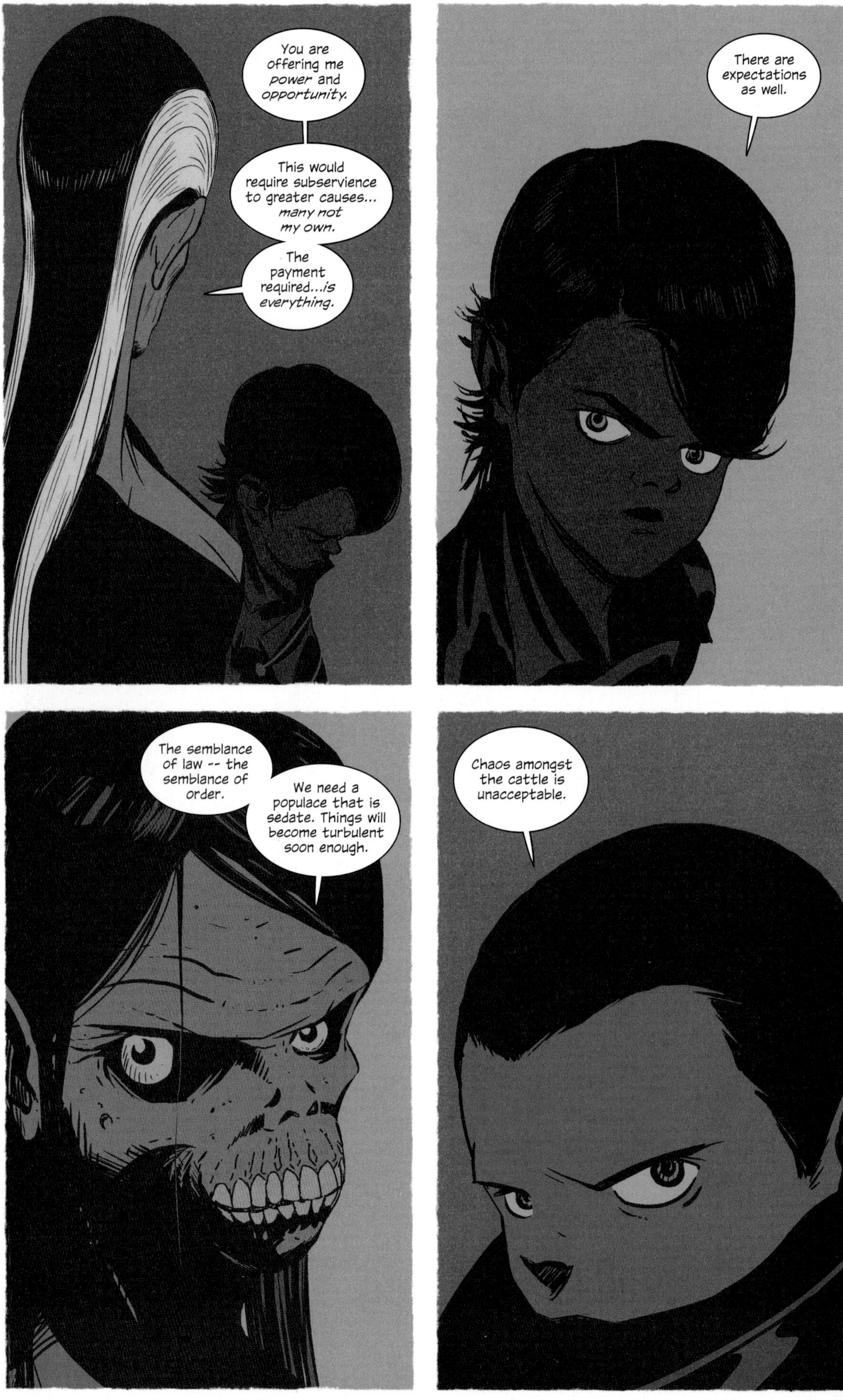

You are offering me *power* and *opportunity.*
This would require subservience to greater causes... *many not my own.*
The payment required...*is everything.*
There are expectations as well.
The semblance of law -- the semblance of order.
We need a populace that is sedate. Things will become turbulent soon enough.
Chaos amongst the cattle is unacceptable.

Control must be absolute and always maintained.

Well?

We need an answer.

You ask me to steal, and I will do so. You ask me to lie for you, and I will forget any truth I have ever known. You ask me to murder...I will murder.

Ask me for my *own life*... and it is *yours*.

If you would have me...*I accept*.

She'll do...

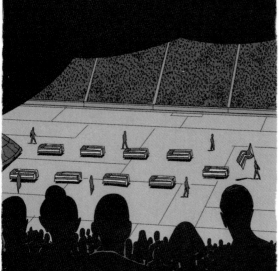

For now.

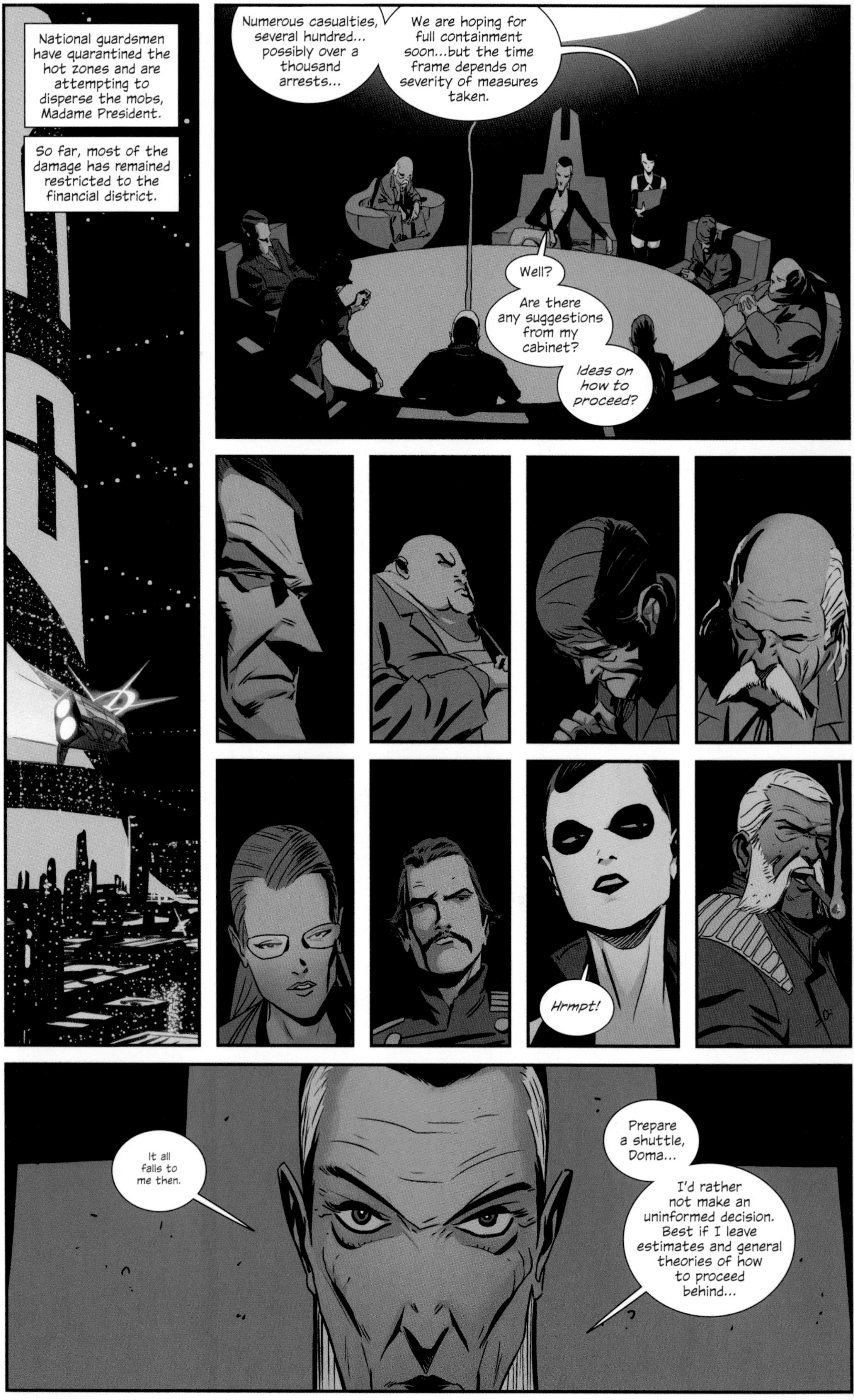
National guardsmen have quarantined the hot zones and are attempting to disperse the mobs, Madame President.
So far, most of the damage has remained restricted to the financial district.
Numerous casualties, several hundred... possibly over a thousand arrests...
We are hoping for full containment soon...but the time frame depends on severity of measures taken.
Well?
Are there any suggestions from my cabinet?
Ideas on how to proceed?
Hrmpt!
It all falls to me then.
Prepare a shuttle, Doma...
I'd rather not make an uninformed decision. Best if I leave estimates and general theories of how to proceed behind...

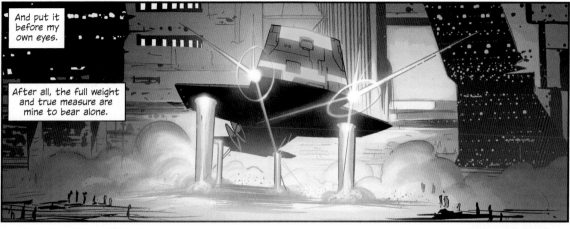

And put it before my own eyes.

After all, the full weight and true measure are mine to bear alone.

Let's see what's happened to my city.

Are they all this young?

It's skewing that way, Madame President.

We're taking DNA samples from all the dead as well as those we've arrested -- there are some that are older, *but most are not.*

We're not finding anything definable as a command structure, but if you apply the term loosely, these four seemed to be of *some* importance.

I want to speak with them.

This way, ma'am.

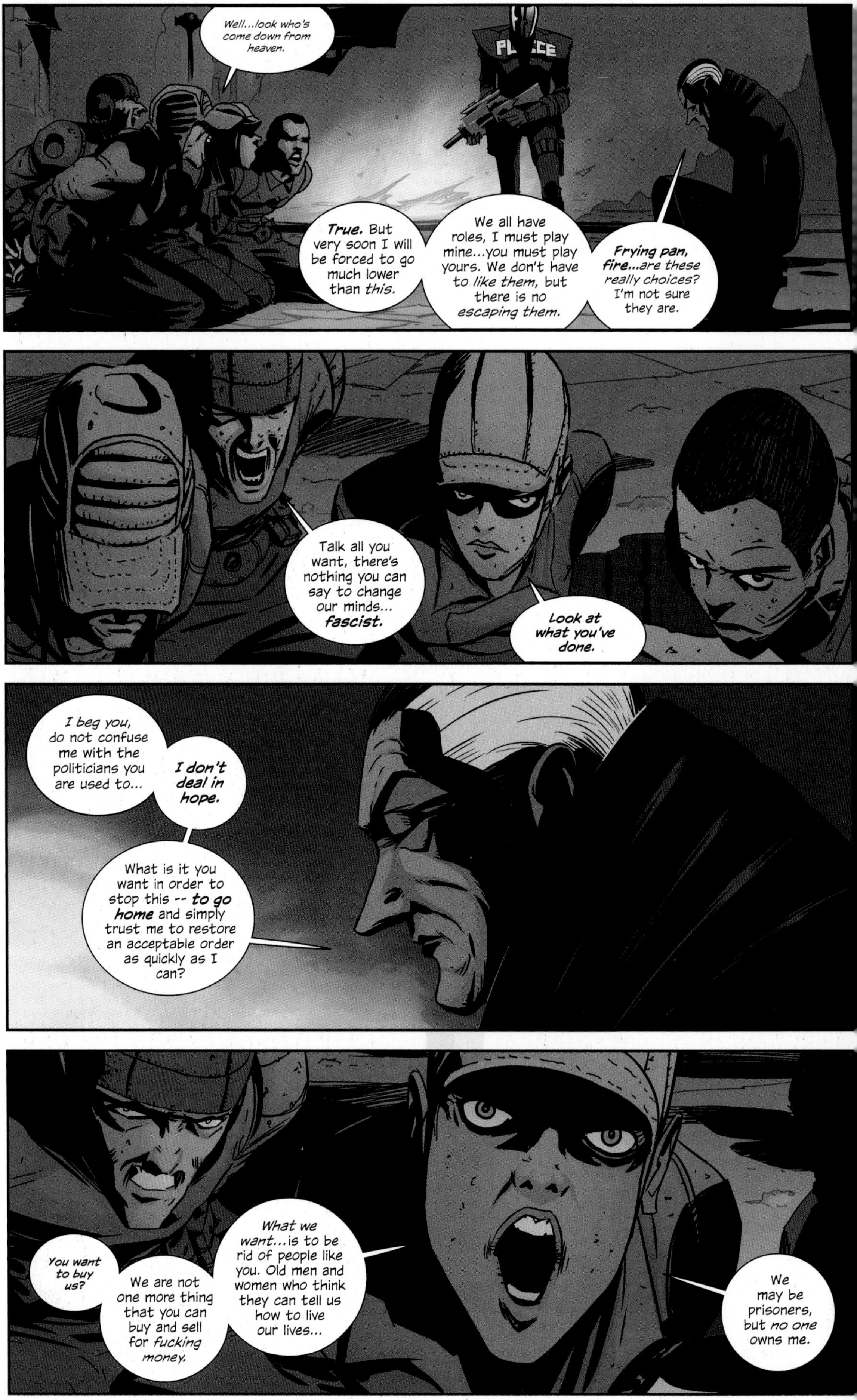
Well...look who's come down from heaven.
True. But very soon I will be forced to go much lower than this.
We all have roles, I must play mine...you must play yours. We don't have to like them, but there is no escaping them.
Frying pan, fire...are these really choices? I'm not sure they are.
Talk all you want, there's nothing you can say to change our minds... fascist.
Look at what you've done.
I beg you, do not confuse me with the politicians you are used to...
I don't deal in hope.
What is it you want in order to stop this -- to go home and simply trust me to restore an acceptable order as quickly as I can?
You want to buy us?
We are not one more thing that you can buy and sell for fucking money.
What we want...is to be rid of people like you. Old men and women who think they can tell us how to live our lives...
We may be prisoners, but no one owns me.

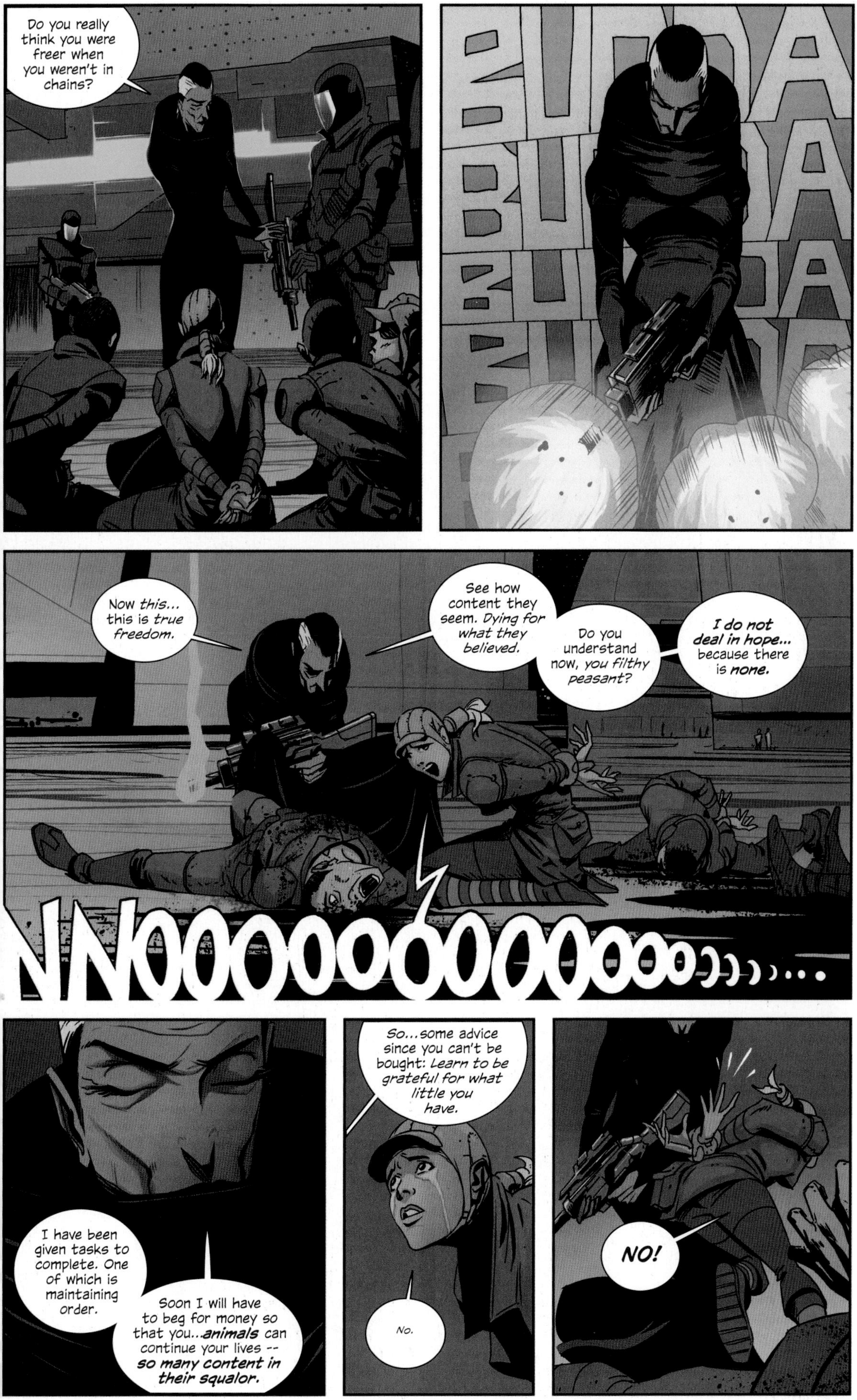
Do you really think you were freer when you weren't in chains?
BUDDA BUDDA BUDDA BUDDA
Now this... this is true freedom.
See how content they seem. Dying for what they believed.
Do you understand now, you filthy peasant?
I do not deal in hope... because there is none.
NNOOOOOOOOOOOOO...
I have been given tasks to complete. One of which is maintaining order.
Soon I will have to beg for money so that you...animals can continue your lives -- so many content in their squalor.
So...some advice since you can't be bought: Learn to be grateful for what little you have.
No.
NO!

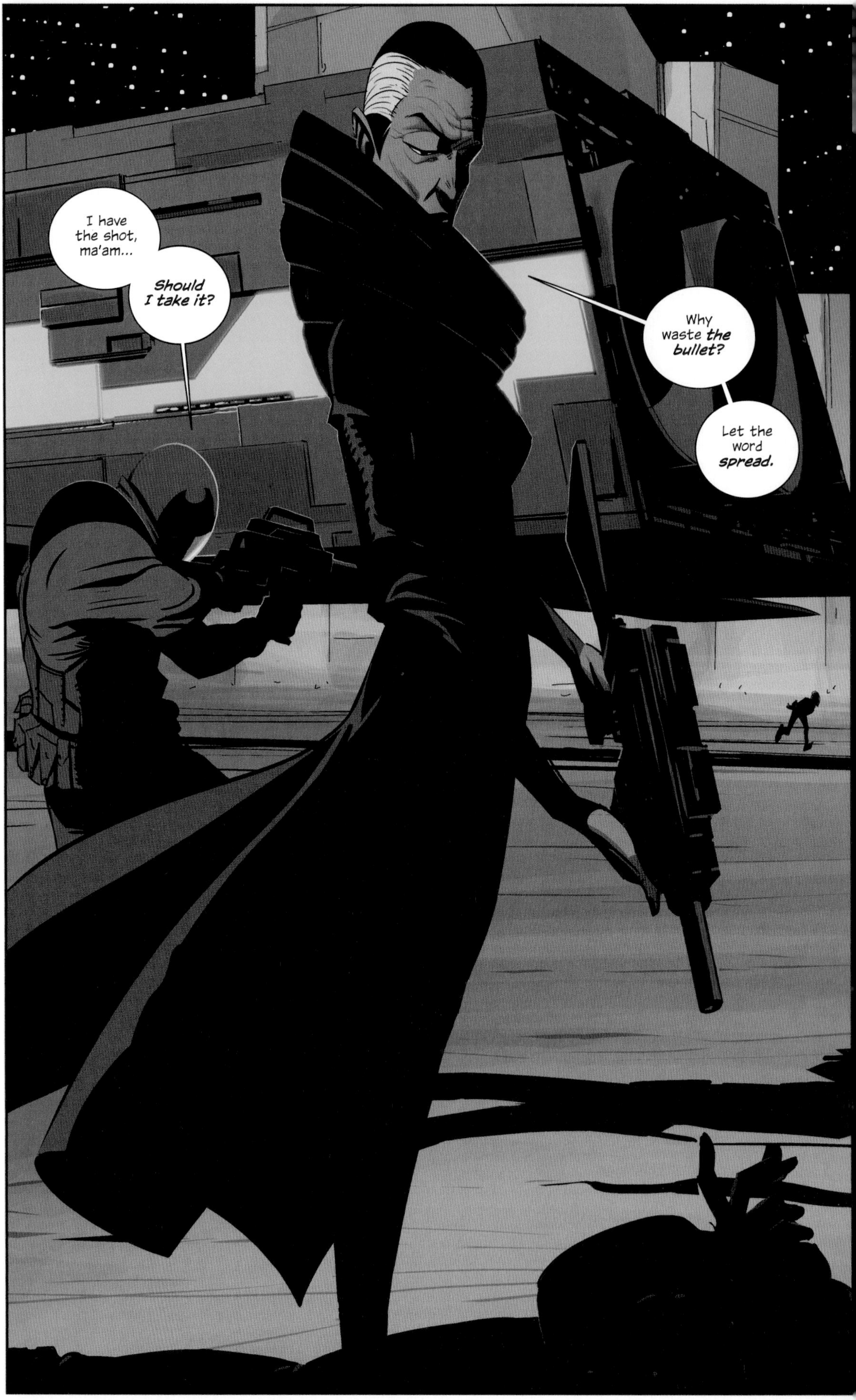
I have the shot, ma'am...
Should I take it?
Why waste ***the bullet?***
Let the word ***spread.***

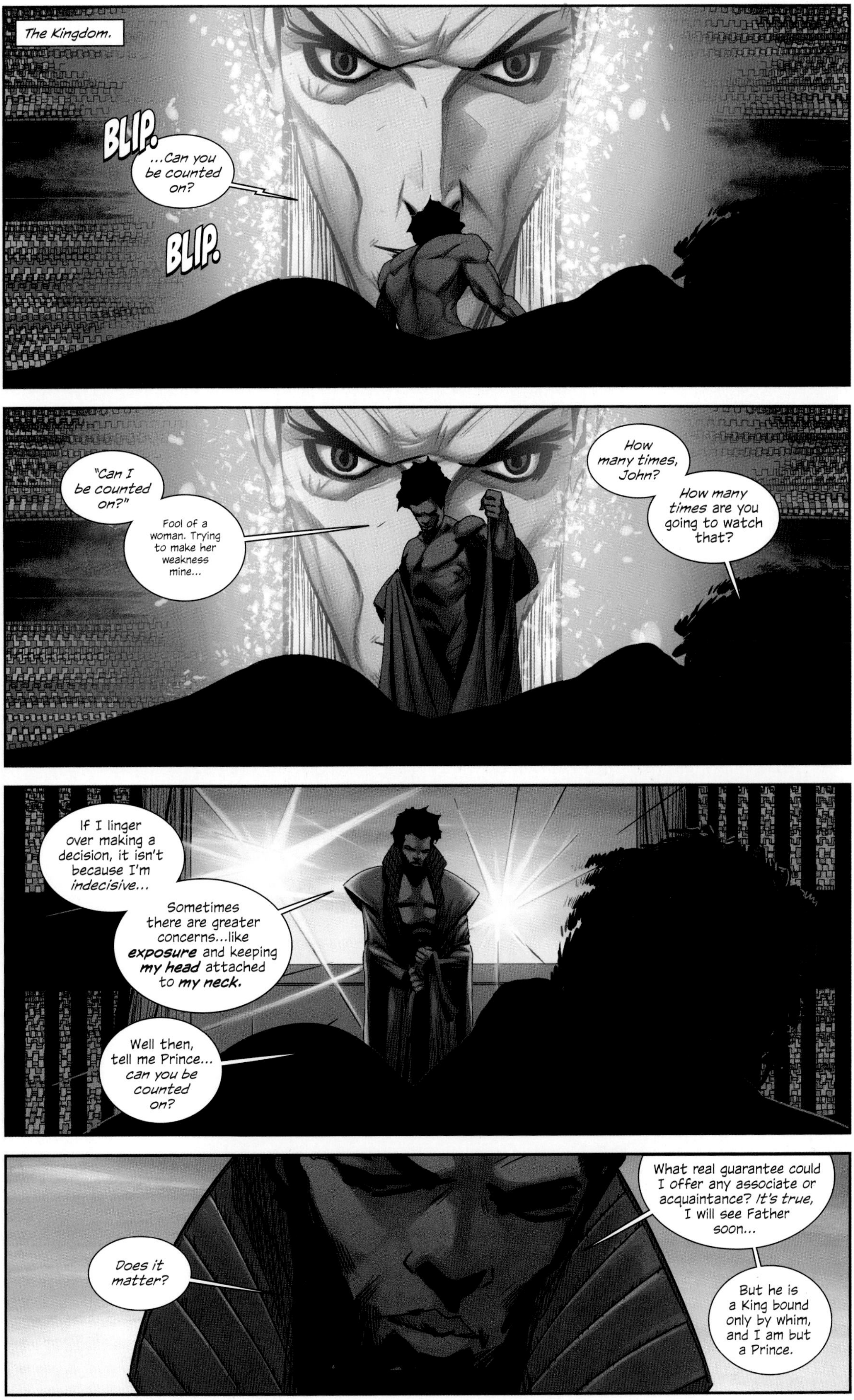
The Kingdom.
BLIP.
...Can you be counted on?
BLIP.
"Can I be counted on?"
Fool of a woman. Trying to make her weakness mine...
How many times, John?
How many times are you going to watch that?
If I linger over making a decision, it isn't because I'm indecisive...
Sometimes there are greater concerns...like exposure and keeping my head attached to my neck.
Well then, tell me Prince... can you be counted on?
Does it matter?
What real guarantee could I offer any associate or acquaintance? It's true, I will see Father soon...
But he is a King bound only by whim, and I am but a Prince.

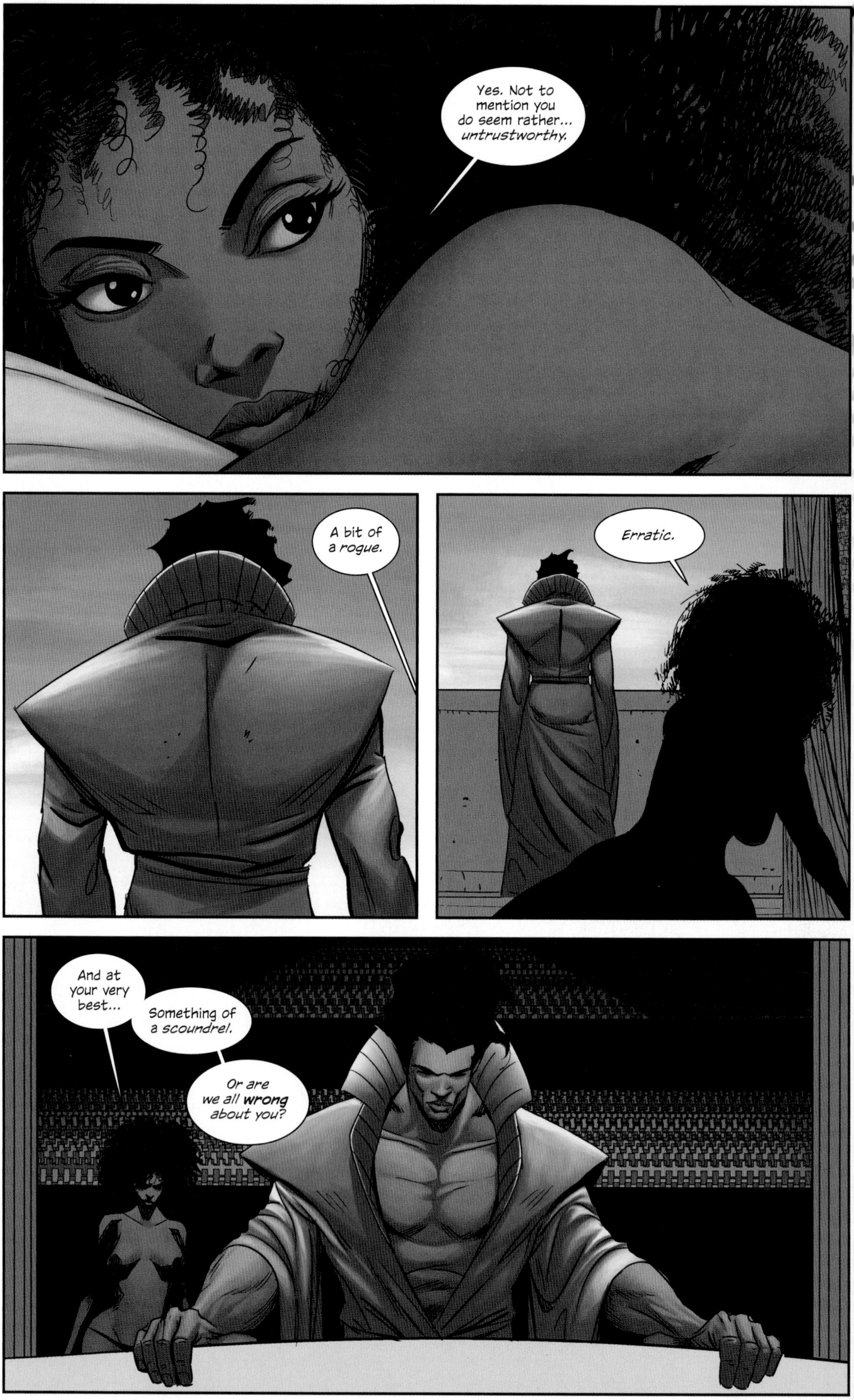
Yes. Not to mention you do seem rather... *untrustworthy.*
A bit of a *rogue.*
Erratic.
And at your very best...
Something of a *scoundrel.*
*Or are we all **wrong** about you?*

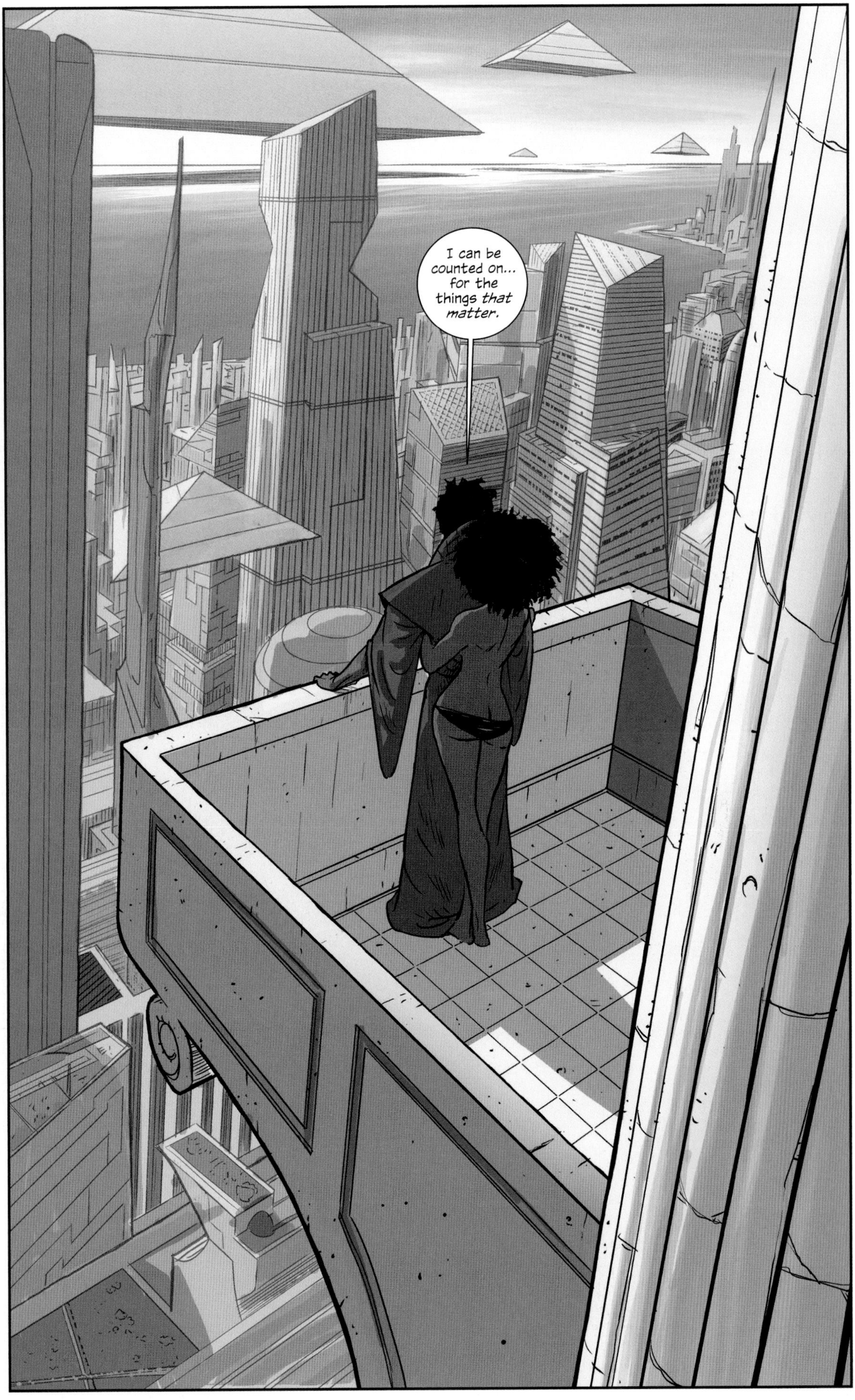
I can be counted on... ...for the things *that matter.*

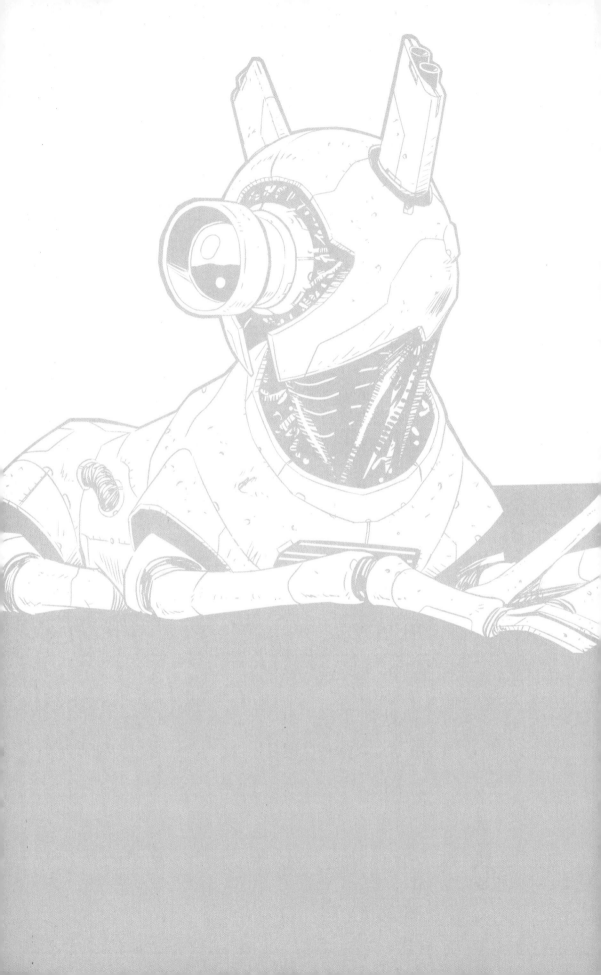

09

NINE: A KINGDOM OF RICHES

WHAT **FAIRNESS** IS THIS?

BLINDNESS IN A WORLD
FULL OF PEOPLE REFUSING TO
USE **THEIR EYES?**

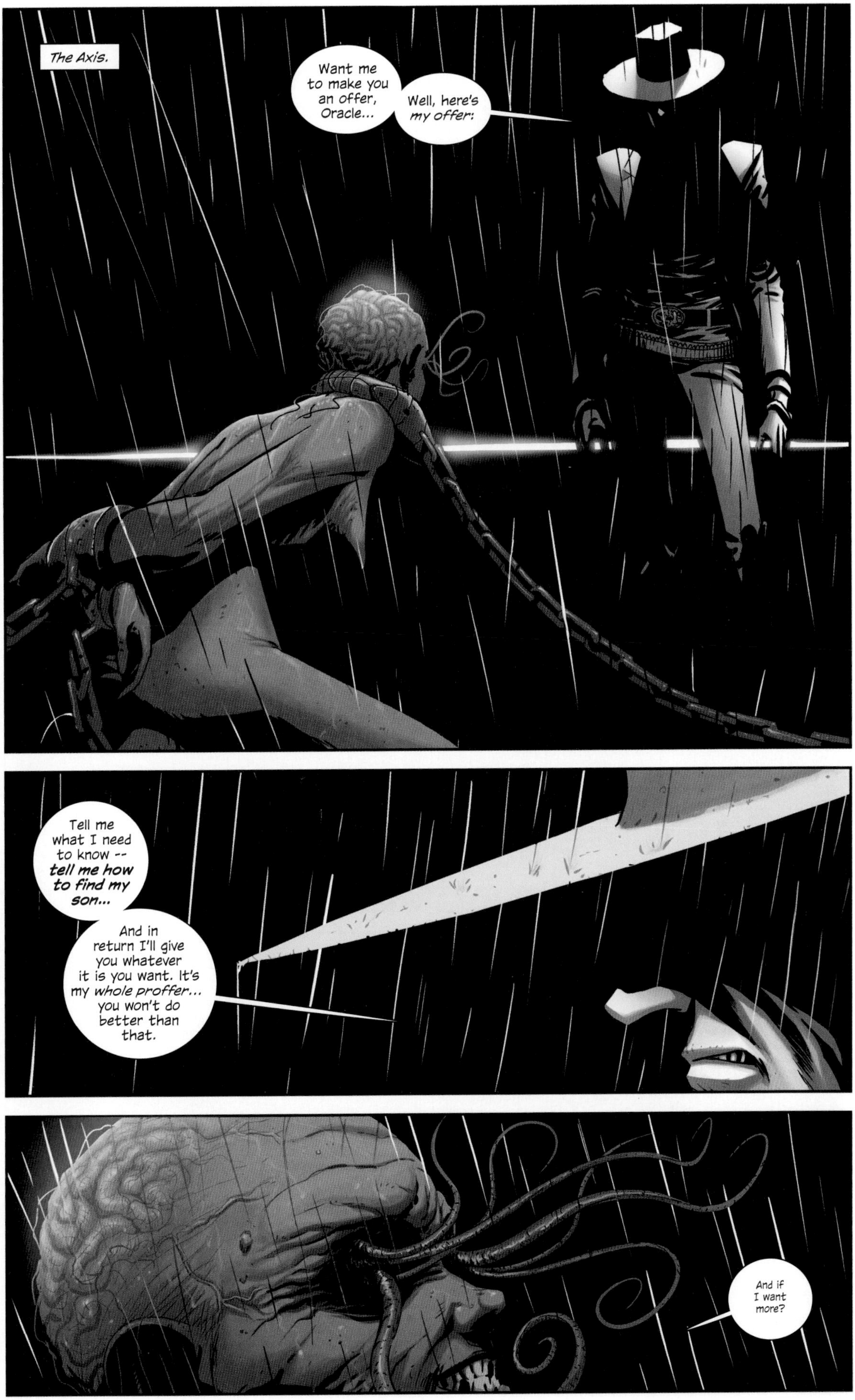
The Axis.
Want me to make you an offer, Oracle...
Well, here's my offer:
Tell me what I need to know -- tell me how to find my son...
And in return I'll give you whatever it is you want. It's my whole proffer... you won't do better than that.
And if I want more?

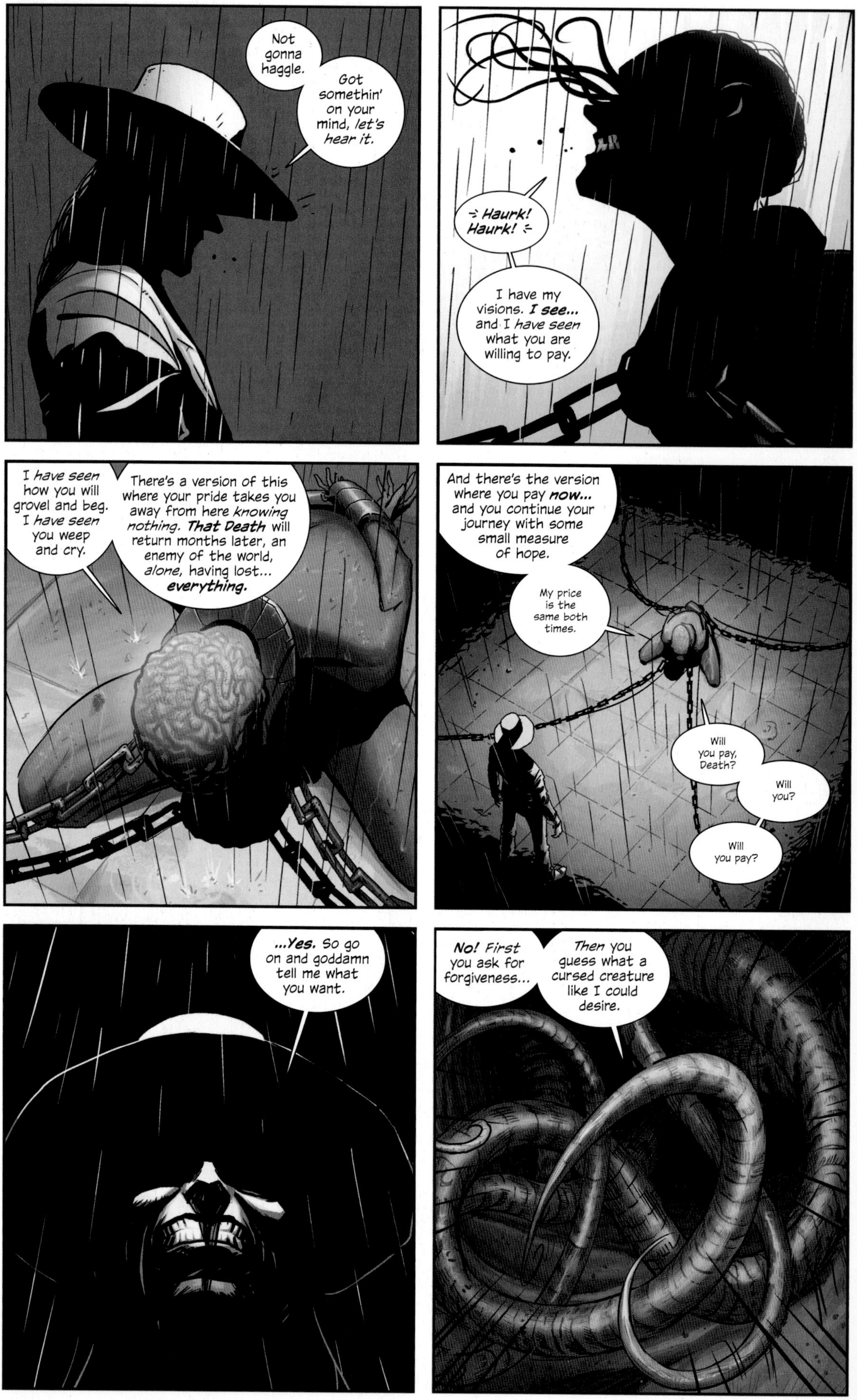
Not gonna haggle.
Got somethin' on your mind, *let's hear it.*
Haurk! Haurk!
I have my visions. ***I see...*** and I *have seen* what you are willing to pay.
I *have seen* how you will grovel and beg. I *have seen* you weep and cry.
There's a version of this where your pride takes you away from here *knowing nothing.* ***That Death*** will return months later, an enemy of the world, *alone,* having lost... ***everything.***
And there's the version where you pay ***now...*** and you continue your journey with some small measure of hope.
My price is the same both times.
Will you pay, Death?
Will you?
Will you pay?
...Yes. So go on and goddamn tell me what you want.
No! *First* you ask for forgiveness...
Then you guess what a cursed creature like I could desire.

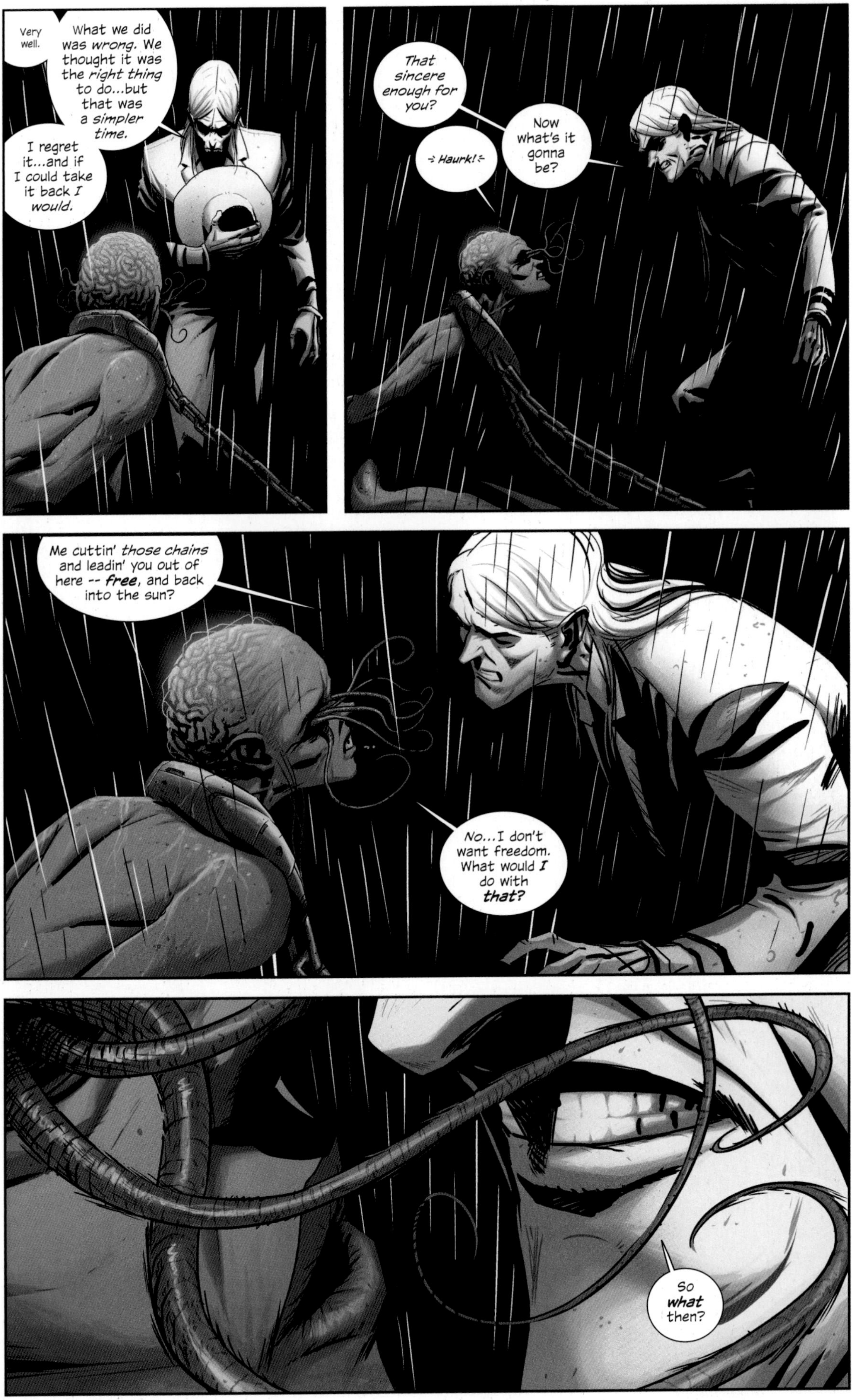
Very well.
What we did was *wrong*. We thought it was the *right thing* to do...but that was a *simpler time*.
I regret it...and if I could take it back *I* would.
That sincere enough for you?
Now what's it gonna be?
Haurk!
Me cuttin' *those chains* and leadin' you out of here -- ***free***, and back into the sun?
No...I don't want freedom. What would *I* do with ***that?***
So ***what*** then?

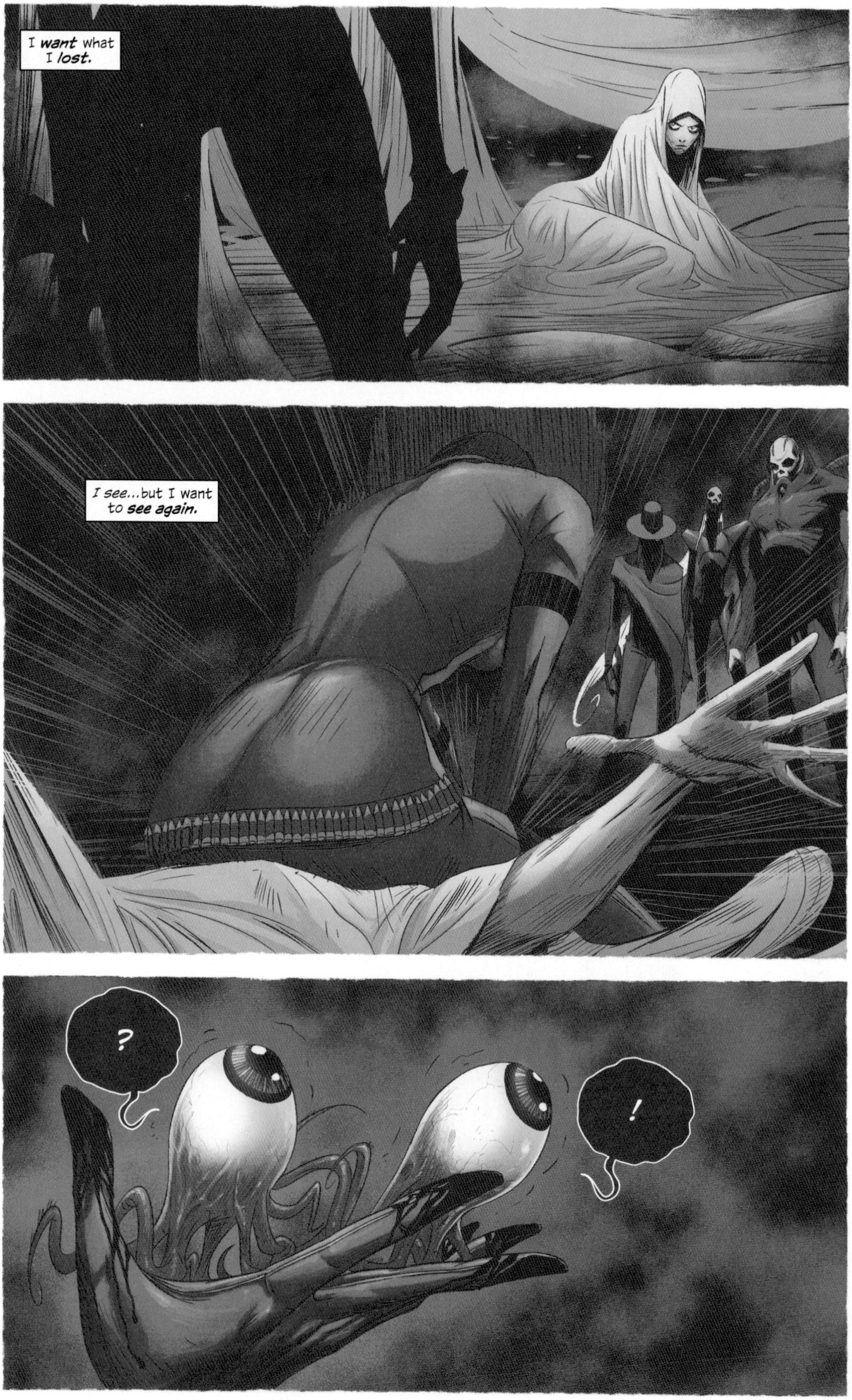
I *want* what I *lost.*
*I see...*but I want to *see again.*
?
!

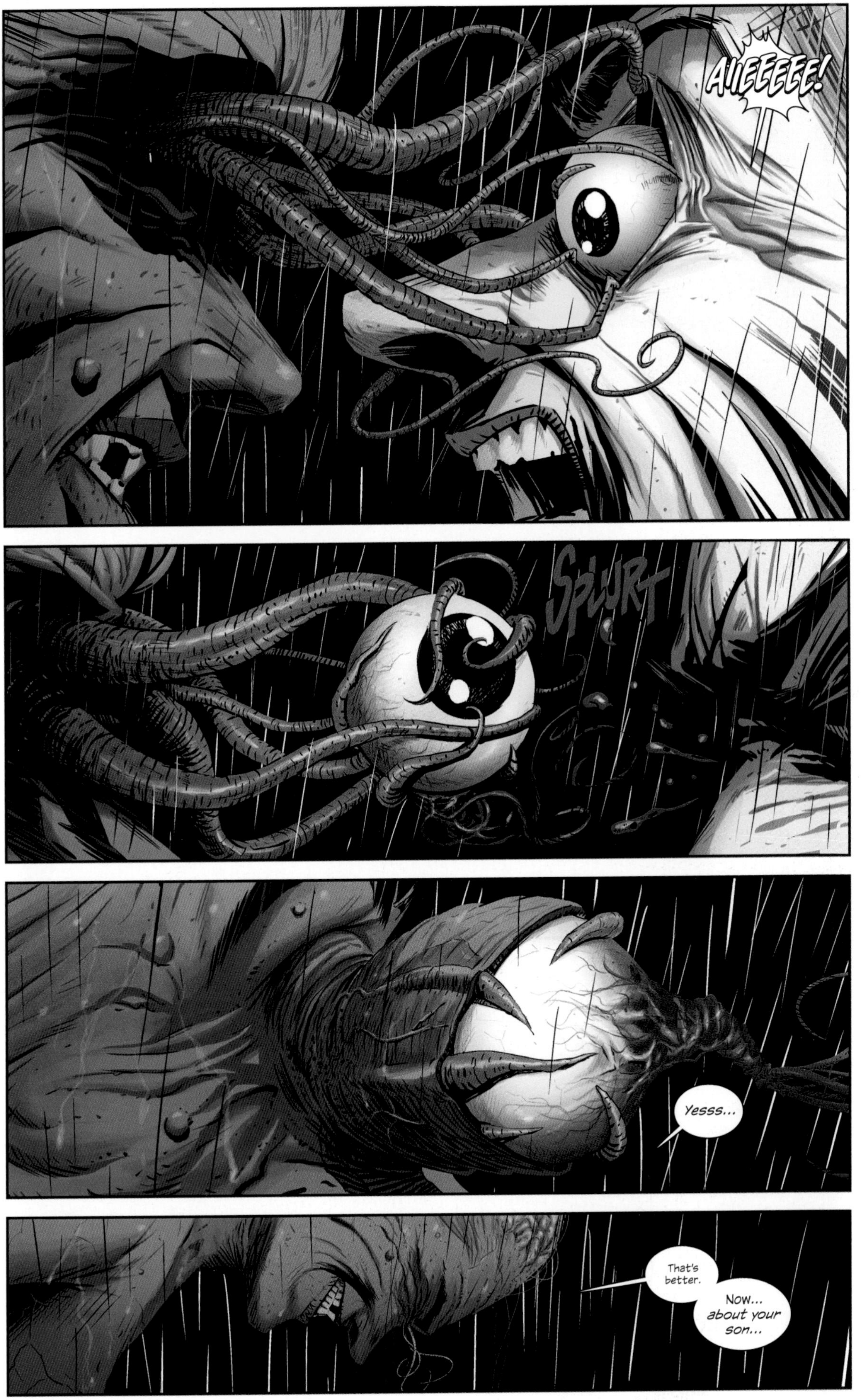
AIIEEEEEE!
SPLURT
Yesss...
That's better.
Now... about your son...

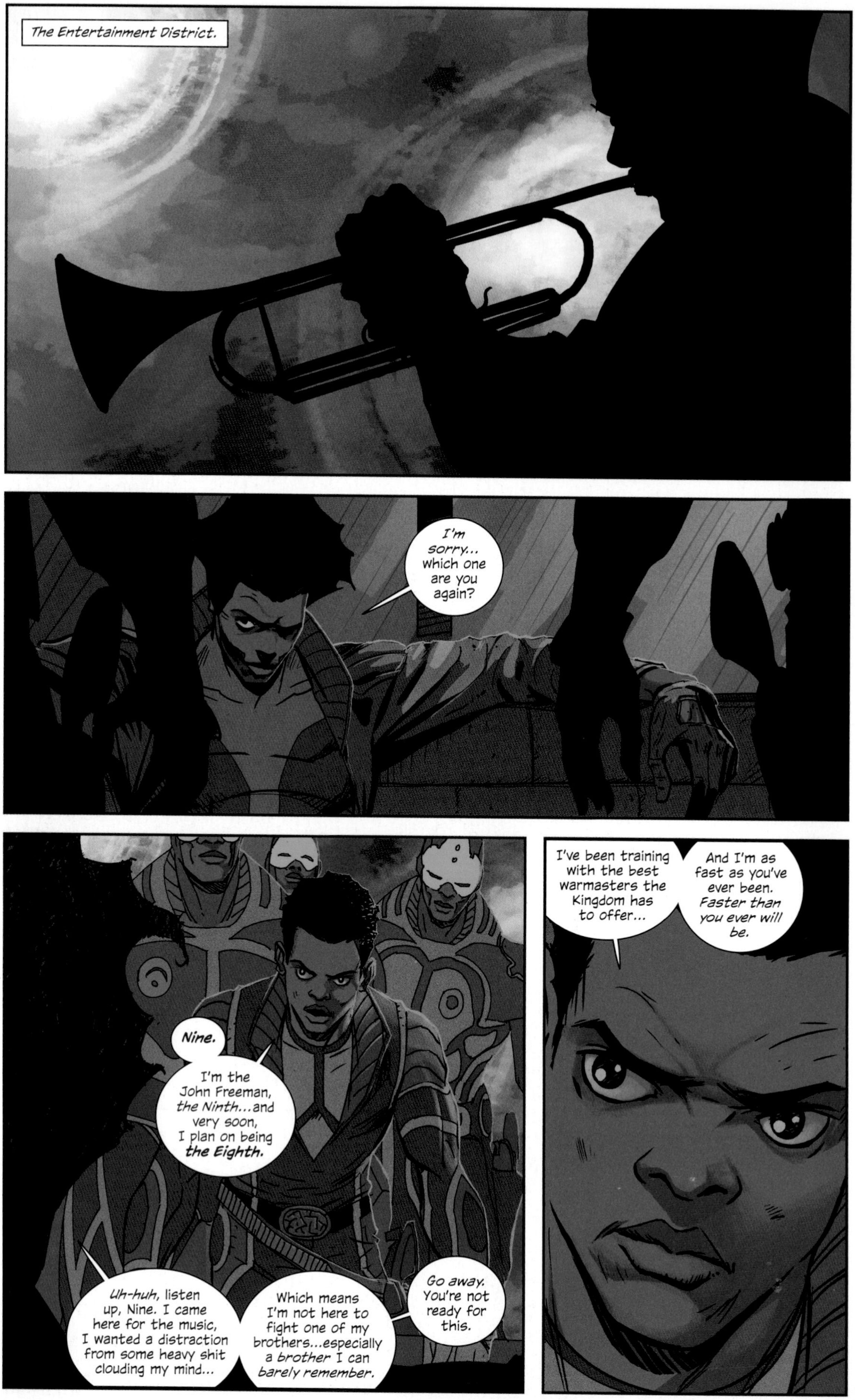

The Entertainment District.
I'm sorry... which one are you again?
Nine.
I'm the John Freeman, *the Ninth*...and very soon, I plan on being ***the Eighth.***
Uh-huh, listen up, Nine. I came here for the music, I wanted a distraction from some heavy shit clouding my mind...
Which means I'm not here to fight one of my brothers...especially a *brother* I can *barely remember.*
Go away. You're not ready for this.
I've been training with the best warmasters the Kingdom has to offer...
And I'm as fast as you've ever been. *Faster than you ever will be.*

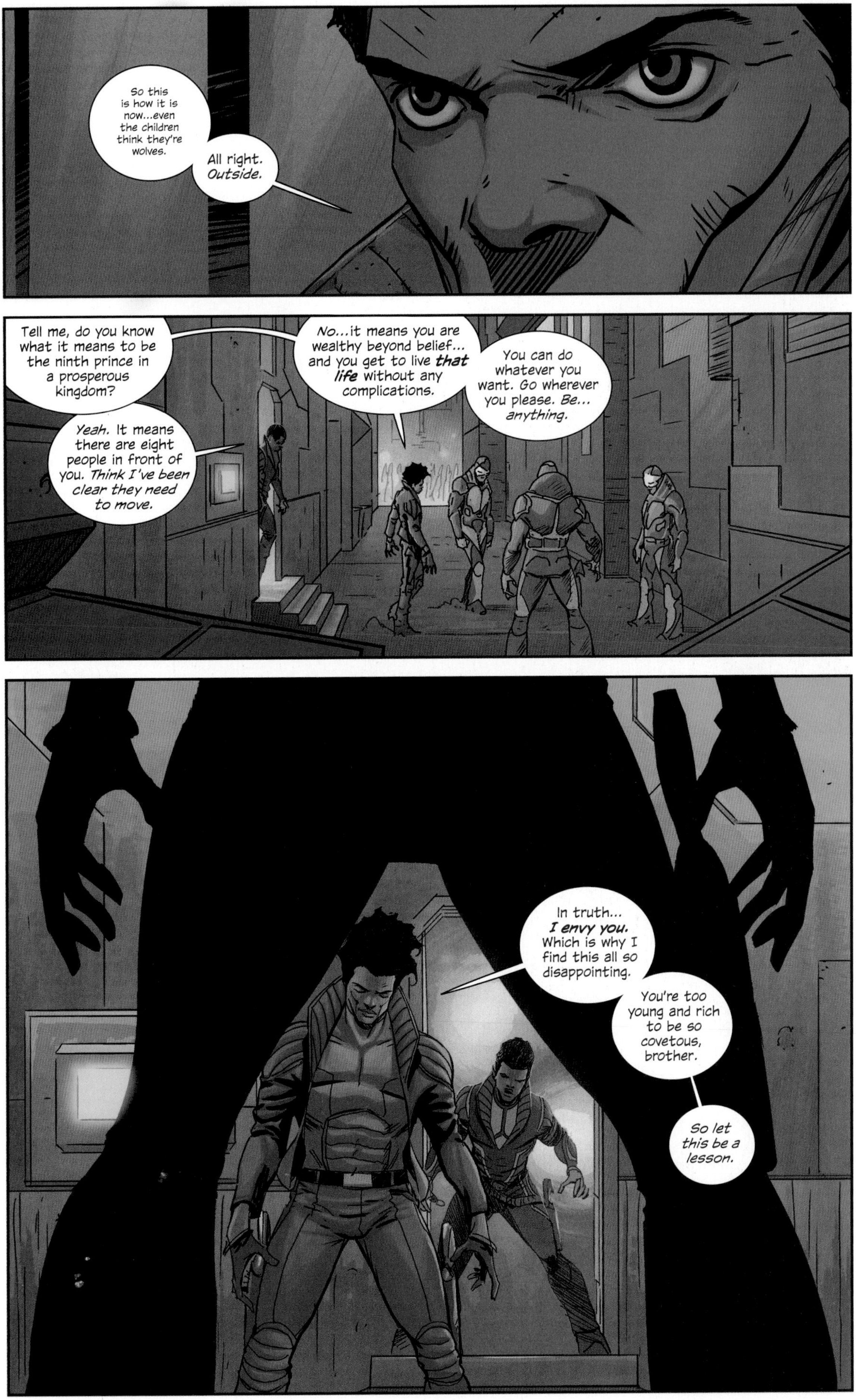
So this is how it is now...even the children think they're wolves.
All right. *Outside.*
Tell me, do you know what it means to be the ninth prince in a prosperous kingdom?
Yeah. It means there are eight people in front of you. *Think I've been clear they need to move.*
*No...*it means you are wealthy beyond belief... and you get to live ***that life*** without any complications.
You can do whatever you want. Go wherever you please. *Be... anything.*
In truth... ***I envy you.*** Which is why I find this all so disappointing.
You're too young and rich to be so covetous, brother.
So let this be a lesson.

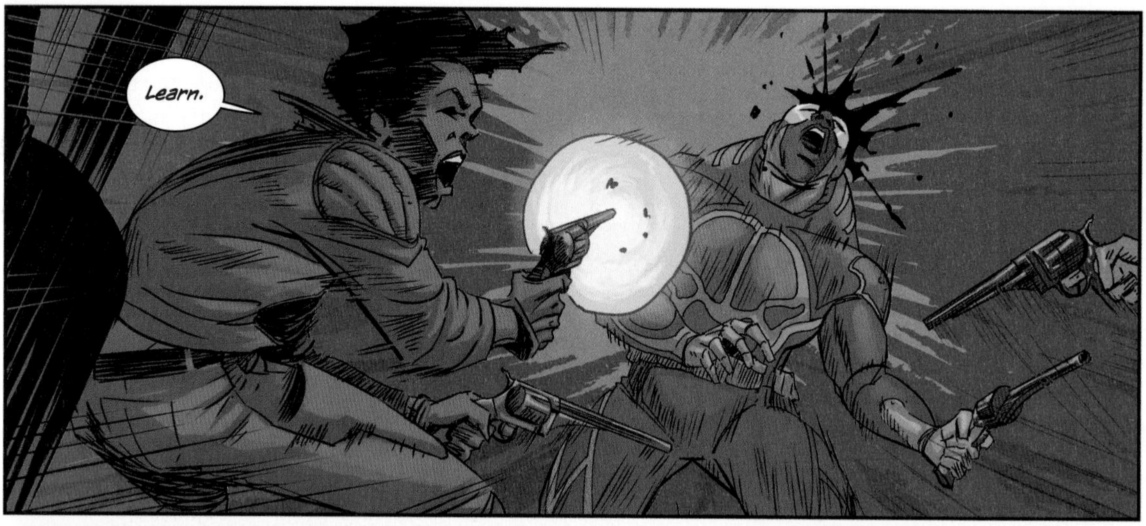
Learn.

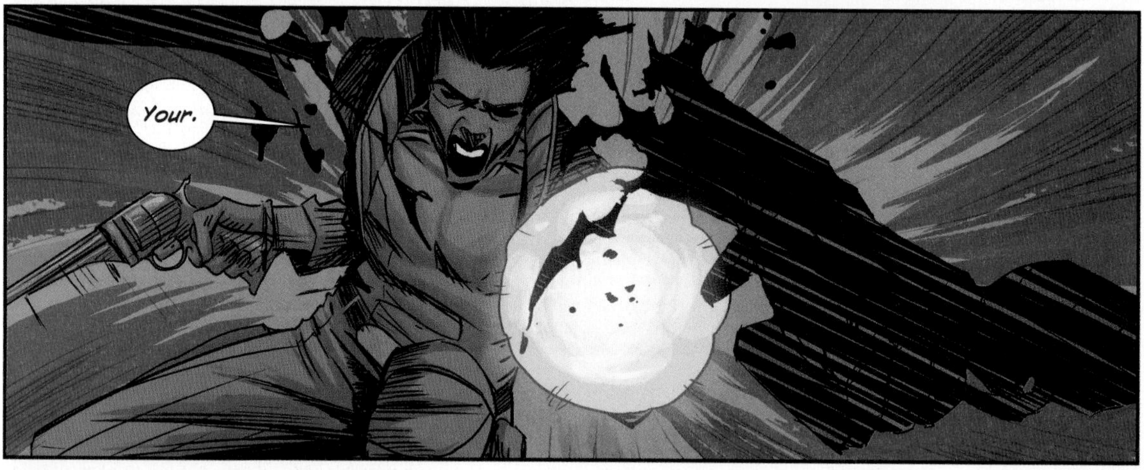
Your.

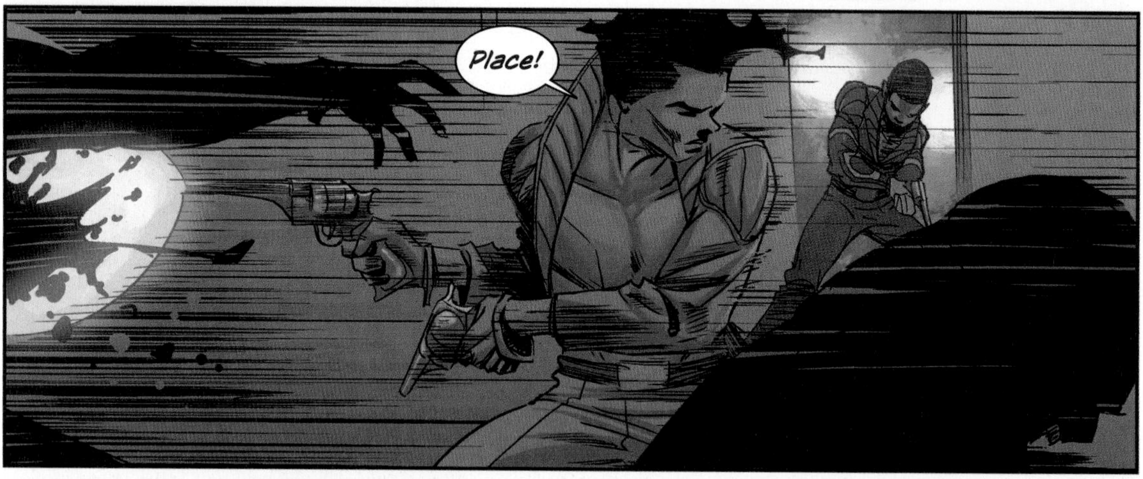
Place!

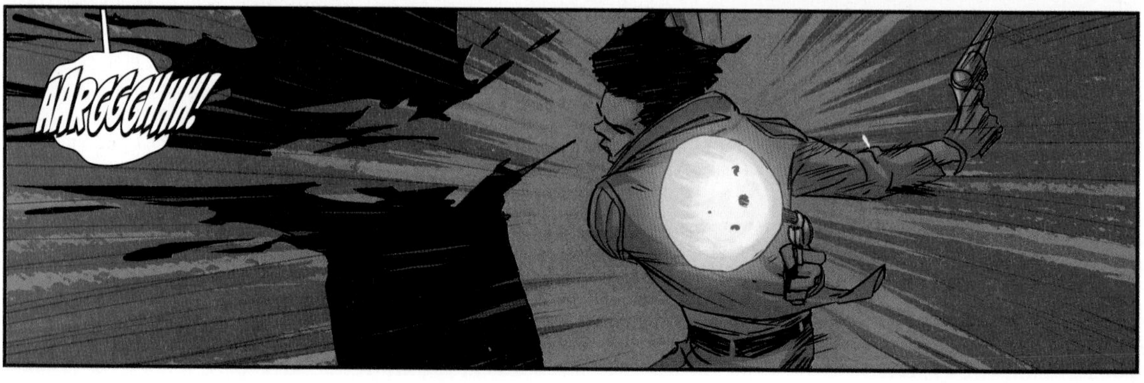
AARGGGHHH!

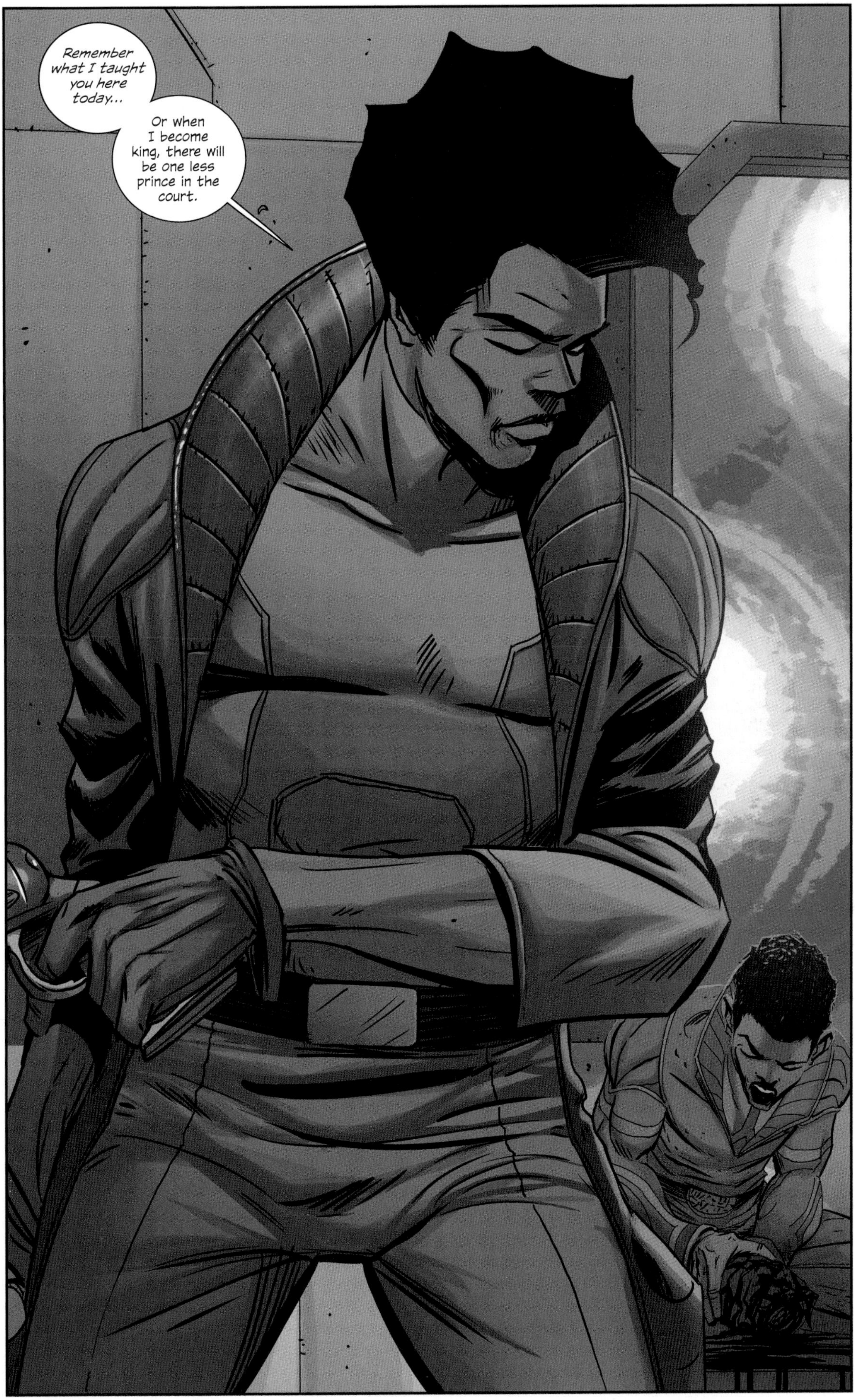
Remember what I taught you here today...
Or when I become king, there will be one less prince in the court.

THERE IS **THE THRONE.**

THEN THERE IS **EVERYTHING ELSE.**

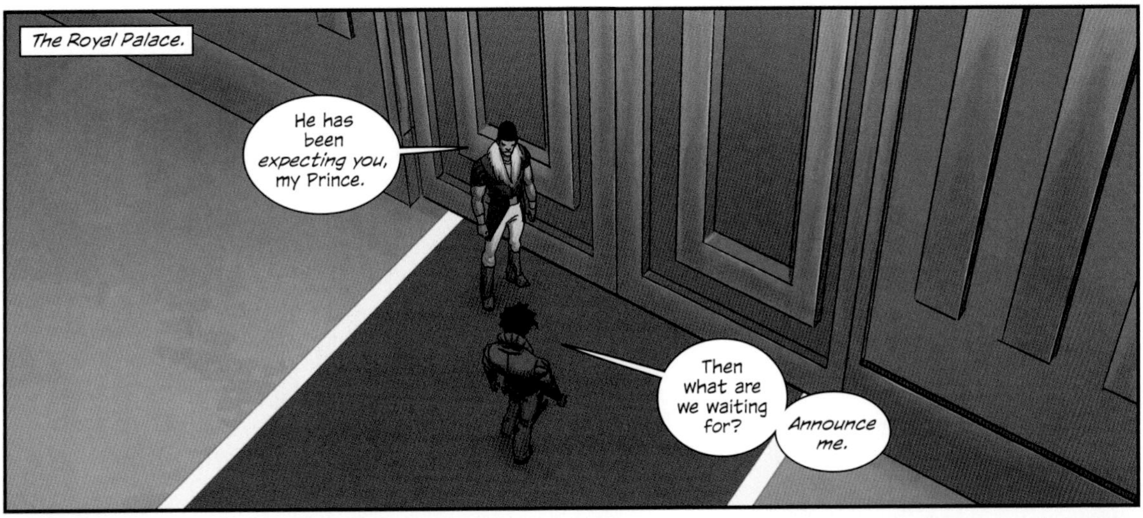
The Royal Palace.
He has been expecting you, my Prince.
Then what are we waiting for?
Announce me.

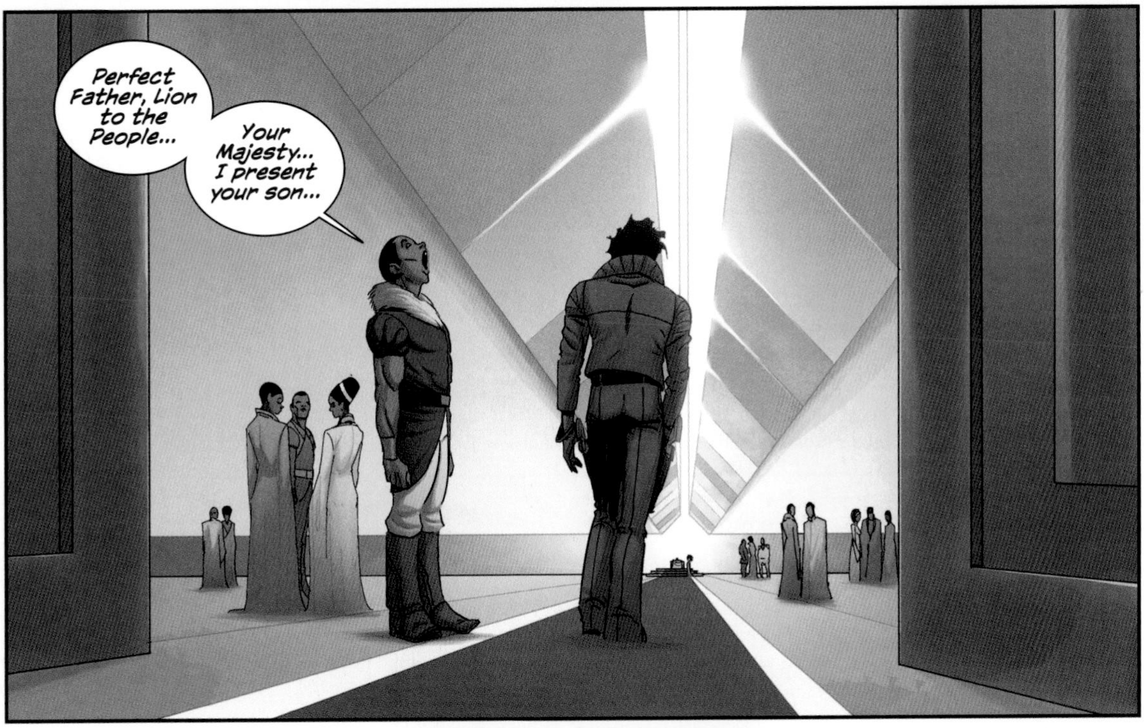
Perfect Father, Lion to the People...
Your Majesty... I present your son...

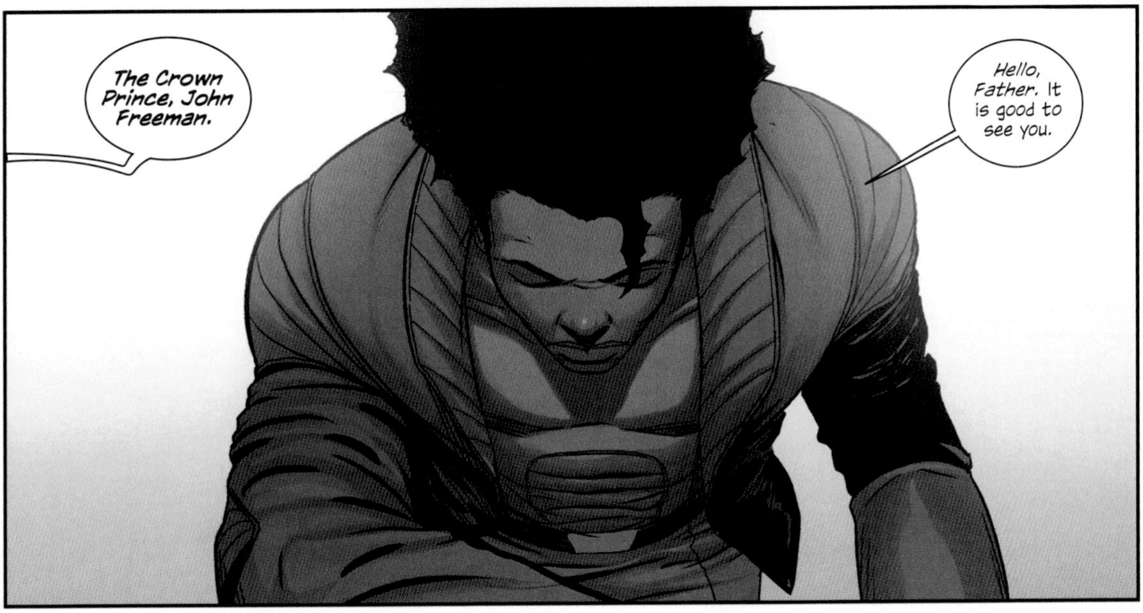
The Crown Prince, John Freeman.
Hello, Father. It is good to see you.

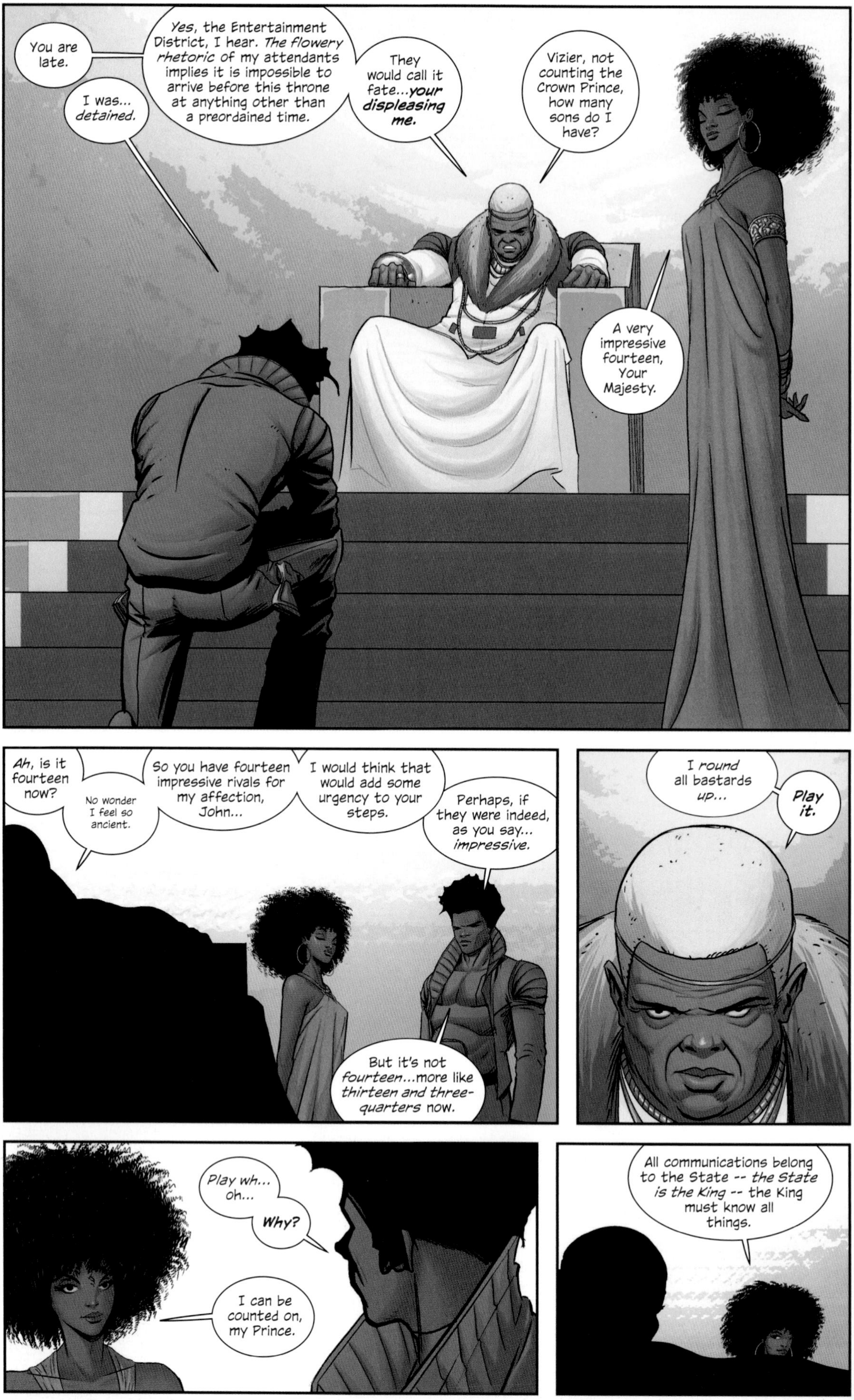

You are late.
Yes, the Entertainment District, I hear. *The flowery rhetoric* of my attendants implies it is impossible to arrive before this throne at anything other than a preordained time.
I was... *detained.*
They would call it fate...***your displeasing me.***
Vizier, not counting the Crown Prince, how many sons do I have?
A very impressive fourteen, Your Majesty.
Ah, is it fourteen now?
No wonder I feel so ancient.
So you have fourteen impressive rivals for my affection, John...
I would think that would add some urgency to your steps.
Perhaps, if they were indeed, as you say... *impressive.*
But it's not *fourteen*...more like *thirteen and three-quarters* now.
I *round* all bastards *up...*
Play it.
Play wh... oh...
Why?
I can be counted on, my Prince.
All communications belong to the State -- *the State is the King* -- the King must know all things.

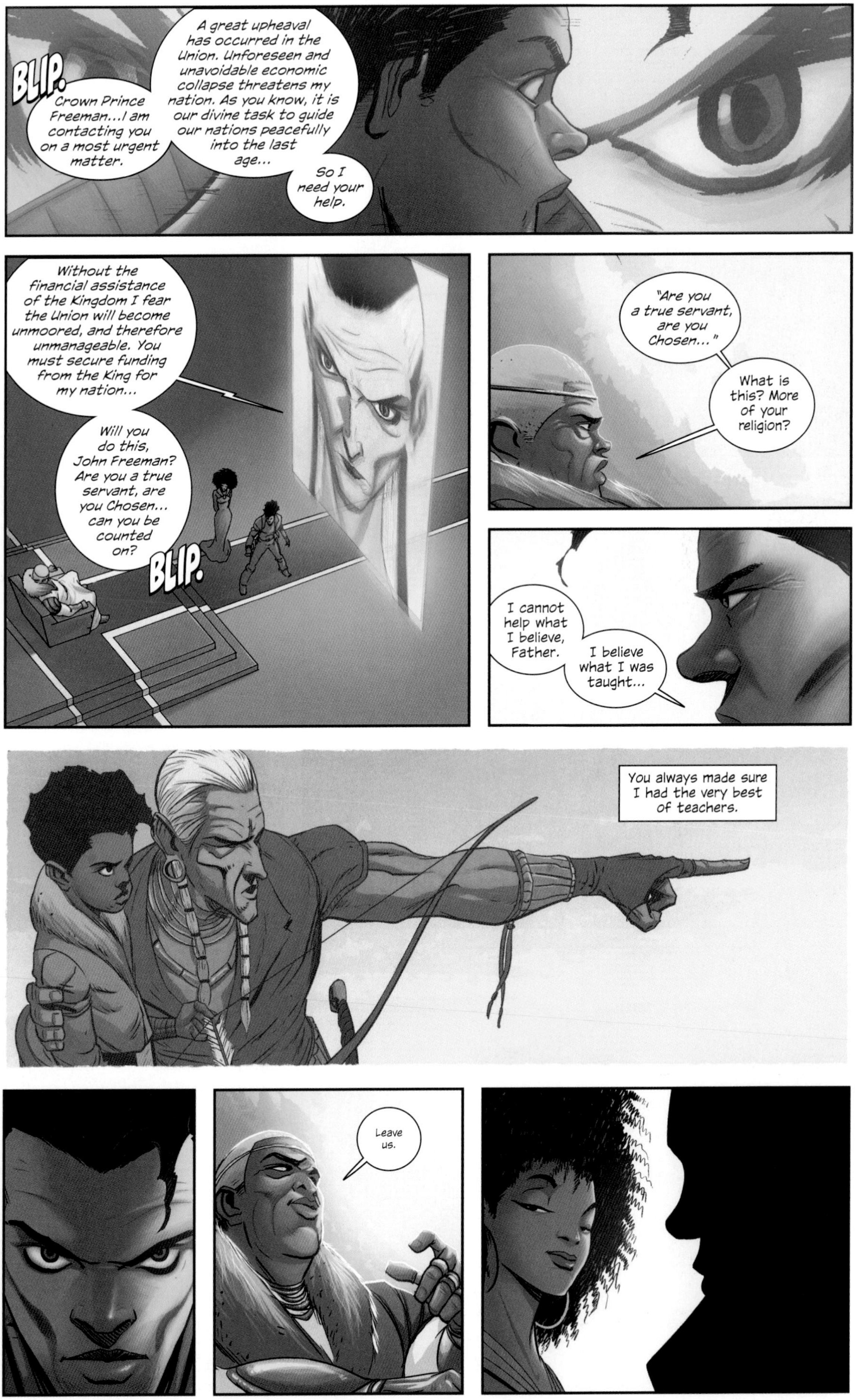
BLIP.
Crown Prince Freeman...I am contacting you on a most urgent matter.
A great upheaval has occurred in the Union. Unforeseen and unavoidable economic collapse threatens my nation. As you know, it is our divine task to guide our nations peacefully into the last age...
So I need your help.
Without the financial assistance of the Kingdom I fear the Union will become unmoored, and therefore unmanageable. You must secure funding from the King for my nation...
Will you do this, John Freeman? Are you a true servant, are you Chosen... can you be counted on?
BLIP.
"Are you a true servant, are you Chosen..."
What is this? More of your religion?
I cannot help what I believe, Father.
I believe what I was taught...
You always made sure I had the very best of teachers.
Leave us.

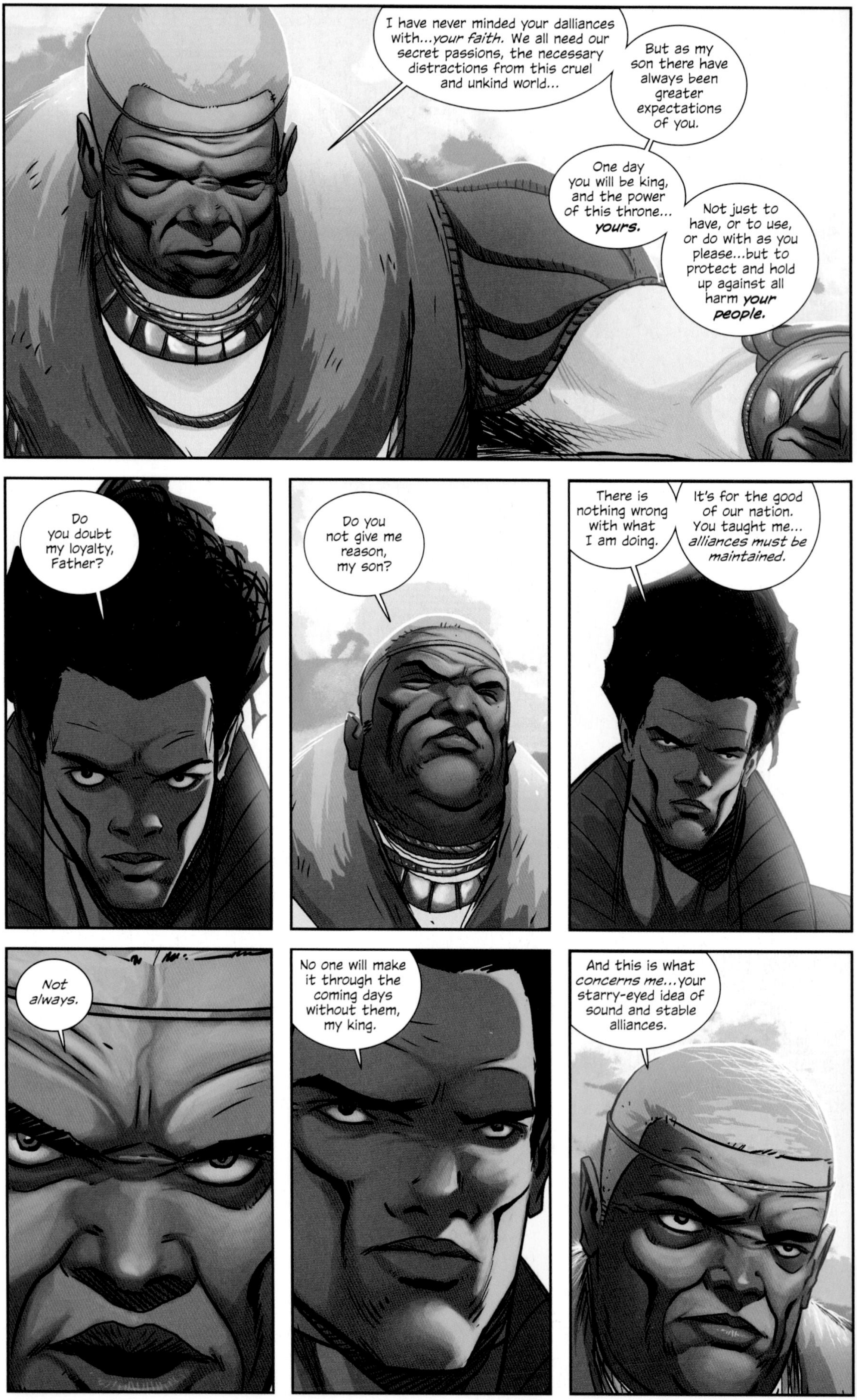
I have never minded your dalliances with...*your faith.* We all need our secret passions, the necessary distractions from this cruel and unkind world...
But as my son there have always been greater expectations of you.
One day you will be king, and the power of this throne... ***yours.***
Not just to have, or to use, or do with as you please...but to protect and hold up against all harm ***your people.***
Do you doubt my loyalty, Father?
Do you not give me reason, my son?
There is nothing wrong with what I am doing.
It's for the good of our nation. You taught me... *alliances must be maintained.*
Not always.
No one will make it through the coming days without them, my king.
And this is what *concerns me*...your starry-eyed idea of sound and stable alliances.

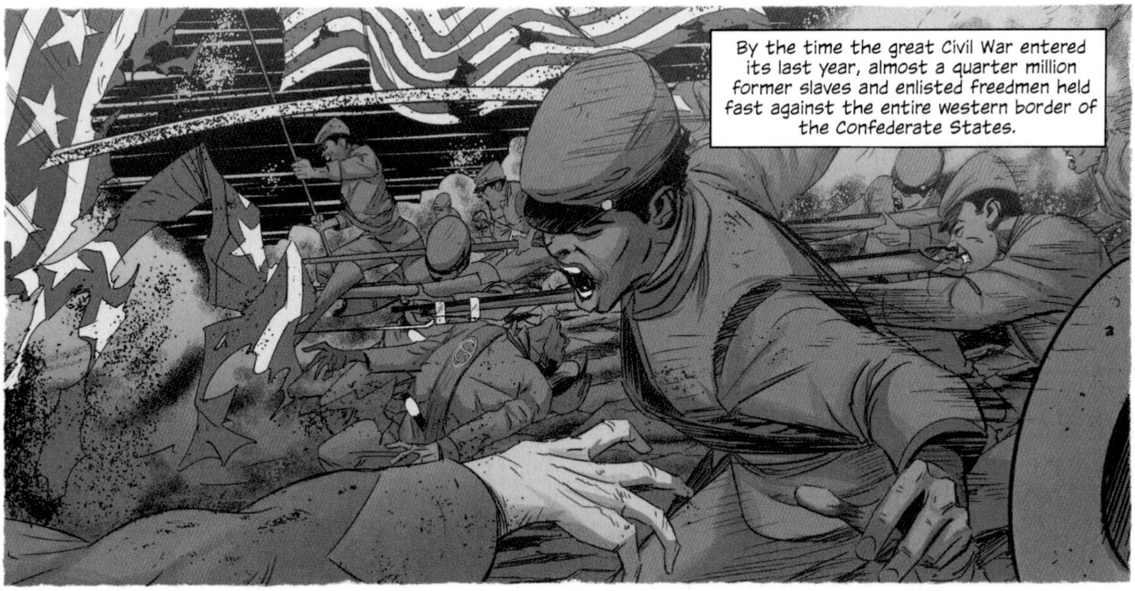
By the time the great Civil War entered its last year, almost a quarter million former slaves and enlisted freedmen held fast against the entire western border of the Confederate States.

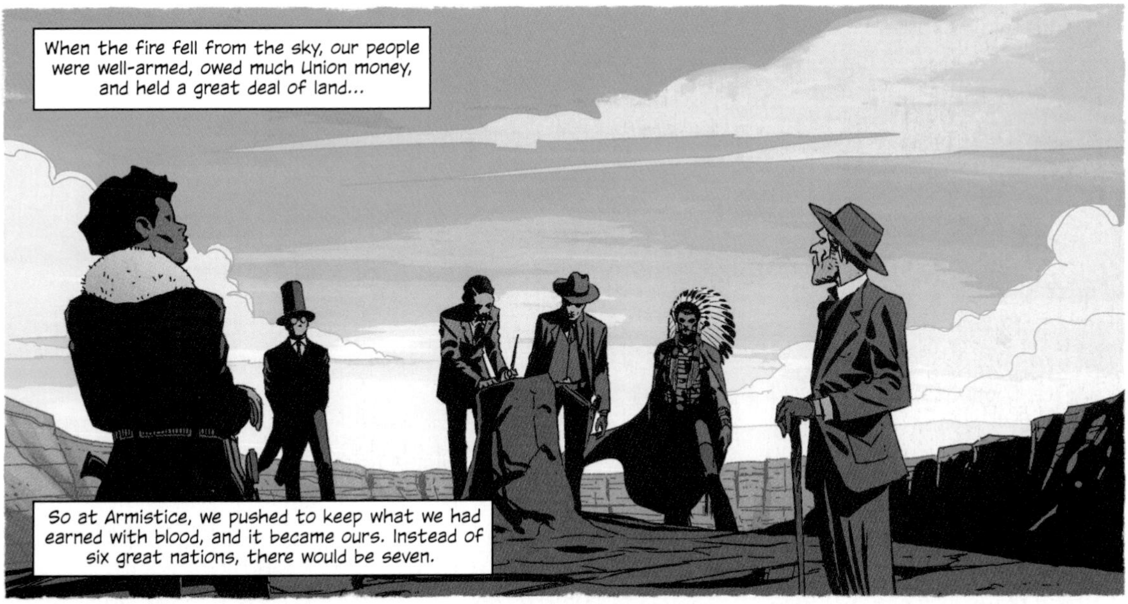
When the fire fell from the sky, our people were well-armed, owed much Union money, and held a great deal of land...
So at Armistice, we pushed to keep what we had earned with blood, and it became ours. Instead of six great nations, there would be seven.

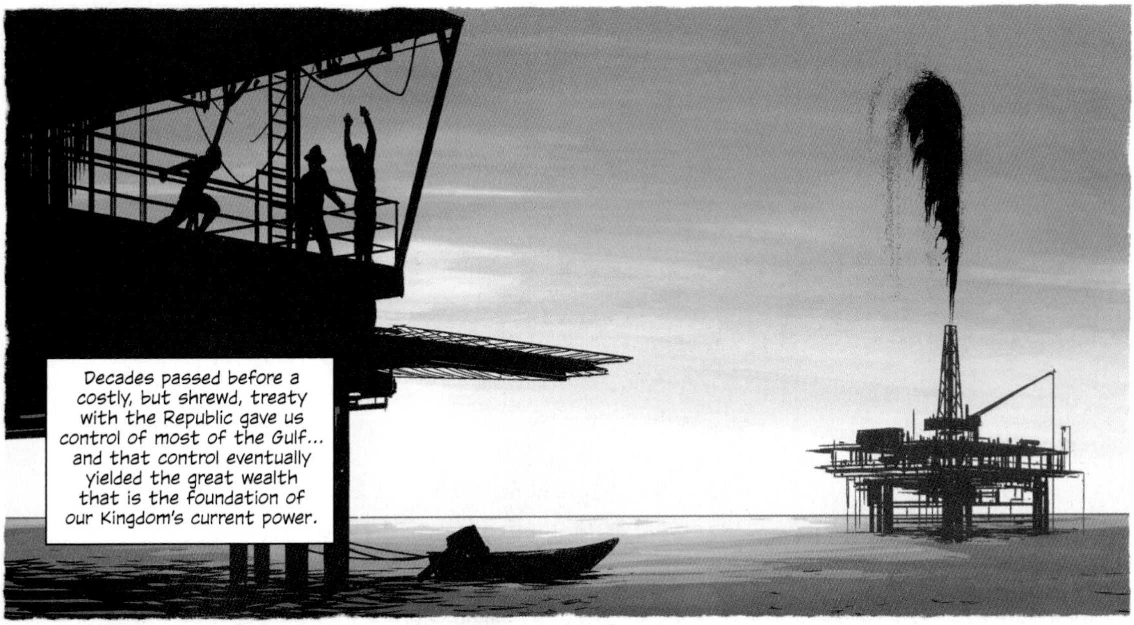
Decades passed before a costly, but shrewd, treaty with the Republic gave us control of most of the Gulf... and that control eventually yielded the great wealth that is the foundation of our Kingdom's current power.

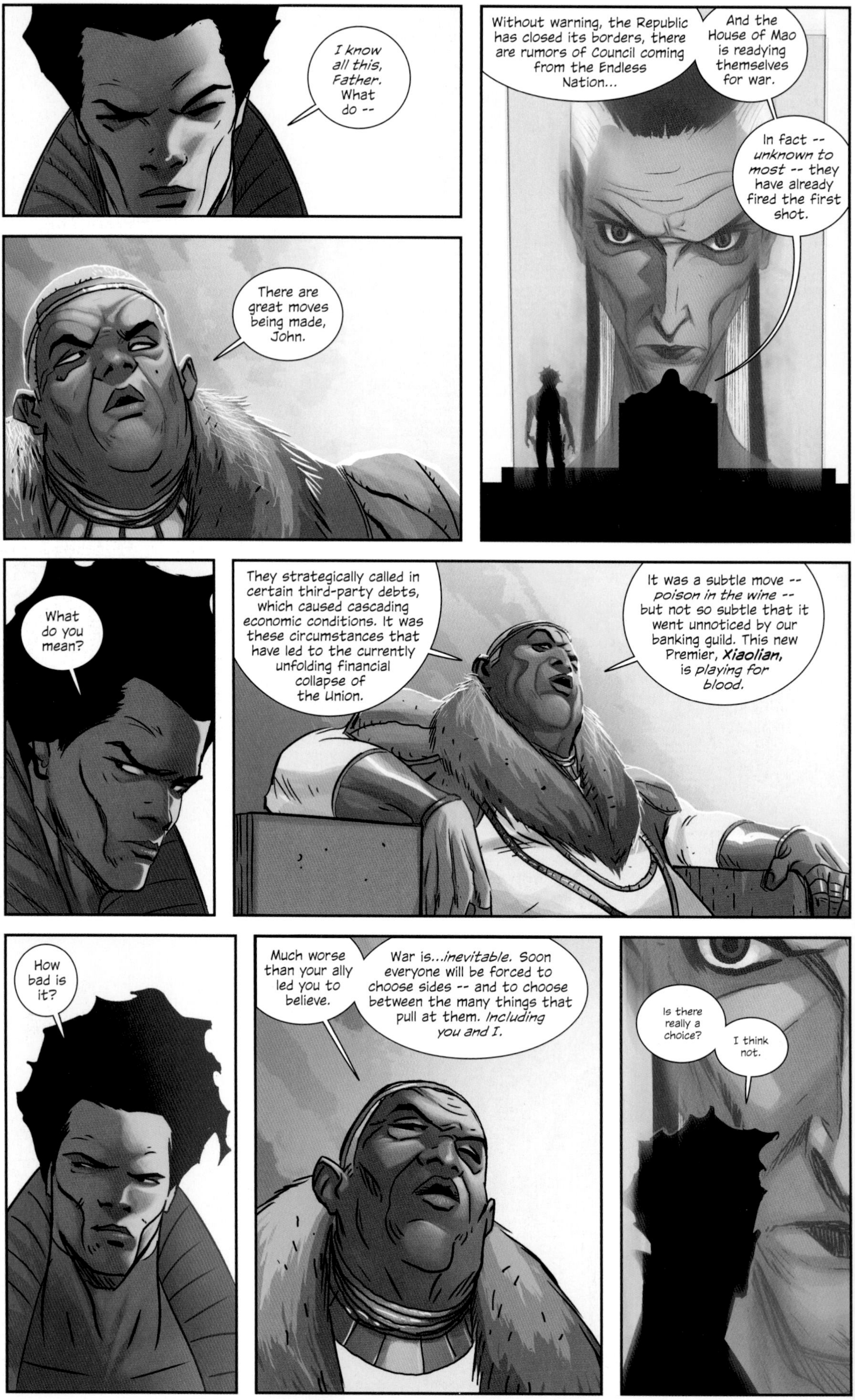

I know all this, Father. What do --
There are great moves being made, John.
Without warning, the Republic has closed its borders, there are rumors of Council coming from the Endless Nation...
And the House of Mao is readying themselves for war.
In fact -- unknown to most -- they have already fired the first shot.
What do you mean?
They strategically called in certain third-party debts, which caused cascading economic conditions. It was these circumstances that have led to the currently unfolding financial collapse of the Union.
It was a subtle move -- poison in the wine -- but not so subtle that it went unnoticed by our banking guild. This new Premier, Xiaolian, is playing for blood.
How bad is it?
Much worse than your ally led you to believe.
War is...inevitable. Soon everyone will be forced to choose sides -- and to choose between the many things that pull at them. Including you and I.
Is there really a choice?
I think not.

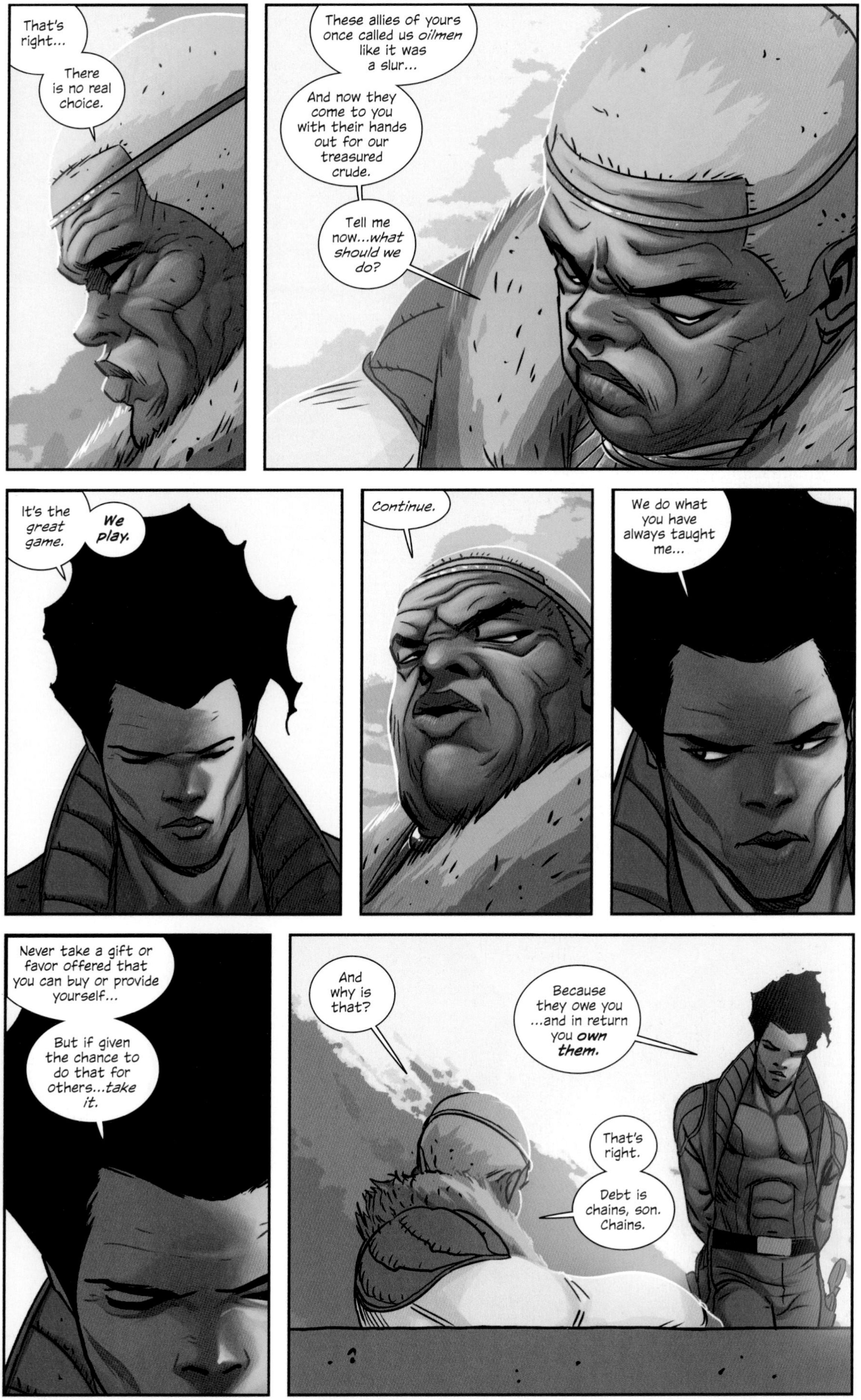
That's right...
There is no real choice.
These allies of yours once called us *oilmen* like it was a slur...
And now they come to you with their hands out for our treasured crude.
Tell me now...*what should we do?*
It's the *great game.*
We play.
Continue.
We do what you have always taught me...
Never take a gift or favor offered that you can buy or provide yourself...
But if given the chance to do that for others...*take it.*
And why is that?
Because they owe you ...and in return you ***own them.***
That's right.
Debt is chains, son. Chains.

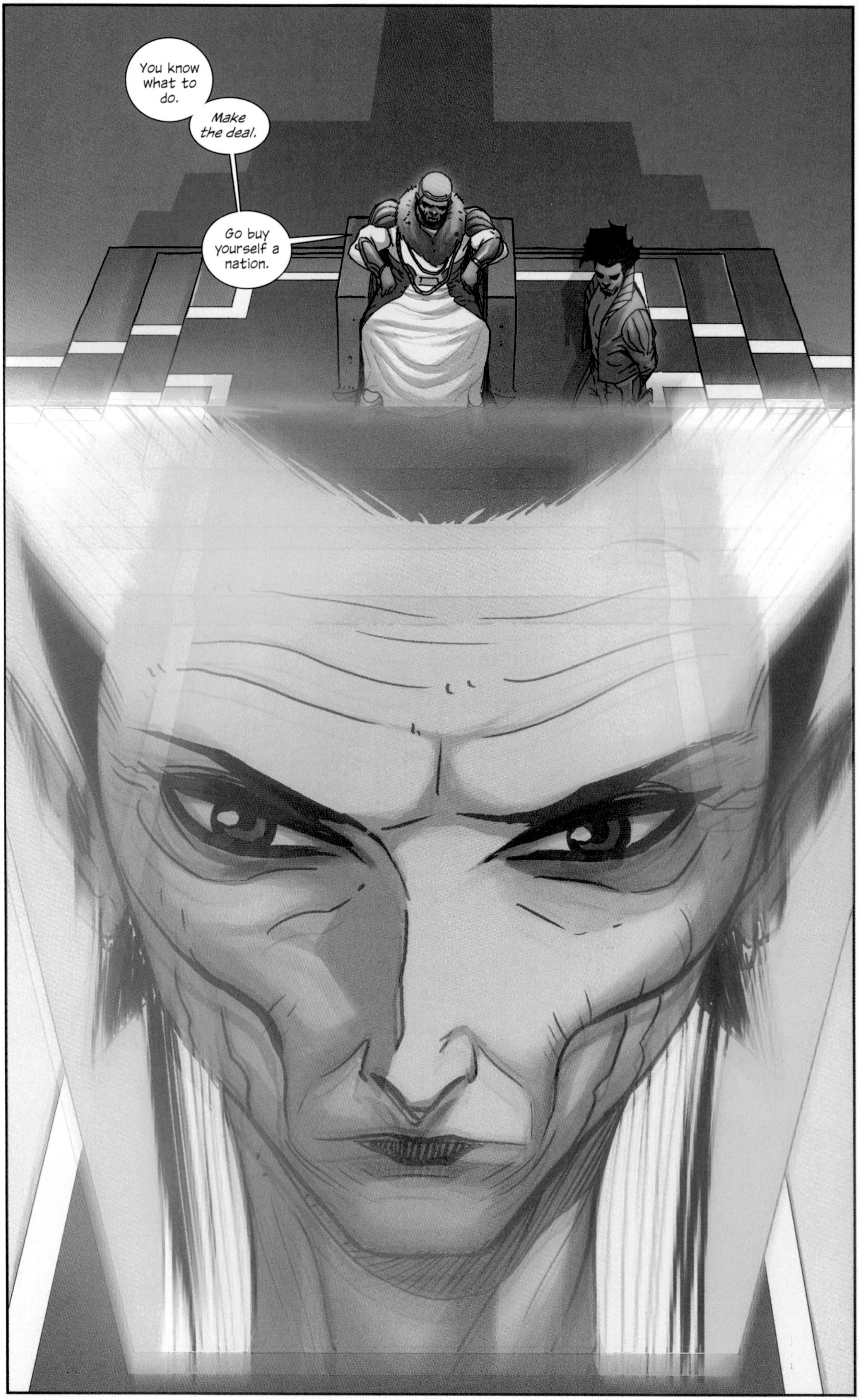
You know what to do.
Make the deal.
Go buy yourself a nation.

YOU SHOULD **FEAR** WHAT THE
FUTURE HOLDS.

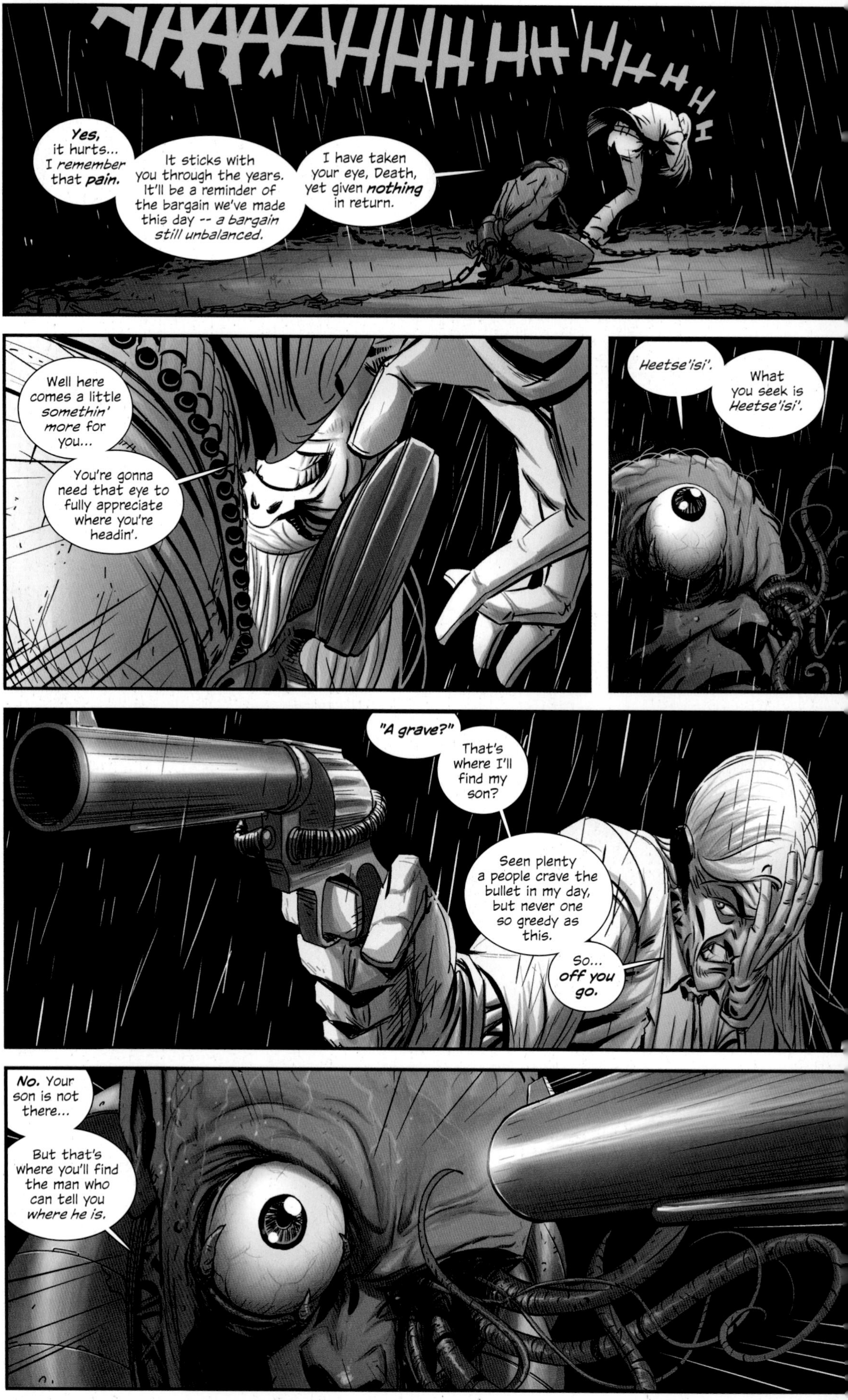
AHHHHHHHHHHHHHHHHH
Yes, it hurts... I remember that pain.
It sticks with you through the years. It'll be a reminder of the bargain we've made this day -- a bargain still unbalanced.
I have taken your eye, Death, yet given nothing in return.
Well here comes a little somethin' more for you...
You're gonna need that eye to fully appreciate where you're headin'.
Heetse'isi'.
What you seek is Heetse'isi'.
"A grave?"
That's where I'll find my son?
Seen plenty a people crave the bullet in my day, but never one so greedy as this.
So... off you go.
No. Your son is not there...
But that's where you'll find the man who can tell you where he is.

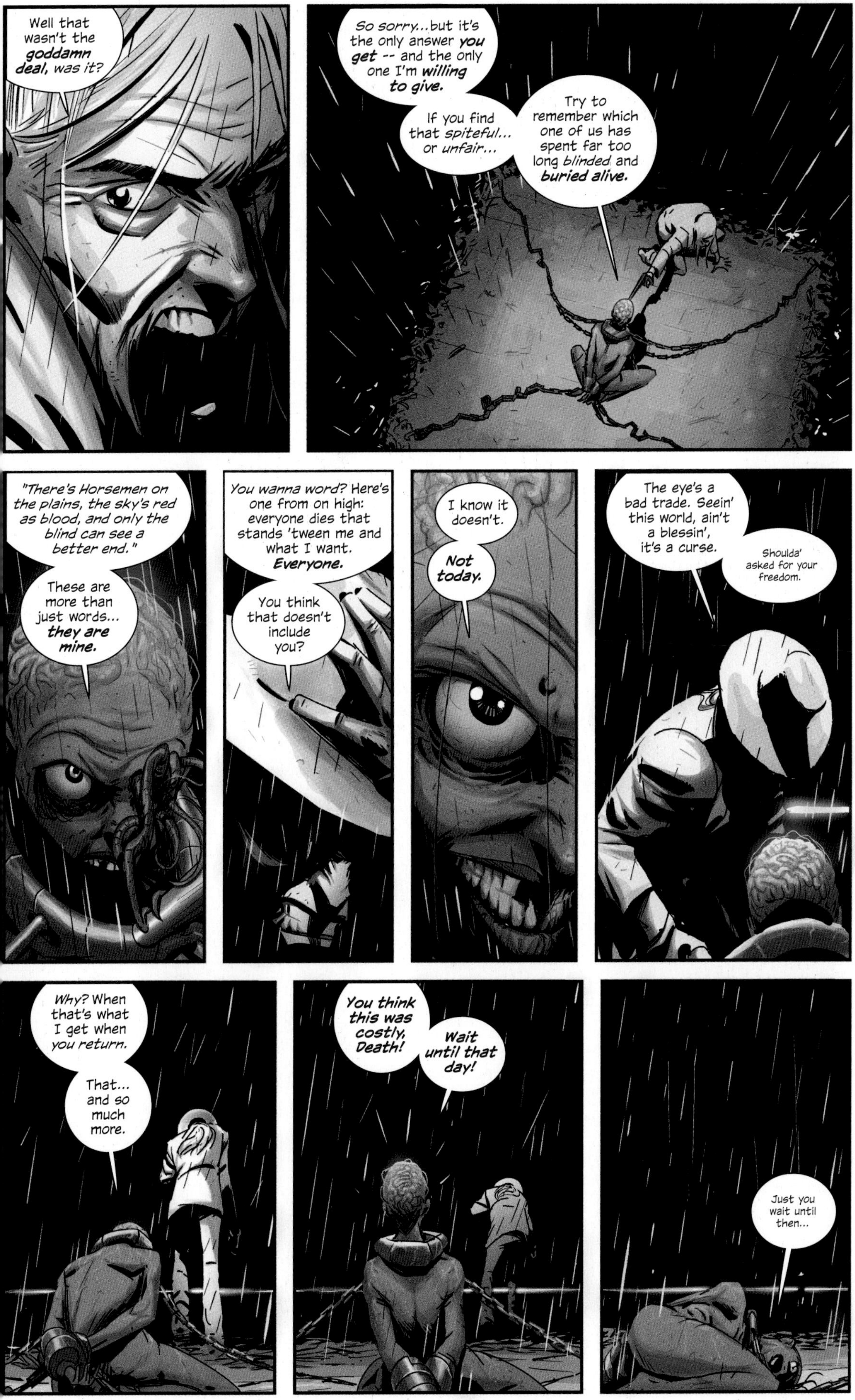
Well that wasn't the goddamn deal, was it?
So sorry...but it's the only answer you get -- and the only one I'm willing to give.
If you find that spiteful... or unfair...
Try to remember which one of us has spent far too long blinded and buried alive.
"There's Horsemen on the plains, the sky's red as blood, and only the blind can see a better end."
These are more than just words... they are mine.
You wanna word? Here's one from on high: everyone dies that stands 'tween me and what I want. Everyone.
You think that doesn't include you?
I know it doesn't.
Not today.
The eye's a bad trade. Seein' this world, ain't a blessin', it's a curse.
Shoulda' asked for your freedom.
Why? When that's what I get when you return.
That... and so much more.
You think this was costly, Death!
Wait until that day!
Just you wait until then...

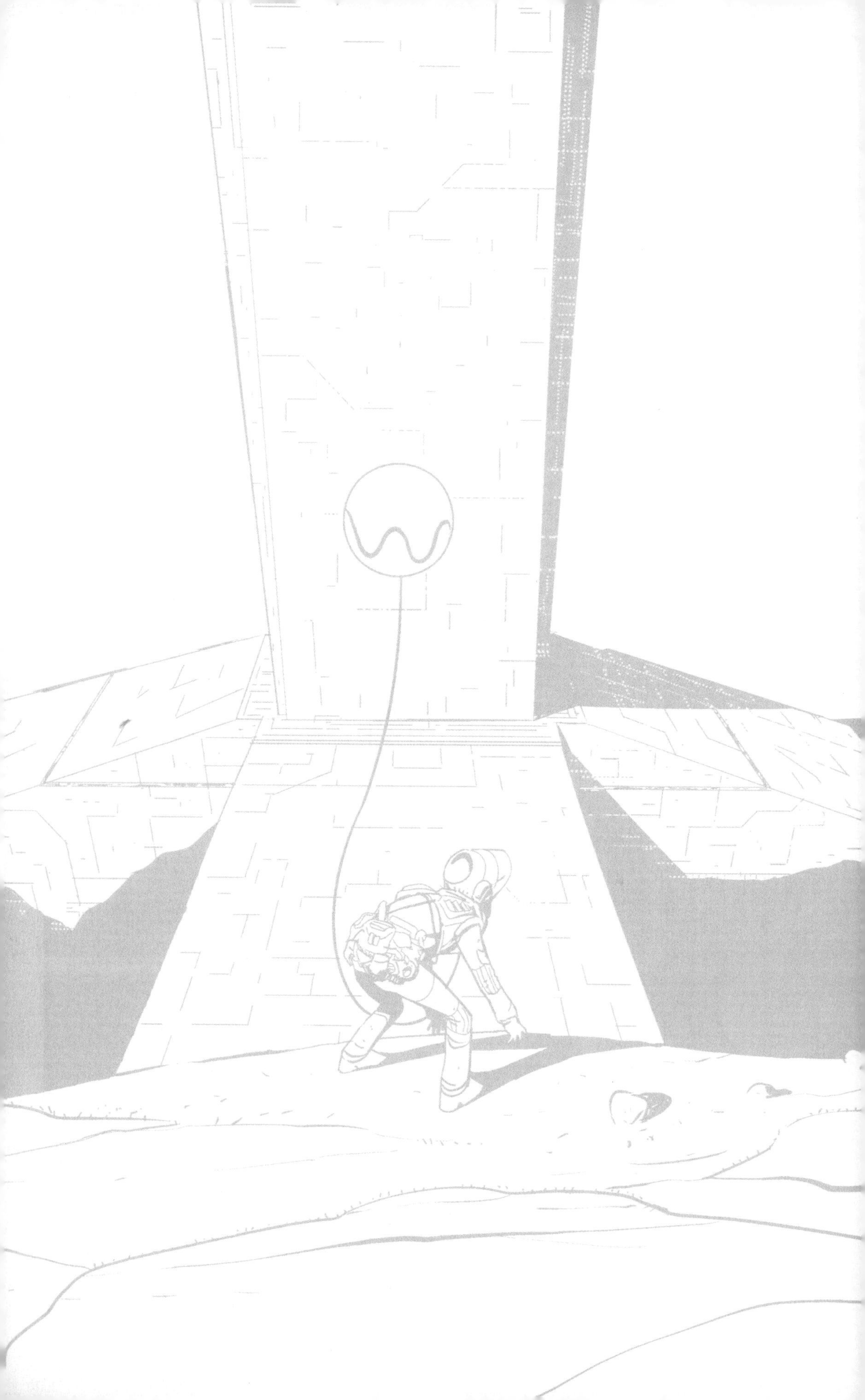

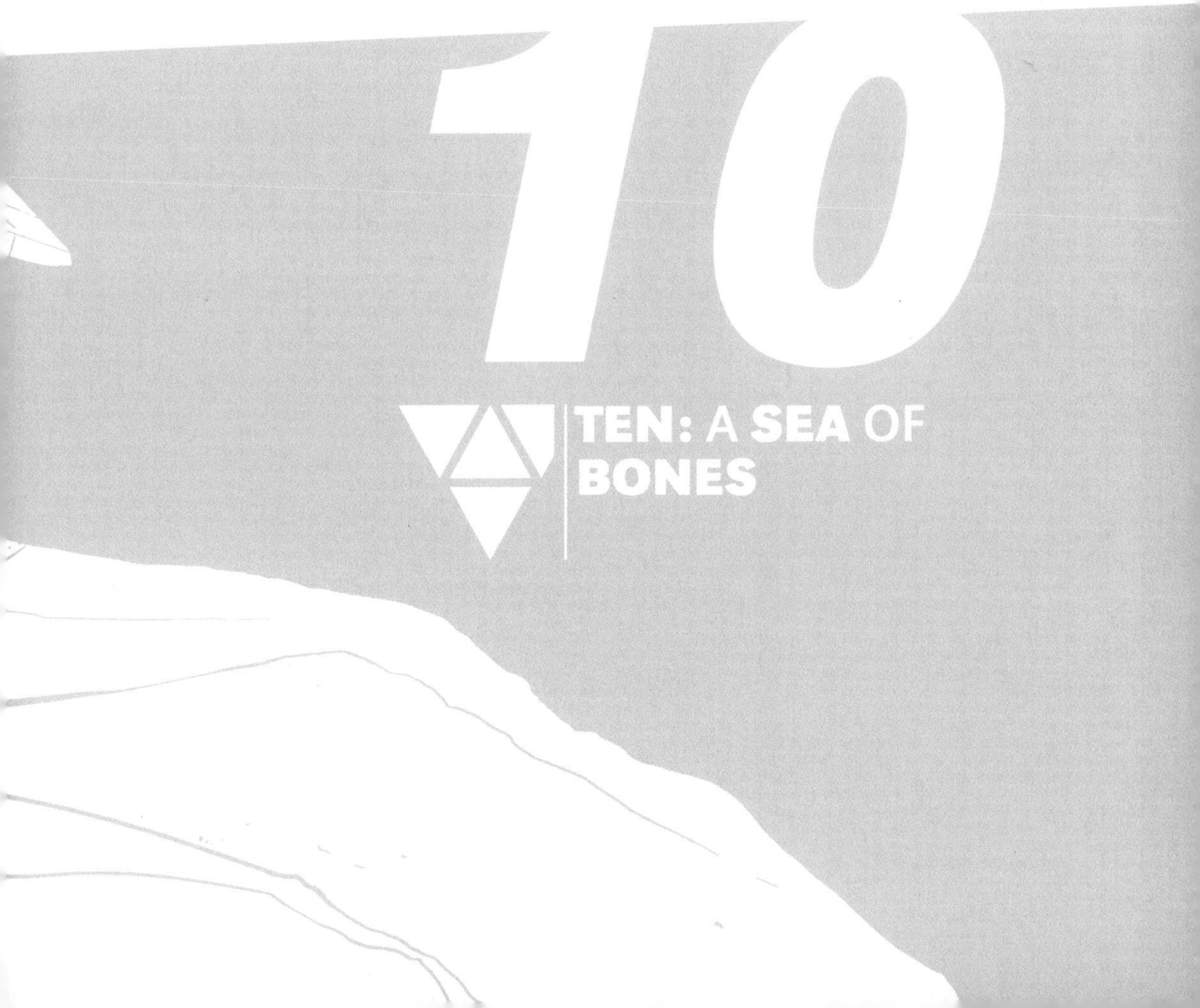

10

TEN: A SEA OF BONES

THEY LIFT THEMSELVES UP AS
YOUR **BETTERS.**

TAKE **JOY** IN WATCHING THEM
FALL.

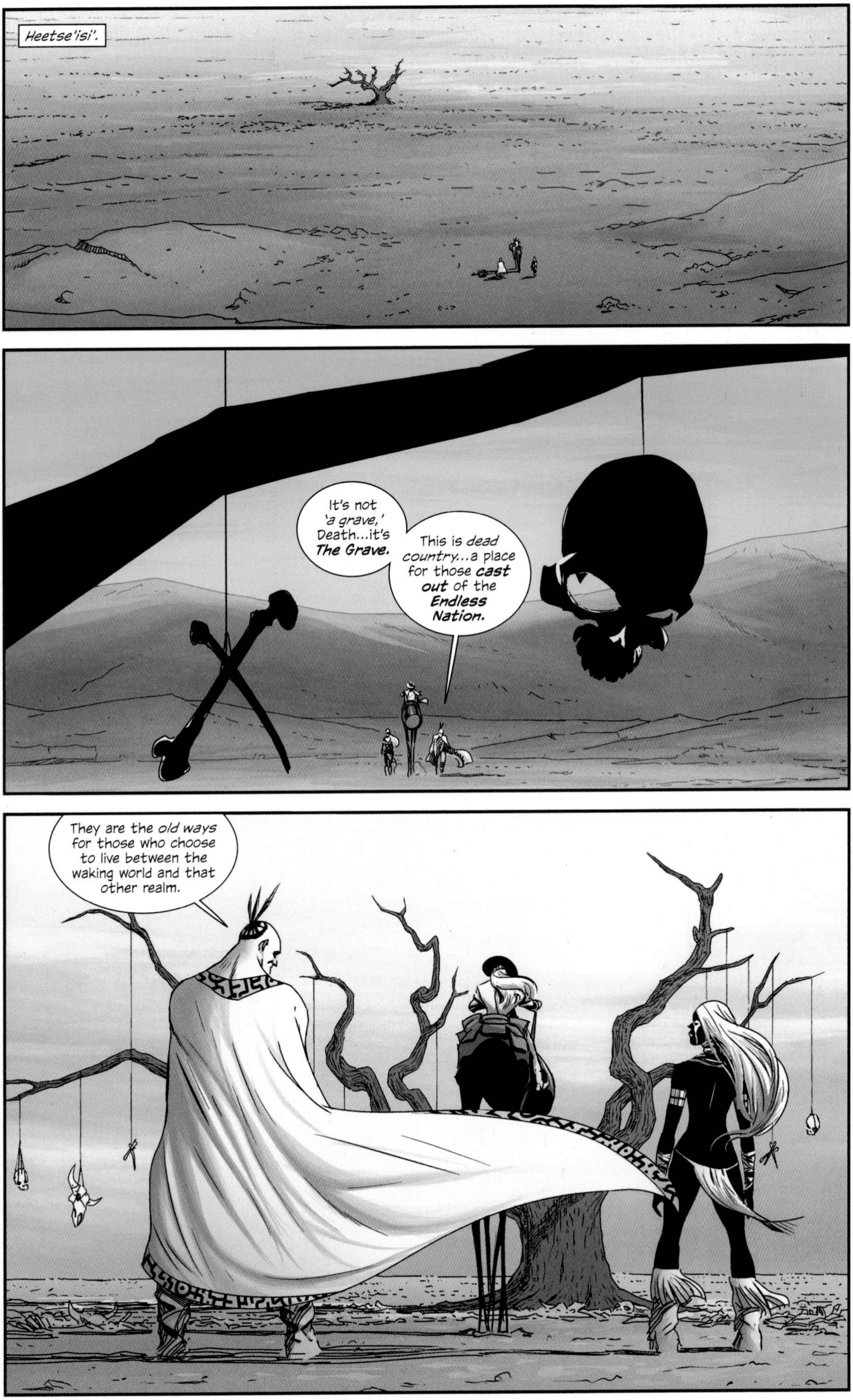
Heetse'isi'.
It's not 'a grave,' Death...it's The Grave.
This is dead country...a place for those cast out of the Endless Nation.
They are the old ways for those who choose to live between the waking world and that other realm.

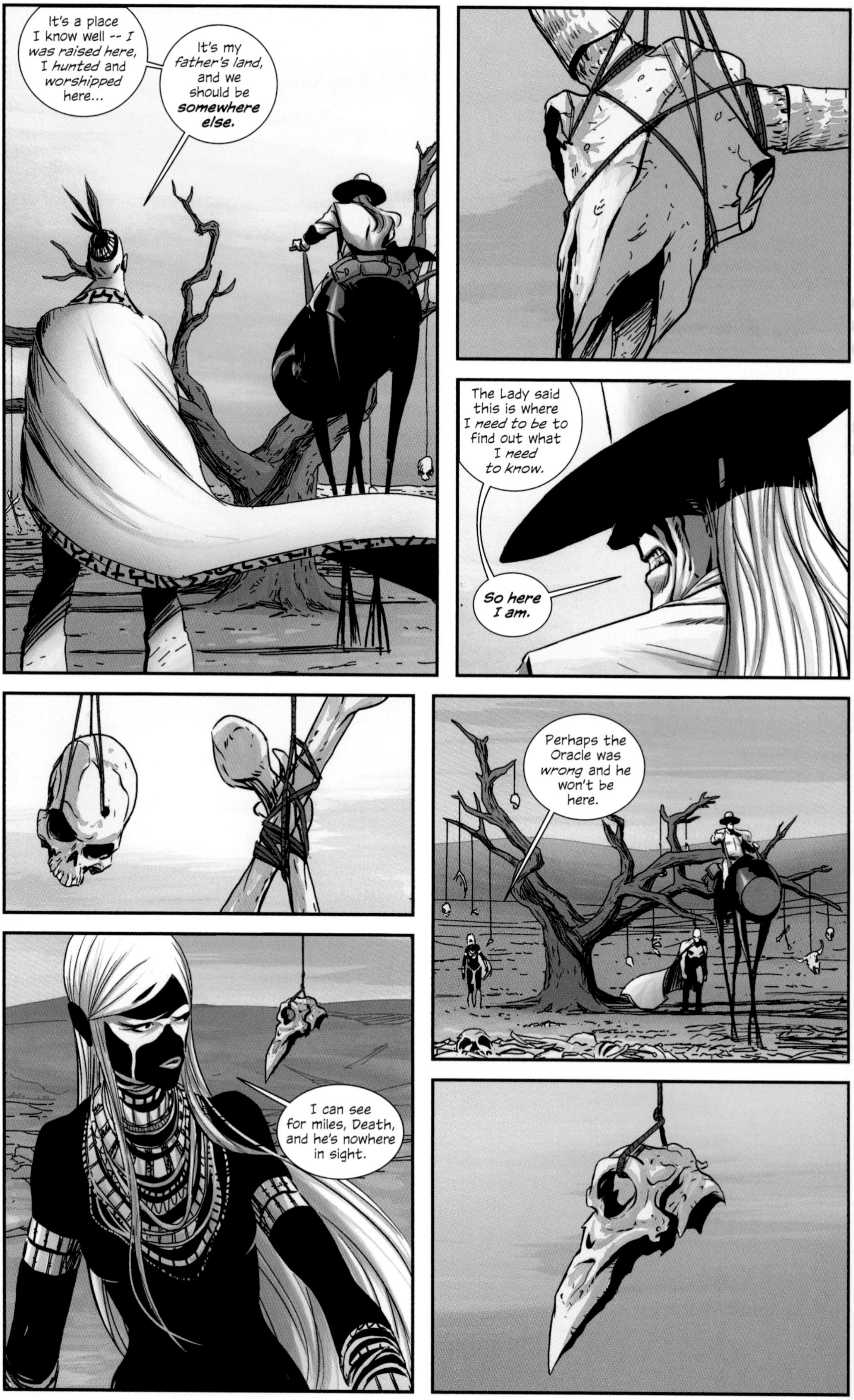
It's a place I know well -- *I was raised here,* I *hunted* and *worshipped* here...
It's my *father's land,* and we should be ***somewhere else.***
The Lady said this is where I *need to be* to find out what I *need to know.*
So here I am.
Perhaps the Oracle was *wrong* and he won't be here.
I can see for miles, Death, and he's nowhere in sight.

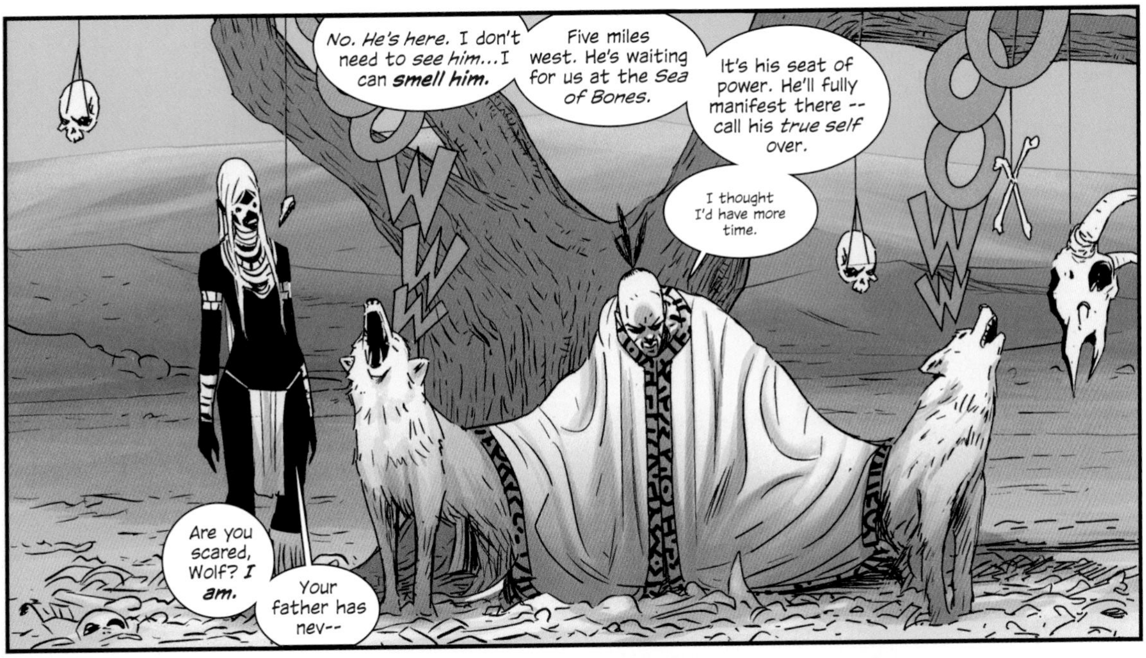
No. *He's here.* I don't need to see *him*...I can ***smell him.***
Five miles west. He's waiting for us at the *Sea of Bones.*
It's his seat of power. He'll fully manifest there -- call his *true self* over.
I thought I'd have more time.
Are you scared, Wolf? ***I am.***
Your father has nev--

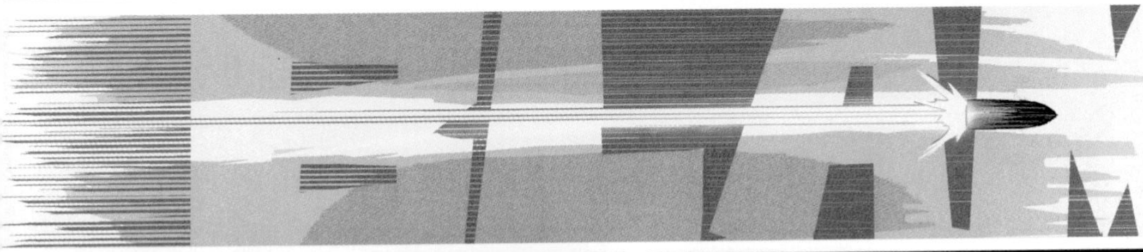

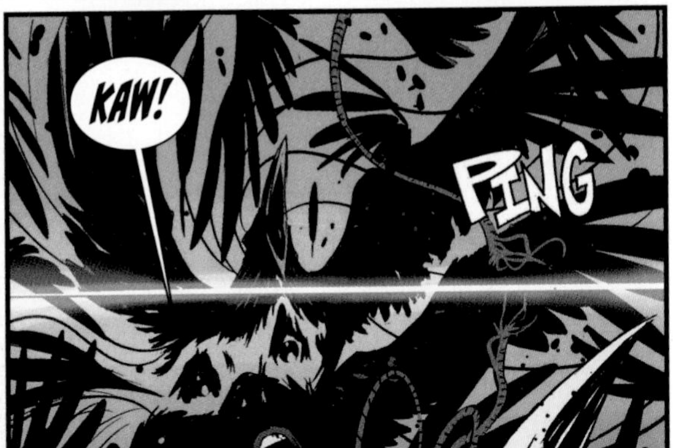
KAW!
PING

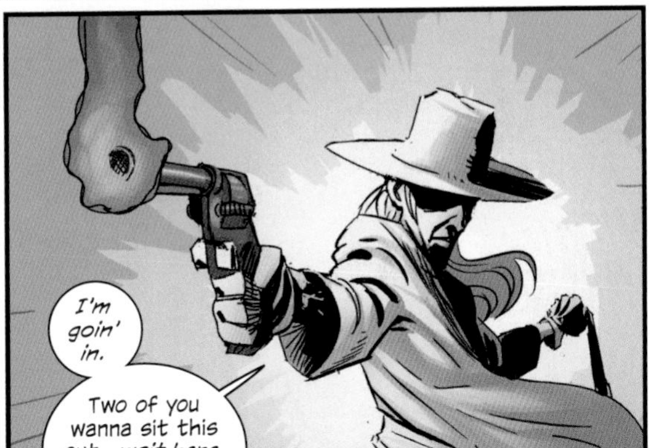
I'm goin' in.
Two of you wanna sit this out...*wait here*, and I'll be back *shortly*.

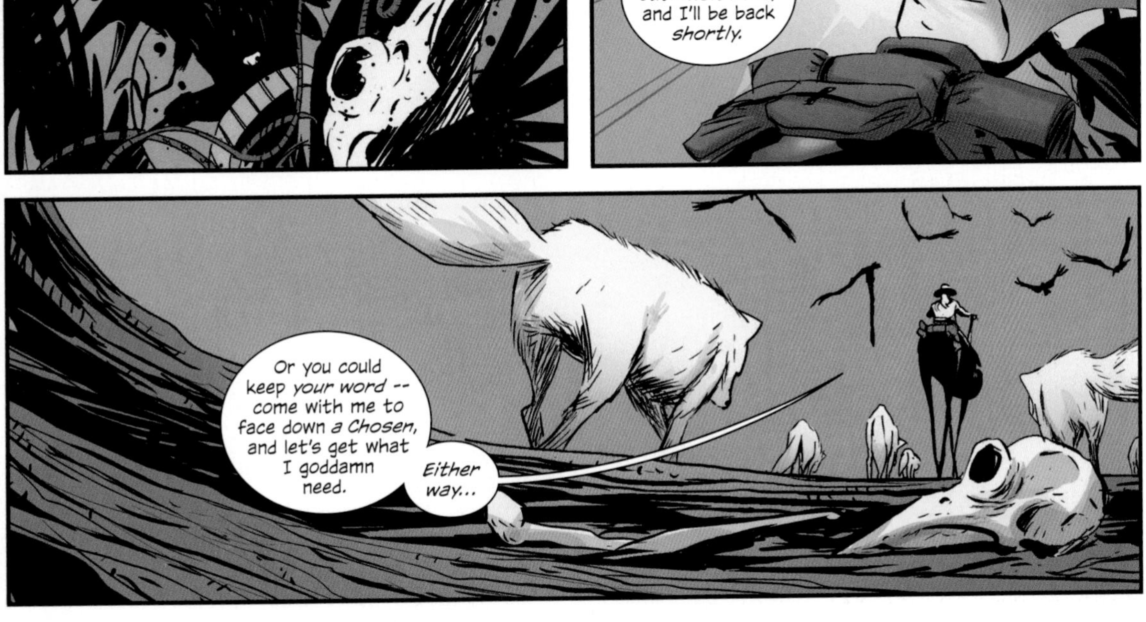
Or you could keep *your word* -- come with me to face down a *Chosen*, and let's get what I goddamn need.
Either way...

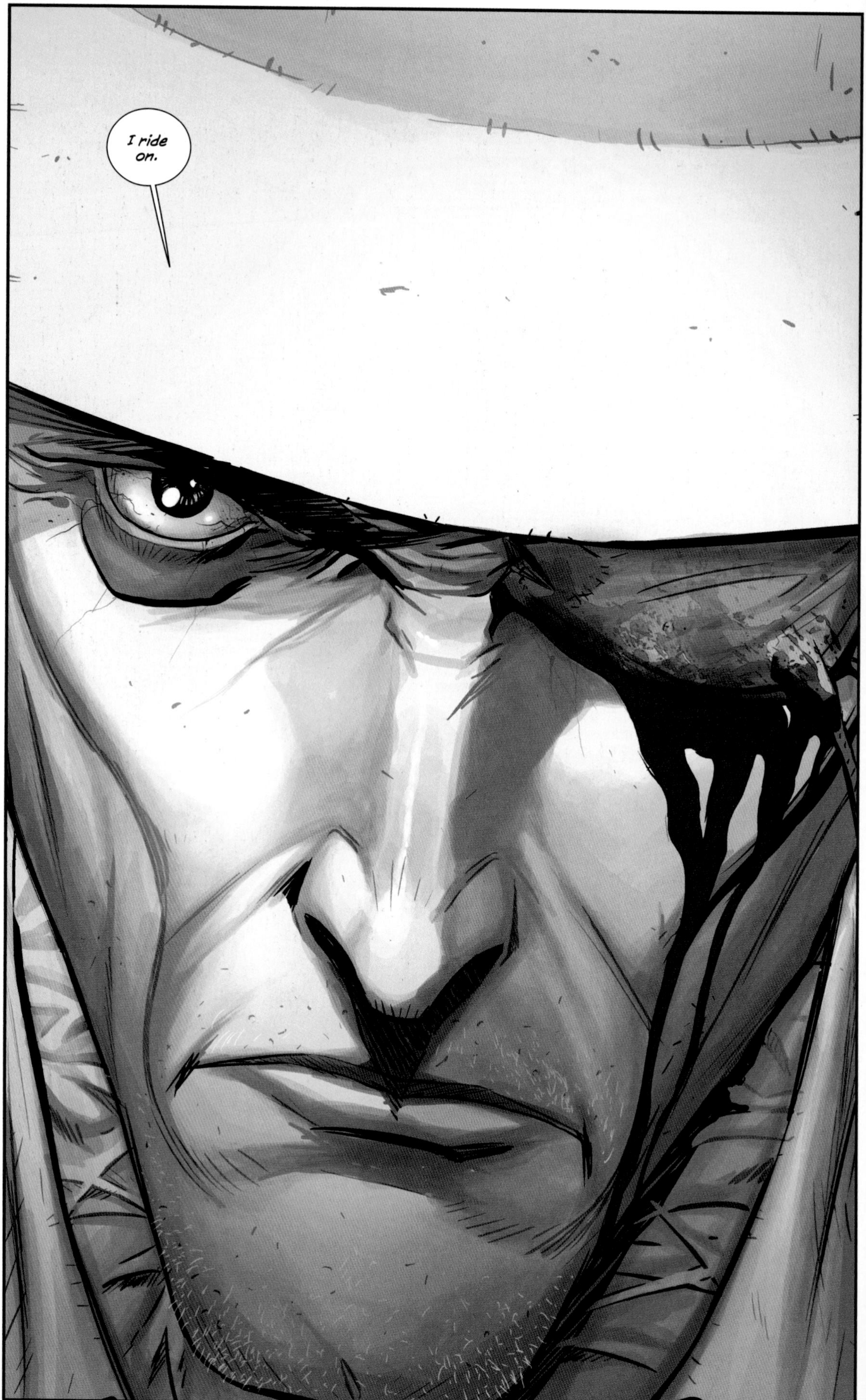
I ride on.

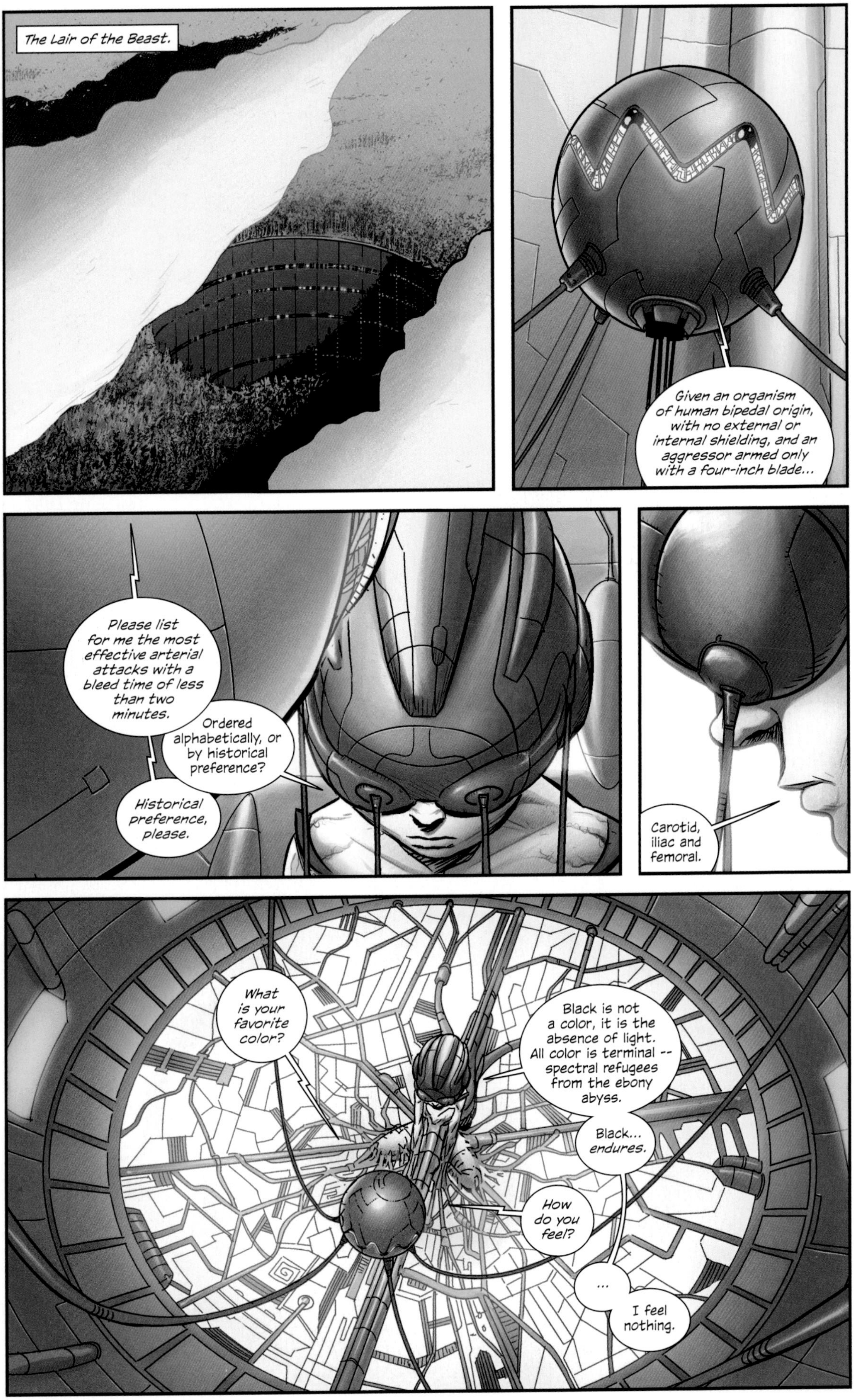
The Lair of the Beast.
Given an organism of human bipedal origin, with no external or internal shielding, and an aggressor armed only with a four-inch blade...
Please list for me the most effective arterial attacks with a bleed time of less than two minutes.
Ordered alphabetically, or by historical preference?
Historical preference, please.
Carotid, iliac and femoral.
What is your favorite color?
Black is not a color, it is the absence of light. All color is terminal -- spectral refugees from the ebony abyss.
Black... endures.
How do you feel?
...
I feel nothing.

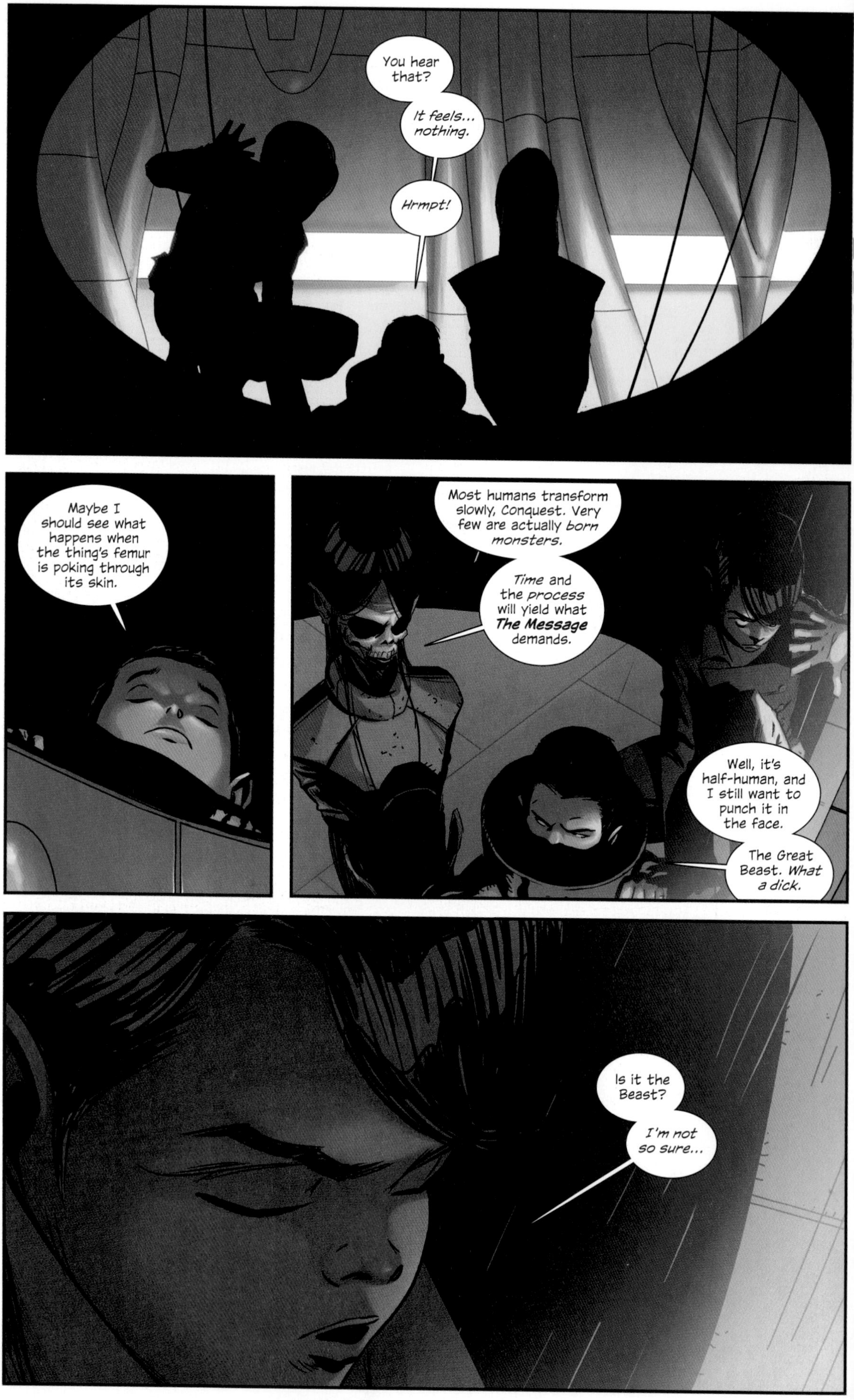

You hear that?
It feels... nothing.
Hrmpt!
Maybe I should see what happens when the thing's femur is poking through its skin.
Most humans transform slowly, Conquest. Very few are actually born monsters.
Time and the process will yield what The Message demands.
Well, it's half-human, and I still want to punch it in the face.
The Great Beast. What a dick.
Is it the Beast?
I'm not so sure...

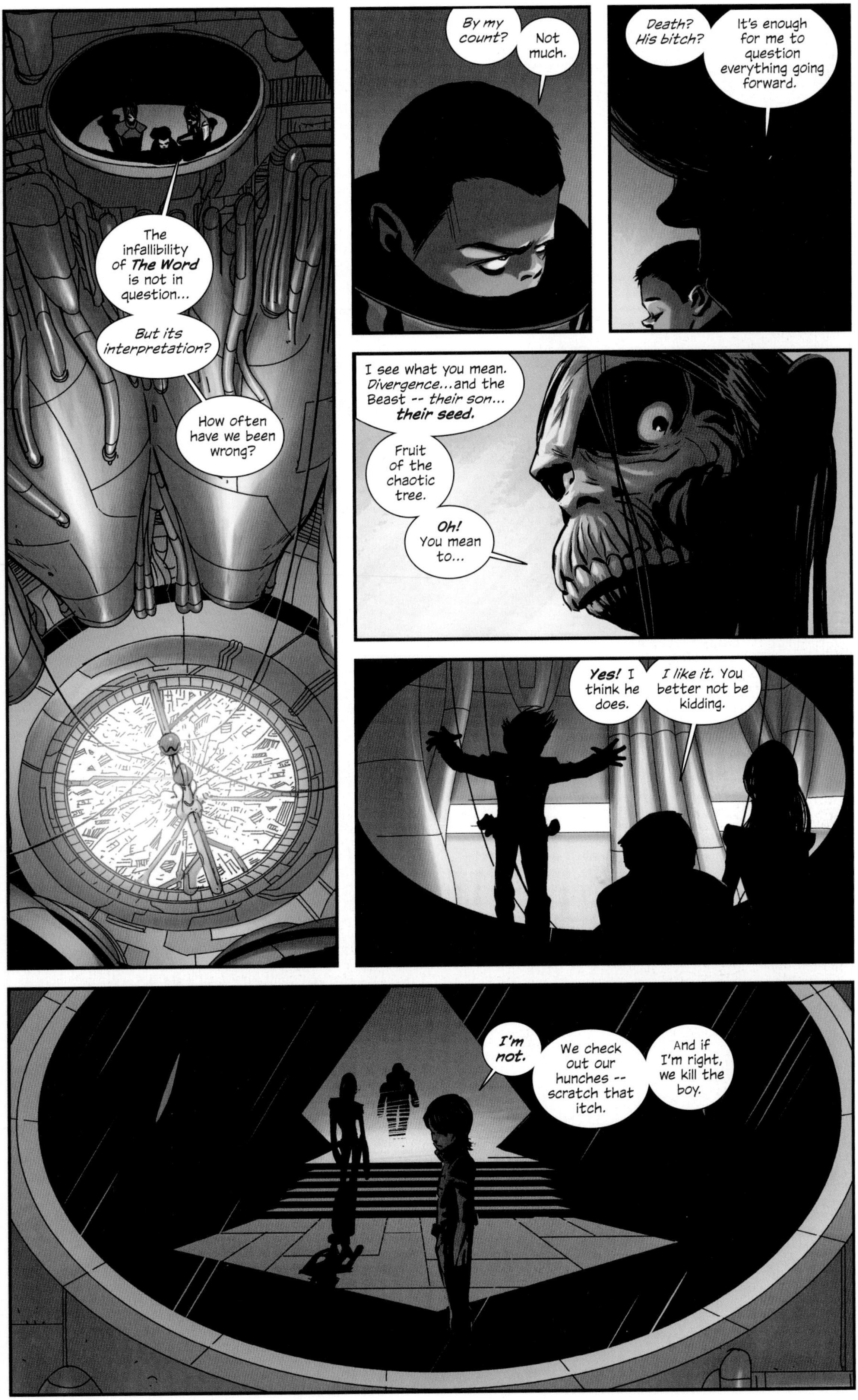
The infallibility of The Word is not in question...
But its interpretation?
How often have we been wrong?
By my count?
Not much.
Death? His bitch?
It's enough for me to question everything going forward.
I see what you mean. Divergence...and the Beast -- their son... their seed.
Fruit of the chaotic tree.
Oh! You mean to...
Yes! I think he does.
I like it. You better not be kidding.
I'm not.
We check out our hunches -- scratch that itch.
And if I'm right, we kill the boy.

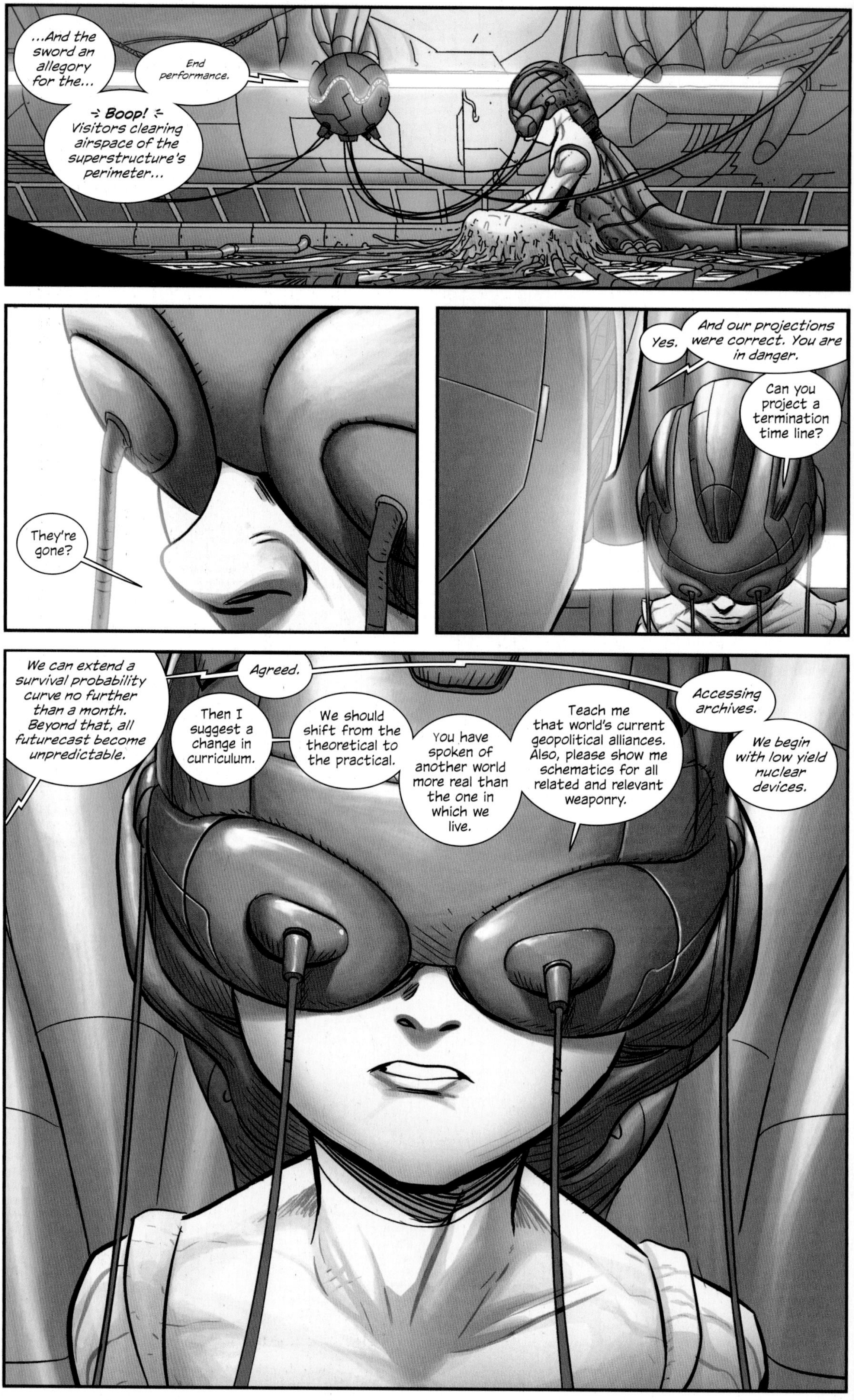
...And the sword an allegory for the...
End performance.
Boop! Visitors clearing airspace of the superstructure's perimeter...
They're gone?
Yes.
And our projections were correct. You are in danger.
Can you project a termination time line?
We can extend a survival probability curve no further than a month. Beyond that, all futurecast become unpredictable.
Agreed.
Then I suggest a change in curriculum.
We should shift from the theoretical to the practical.
You have spoken of another world more real than the one in which we live.
Teach me that world's current geopolitical alliances. Also, please show me schematics for all related and relevant weaponry.
Accessing archives.
We begin with low yield nuclear devices.

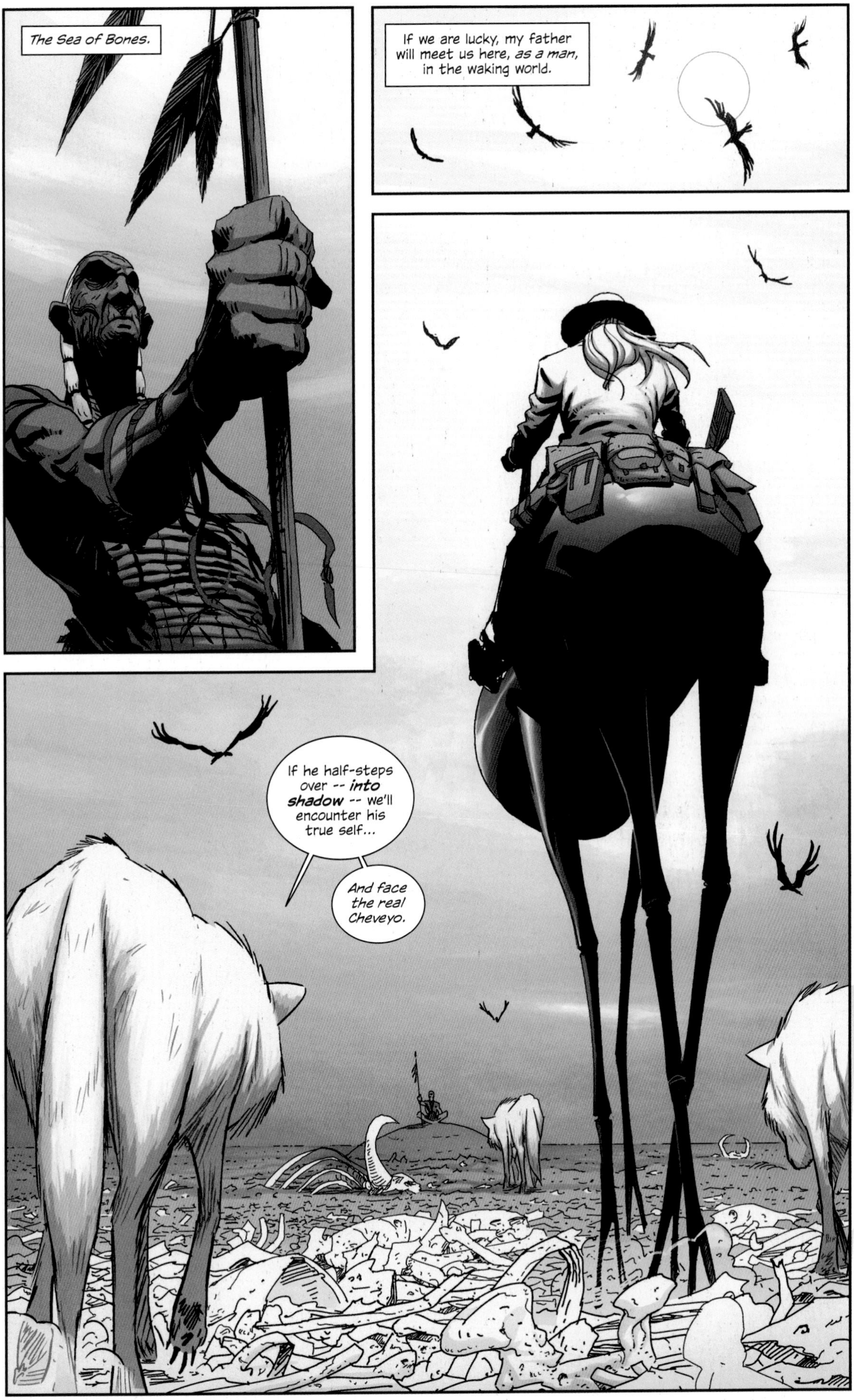
The Sea of Bones.
If we are lucky, my father will meet us here, *as a man*, in the waking world.
If he half-steps over -- ***into shadow*** -- we'll encounter his true self...
And face the real Cheveyo.

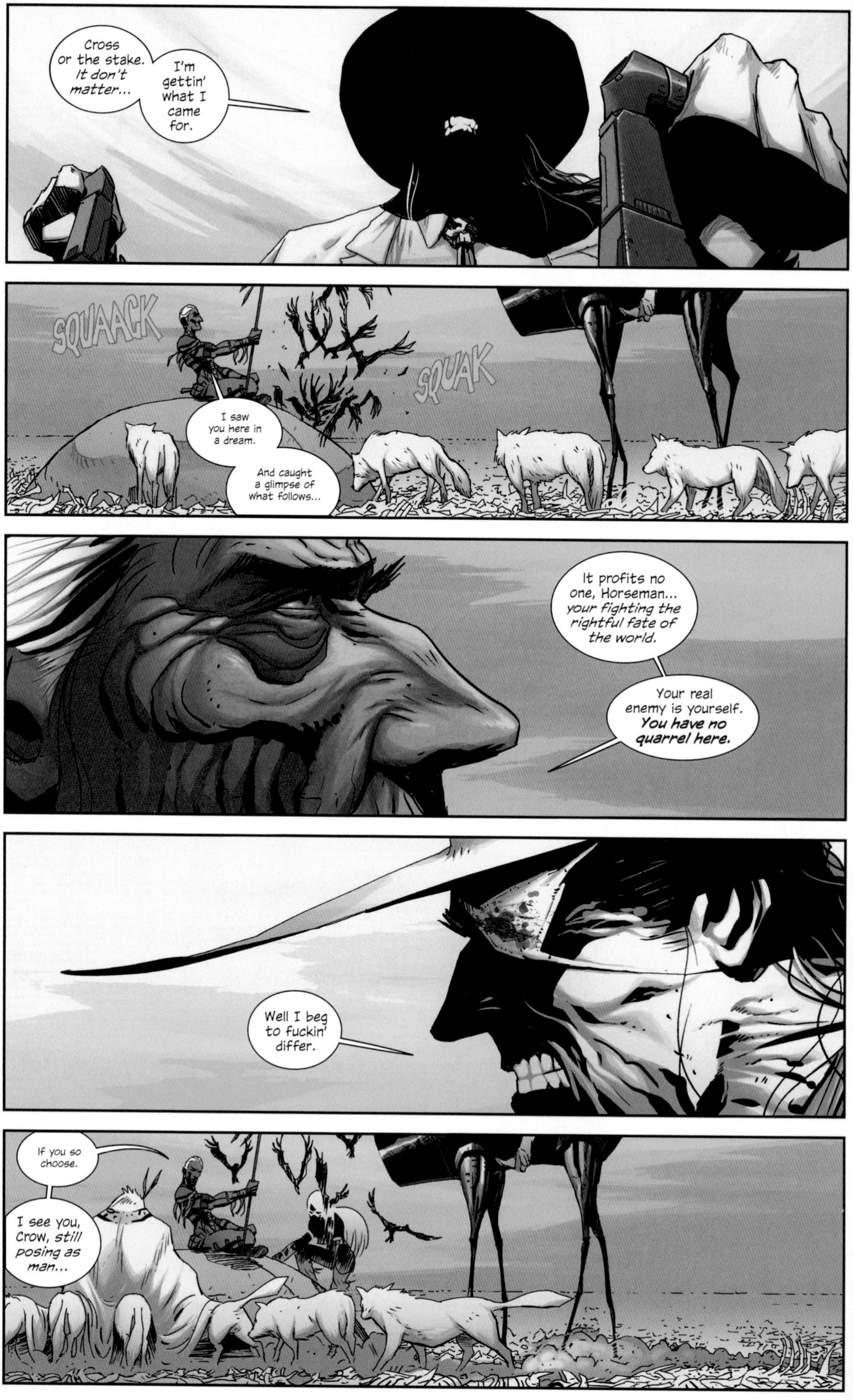
Cross or the stake. It don't matter...
I'm gettin' what I came for.
SQUAACK
SQUAK
I saw you here in a dream.
And caught a glimpse of what follows...
It profits no one, Horseman... your fighting the rightful fate of the world.
Your real enemy is yourself. You have no quarrel here.
Well I beg to fuckin' differ.
If you so choose.
I see you, Crow, still posing as man...

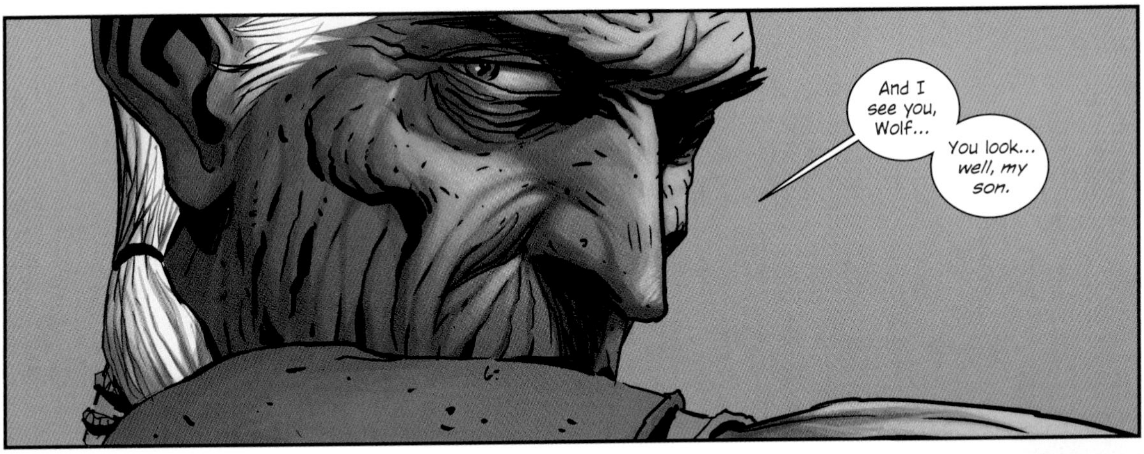
And I see you, Wolf...
You look... *well, my son.*

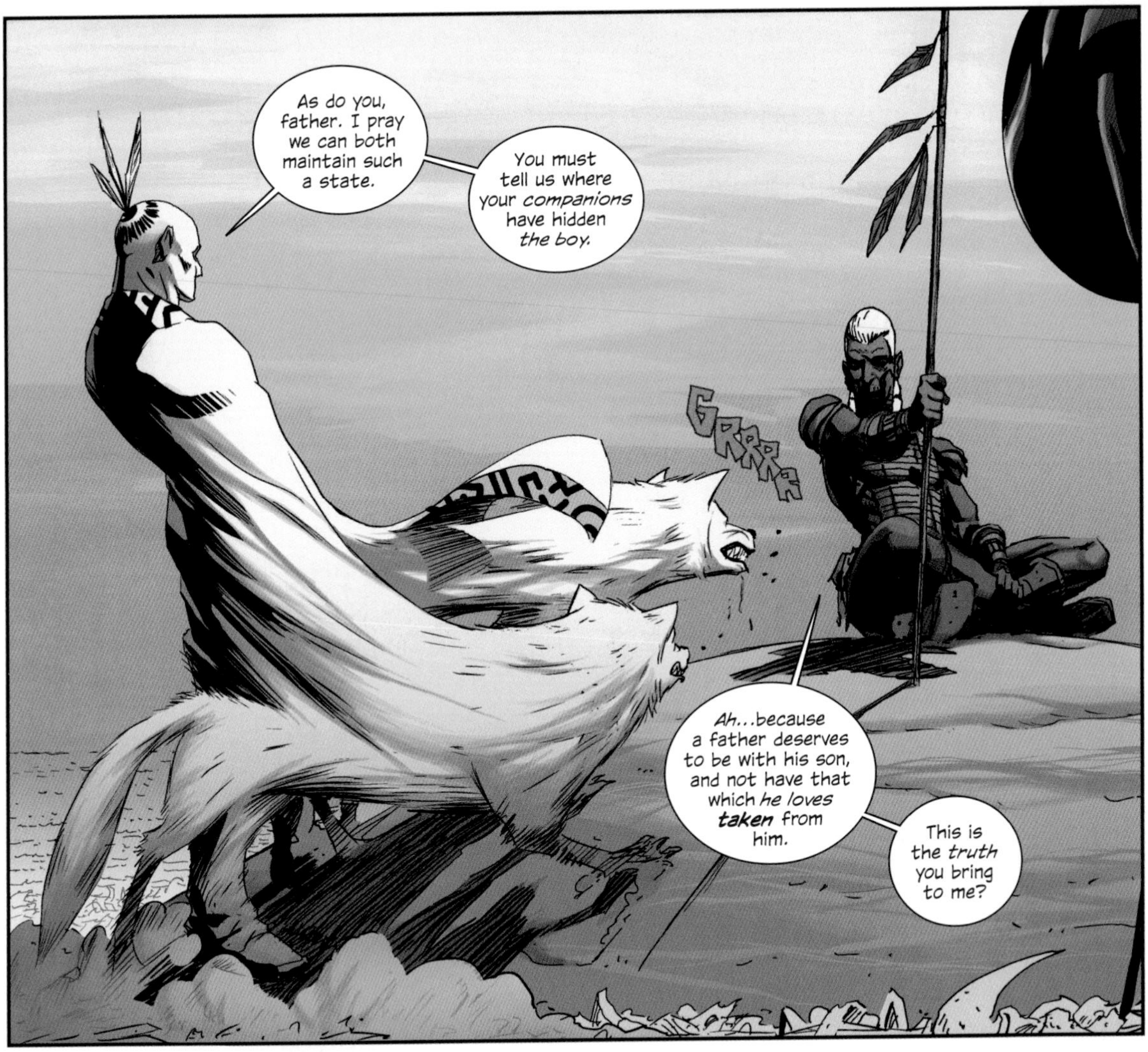
As do you, father. I pray we can both maintain such a state.
You must tell us where your *companions* have hidden *the boy.*
GRRRR
Ah...because a father deserves to be with his son, and not have that which *he loves* ***taken*** from him.
This is the *truth* you bring to me?

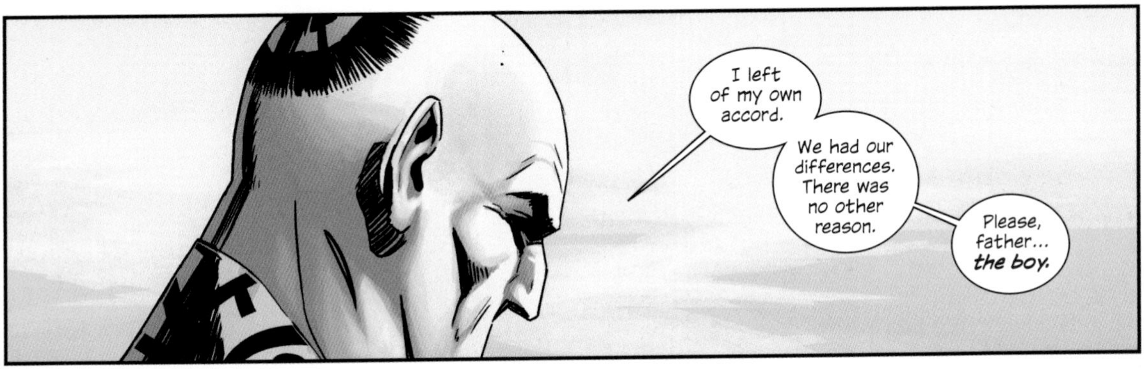
I left of my own accord.
We had our differences. There was no other reason.
Please, father... ***the boy.***

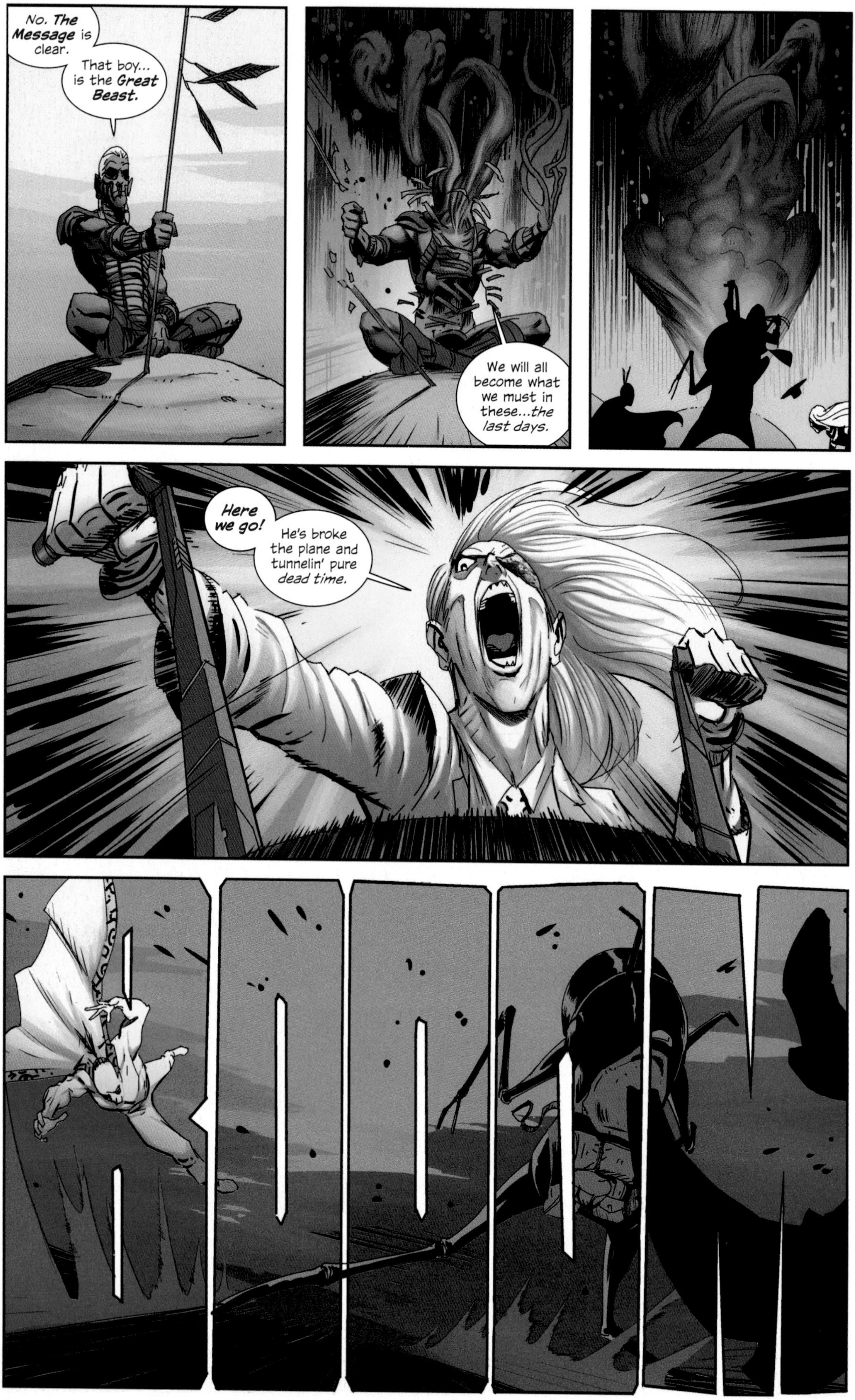
No. The Message is clear.
That boy... is the Great Beast.
We will all become what we must in these...the last days.
Here we go!
He's broke the plane and tunnelin' pure dead time.

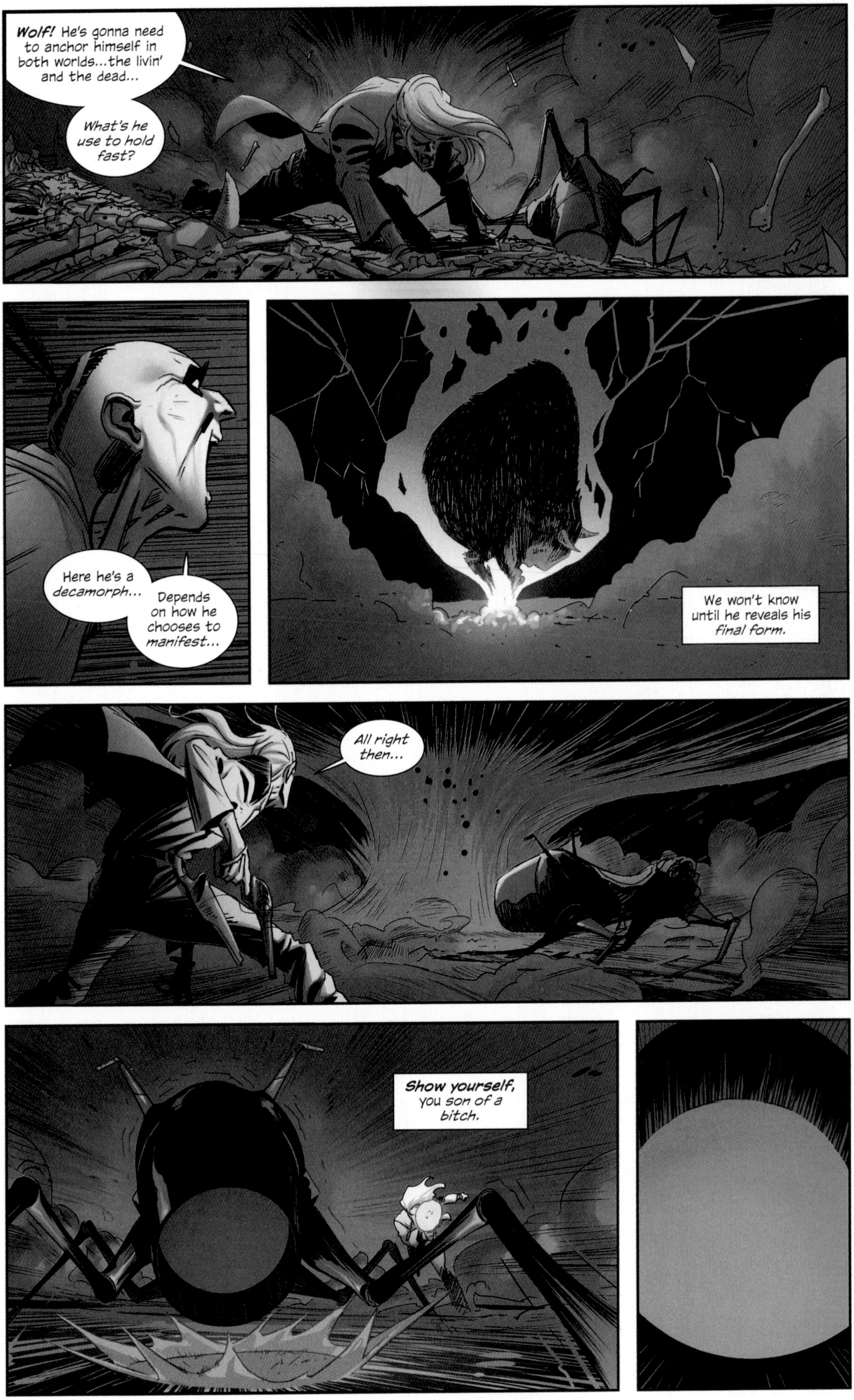
Wolf! He's gonna need to anchor himself in both worlds...the livin' and the dead...
What's he use to hold fast?
Here he's a decamorph...
Depends on how he chooses to manifest...
We won't know until he reveals his final form.
All right then...
Show yourself, you son of a bitch.

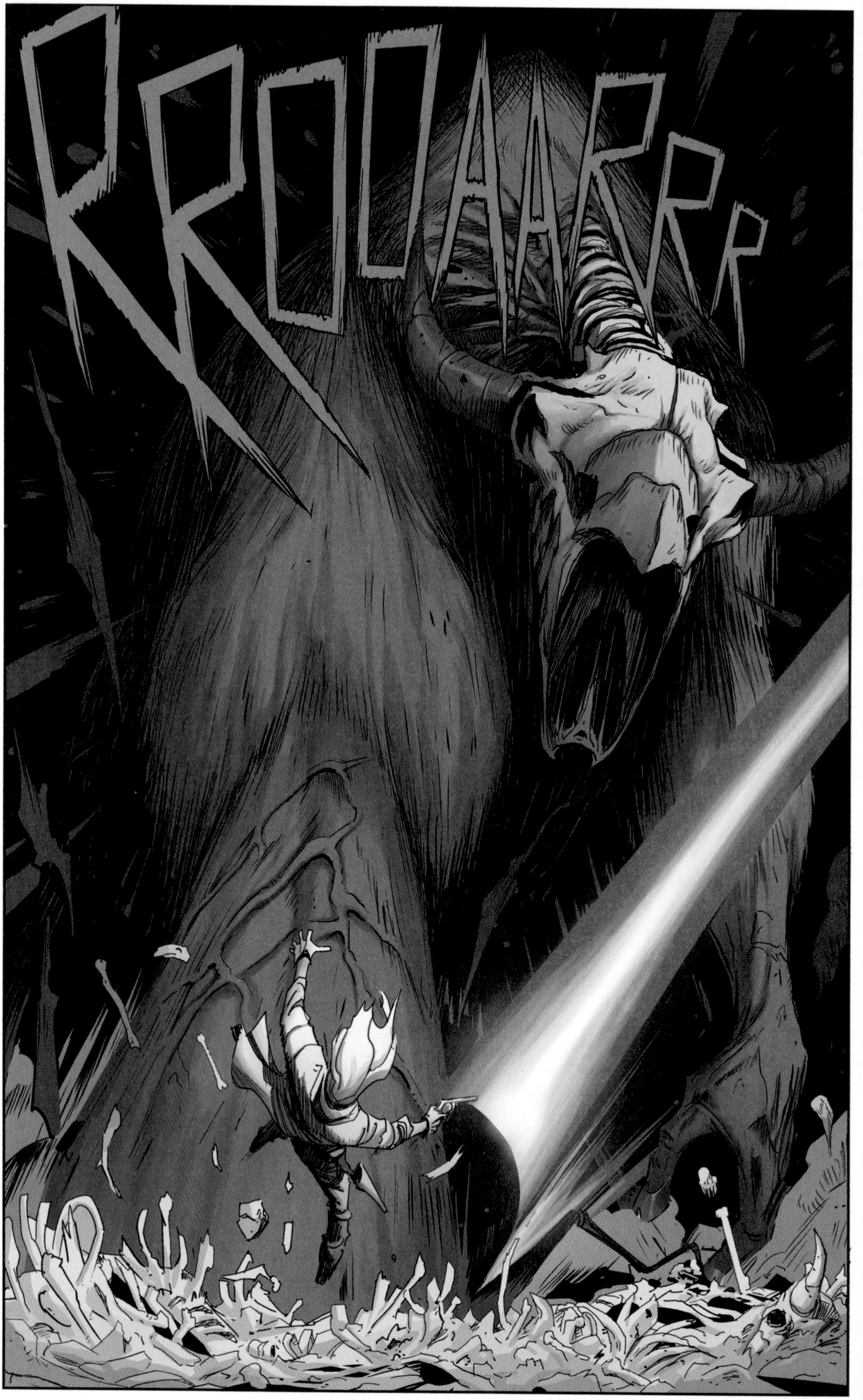
RROOAARRRR

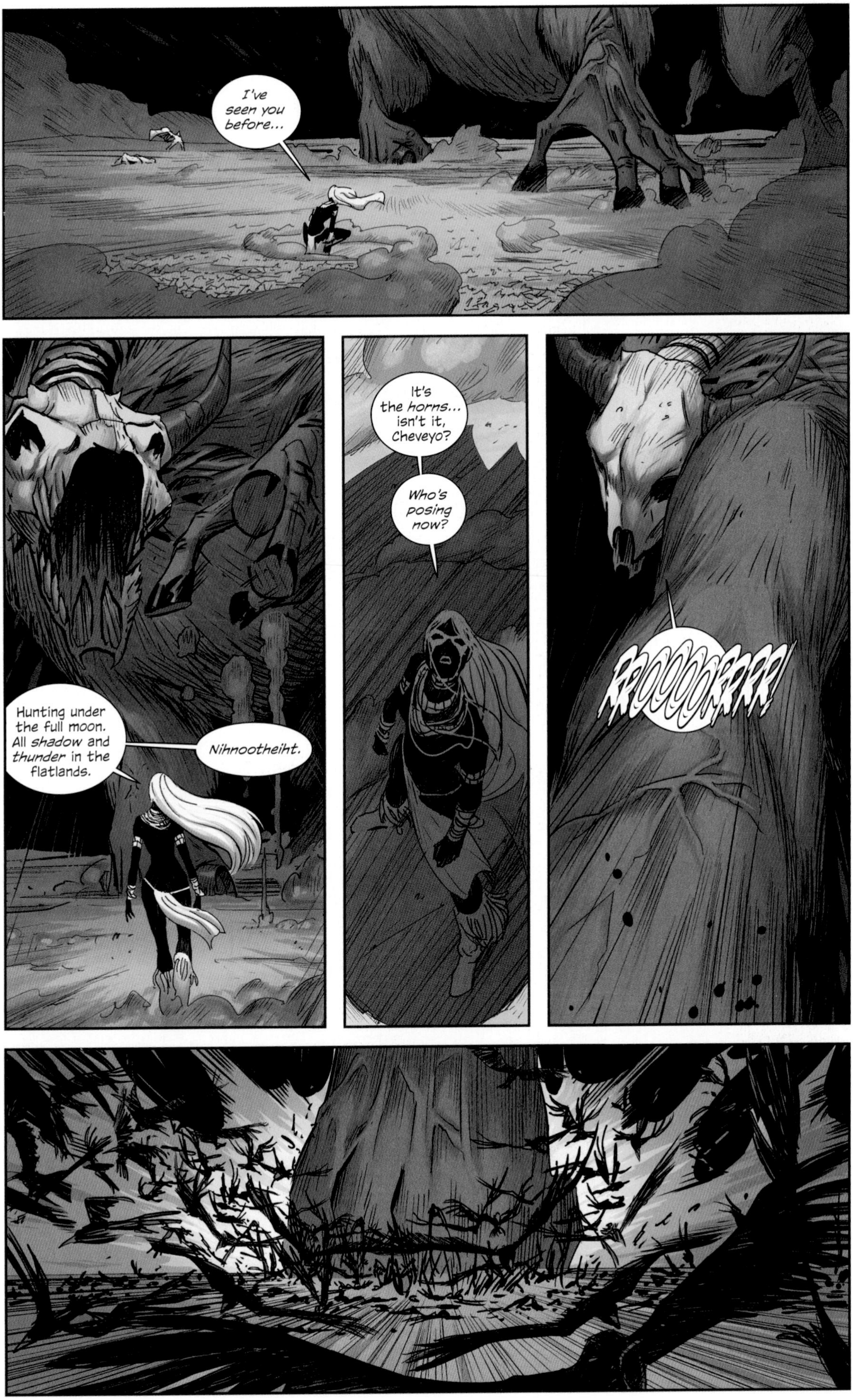
I've seen you before...
Hunting under the full moon. All *shadow* and *thunder* in the flatlands.
Nihnootheiht.
It's the *horns*... isn't it, Cheveyo?
Who's posing now?
RROOOOORRRR!

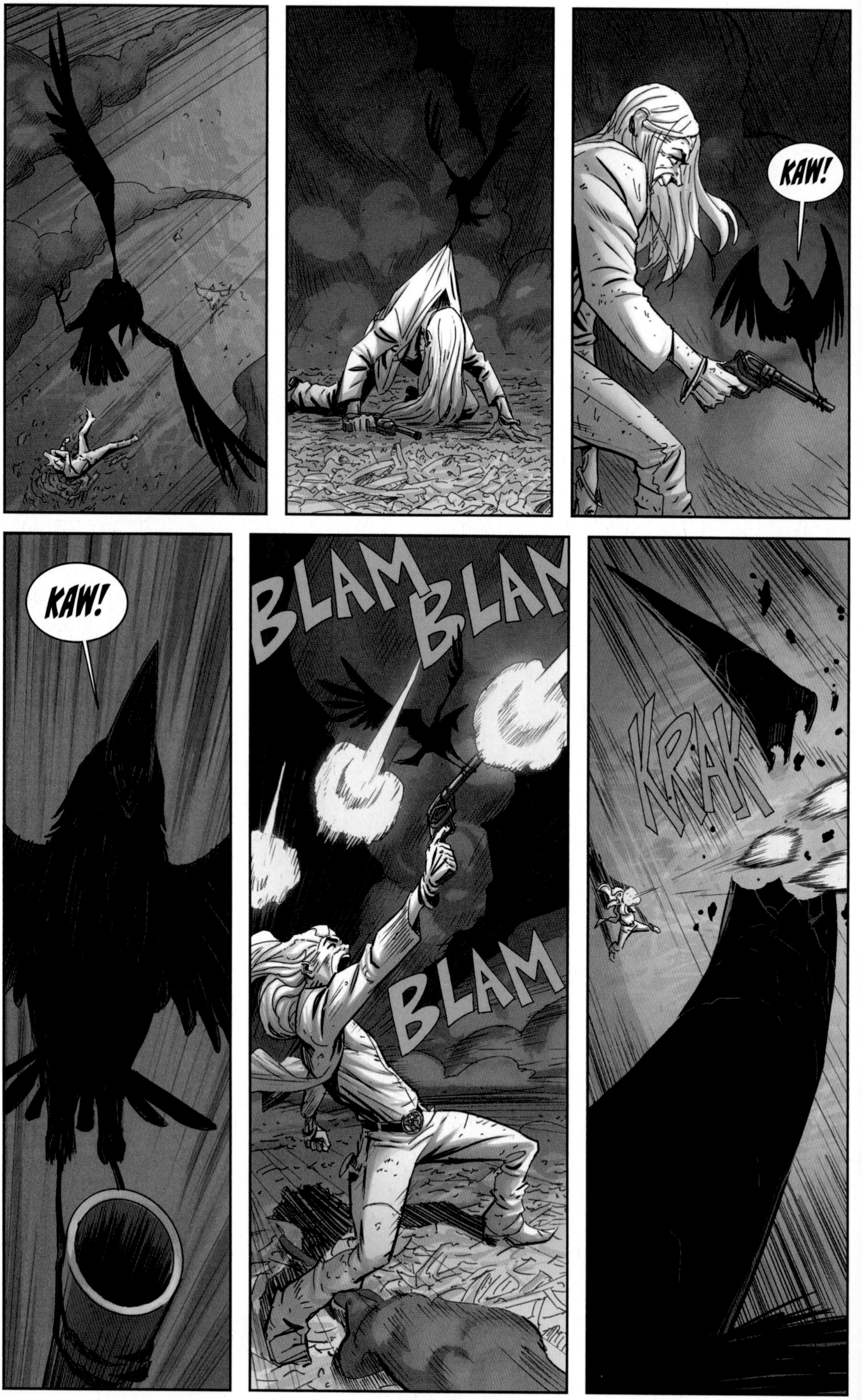
KAW!
KAW!
BLAM
BLAM
BLAM
KRAK

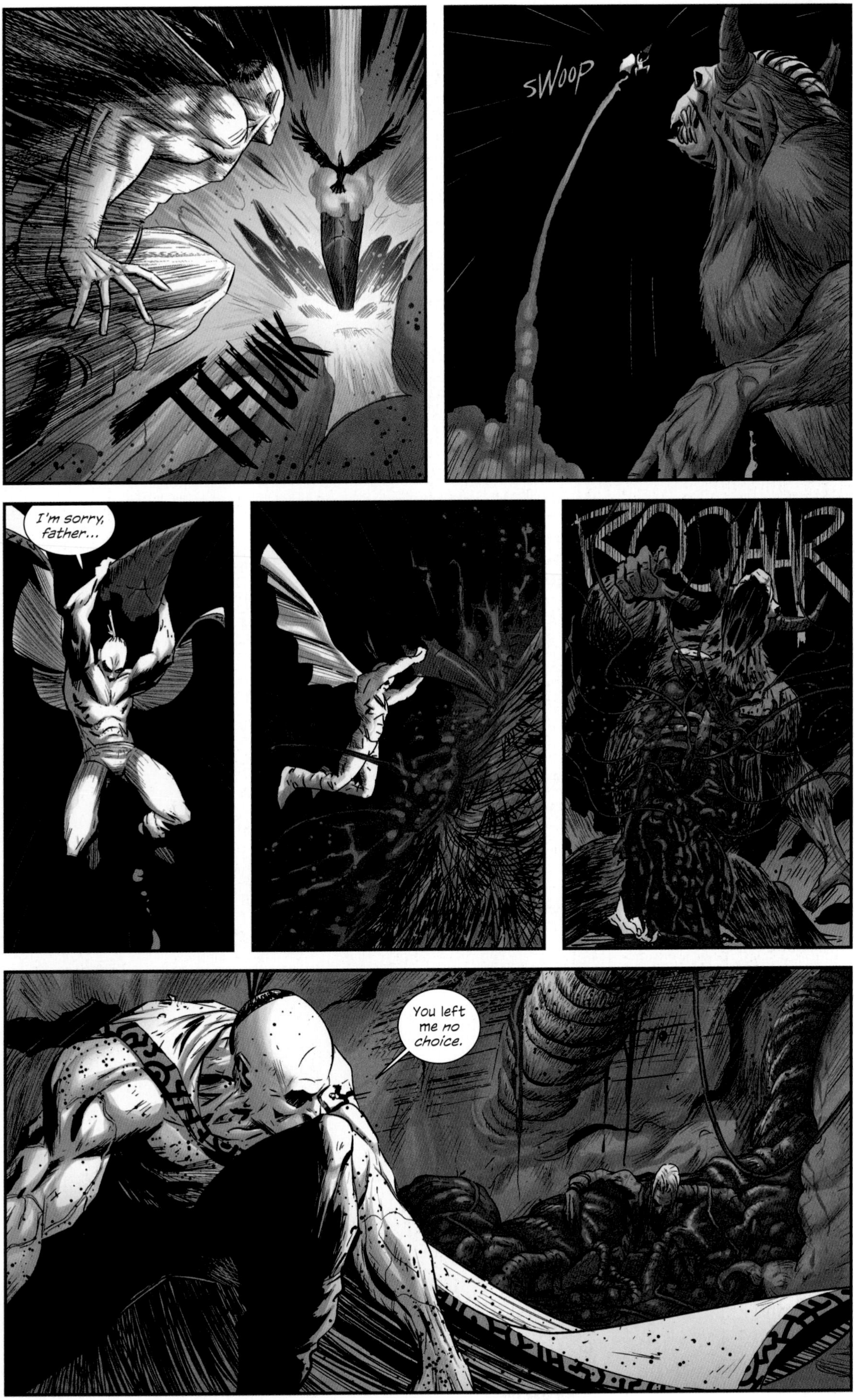
THUNK
SWOOP
I'm sorry, father...
ROOAHR
You left me no choice.

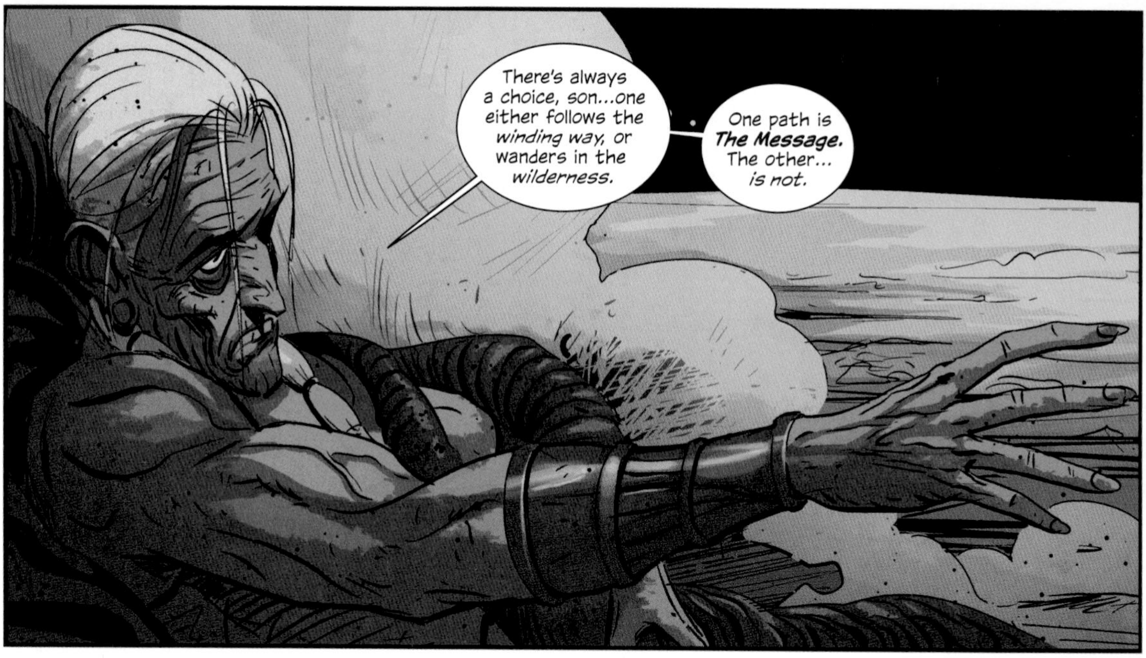
There's always a choice, son...one either follows the *winding way*, or wanders in the *wilderness*.
One path is ***The Message.*** The other... *is not.*

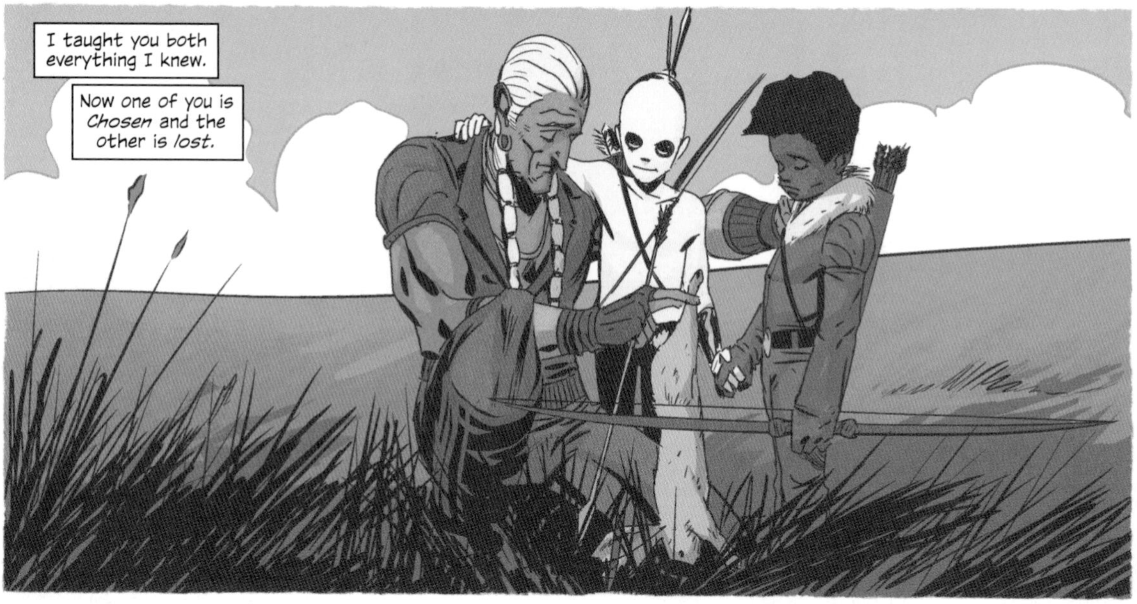
I taught you both everything I knew.
Now one of you is *Chosen* and the other is *lost*.

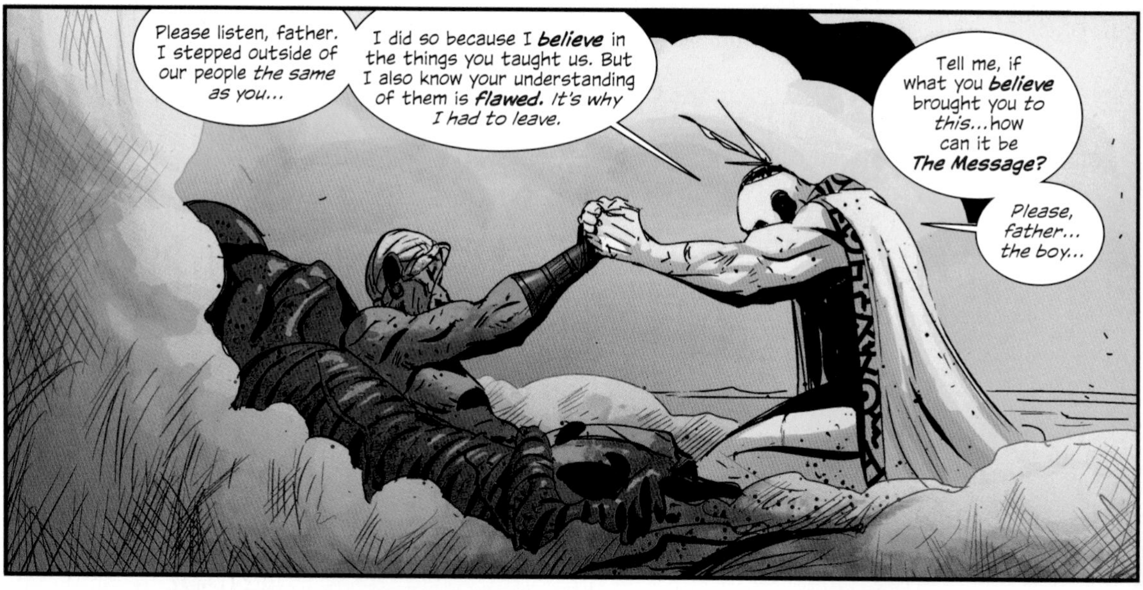
Please listen, father. I stepped outside of our people *the same as you...*
I did so because I ***believe*** in the things you taught us. But I also know your understanding of them is ***flawed.*** *It's why I had to leave.*
Tell me, if what you ***believe*** brought you to *this...*how can it be ***The Message?***
Please, father... the boy...

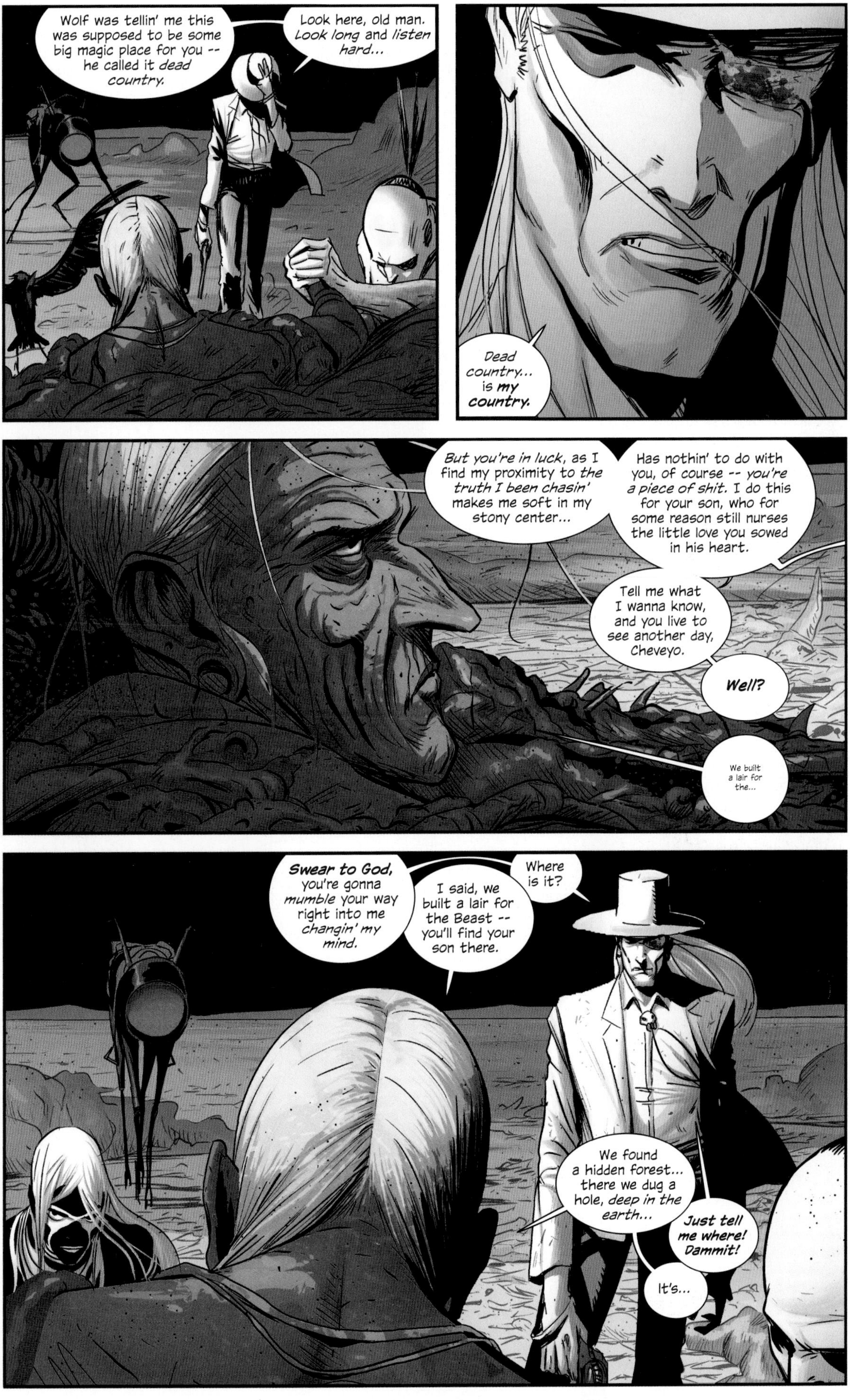
Wolf was tellin' me this was supposed to be some big magic place for you -- he called it *dead country.*
Look here, old man. *Look long* and *listen hard...*
Dead country... is ***my country.***
But you're in luck, as I find my proximity to *the truth I been chasin'* makes me soft in my stony center...
Has nothin' to do with you, of course -- *you're a piece of shit.* I do this for your son, who for some reason still nurses the little love you sowed in his heart.
Tell me what I wanna know, and you live to see another day, Cheveyo.
Well?
We built a lair for the...
Swear to God, you're gonna *mumble* your way right into me *changin' my mind.*
Where is it?
I said, we built a lair for the Beast -- you'll find your son there.
We found a hidden forest... there we dug a hole, *deep in the earth...*
Just tell me where! Dammit!
It's...

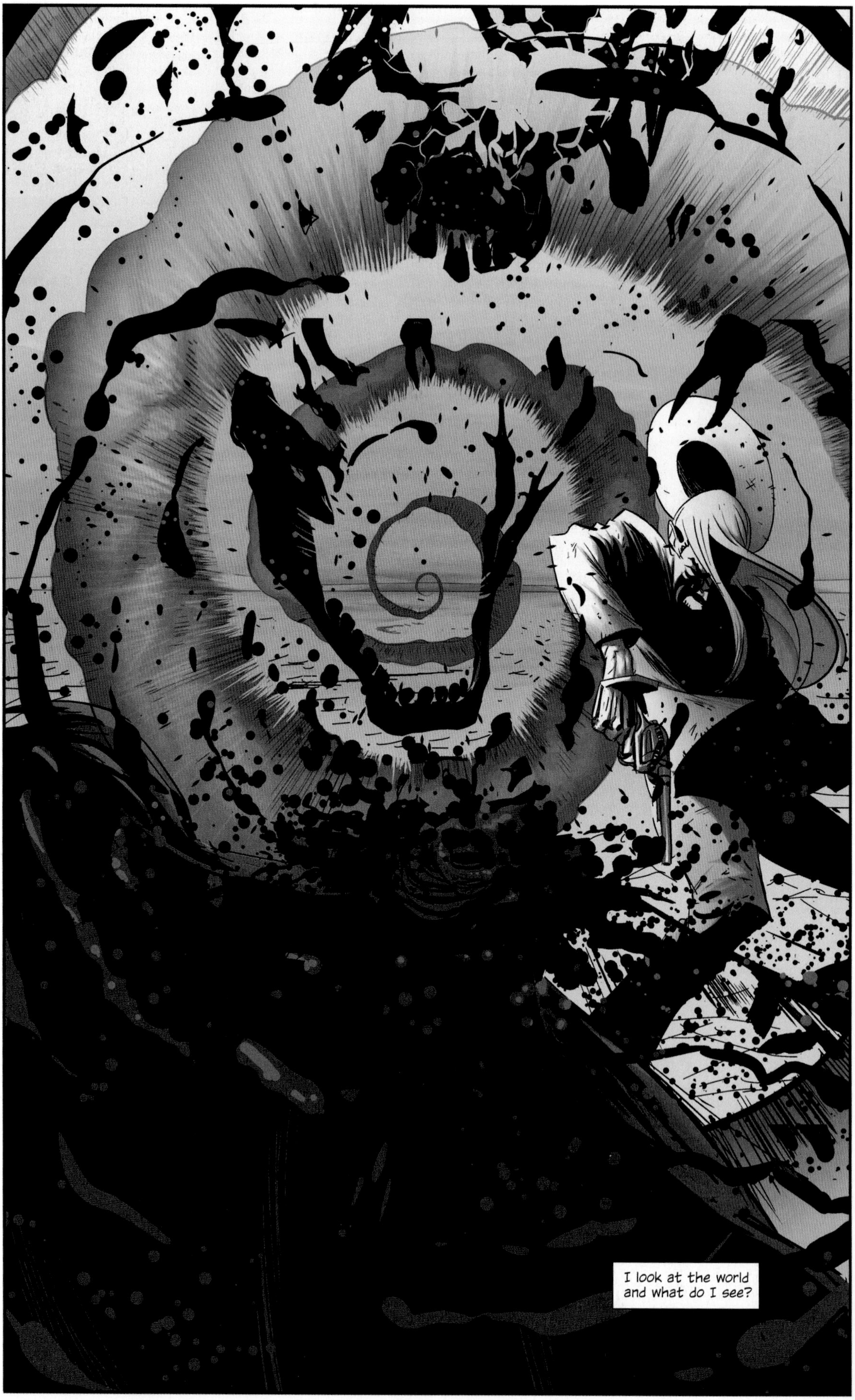
I look at the world and what do I see?

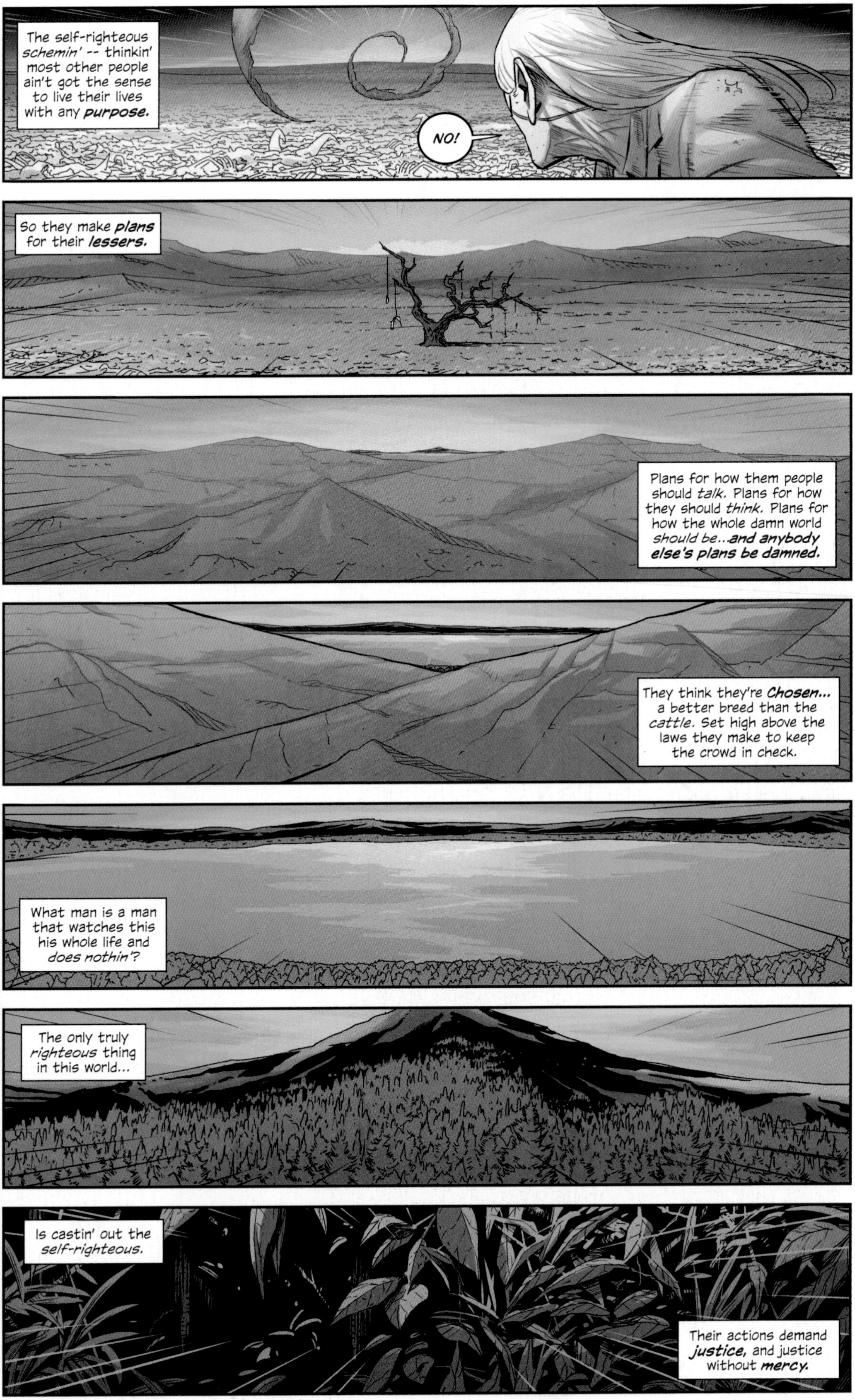
The self-righteous schemin' -- thinkin' most other people ain't got the sense to live their lives with any purpose.
NO!
So they make plans for their lessers.
Plans for how them people should talk. Plans for how they should think. Plans for how the whole damn world should be...and anybody else's plans be damned.
They think they're Chosen... a better breed than the cattle. Set high above the laws they make to keep the crowd in check.
What man is a man that watches this his whole life and does nothin'?
The only truly righteous thing in this world...
Is castin' out the self-righteous.
Their actions demand justice, and justice without mercy.

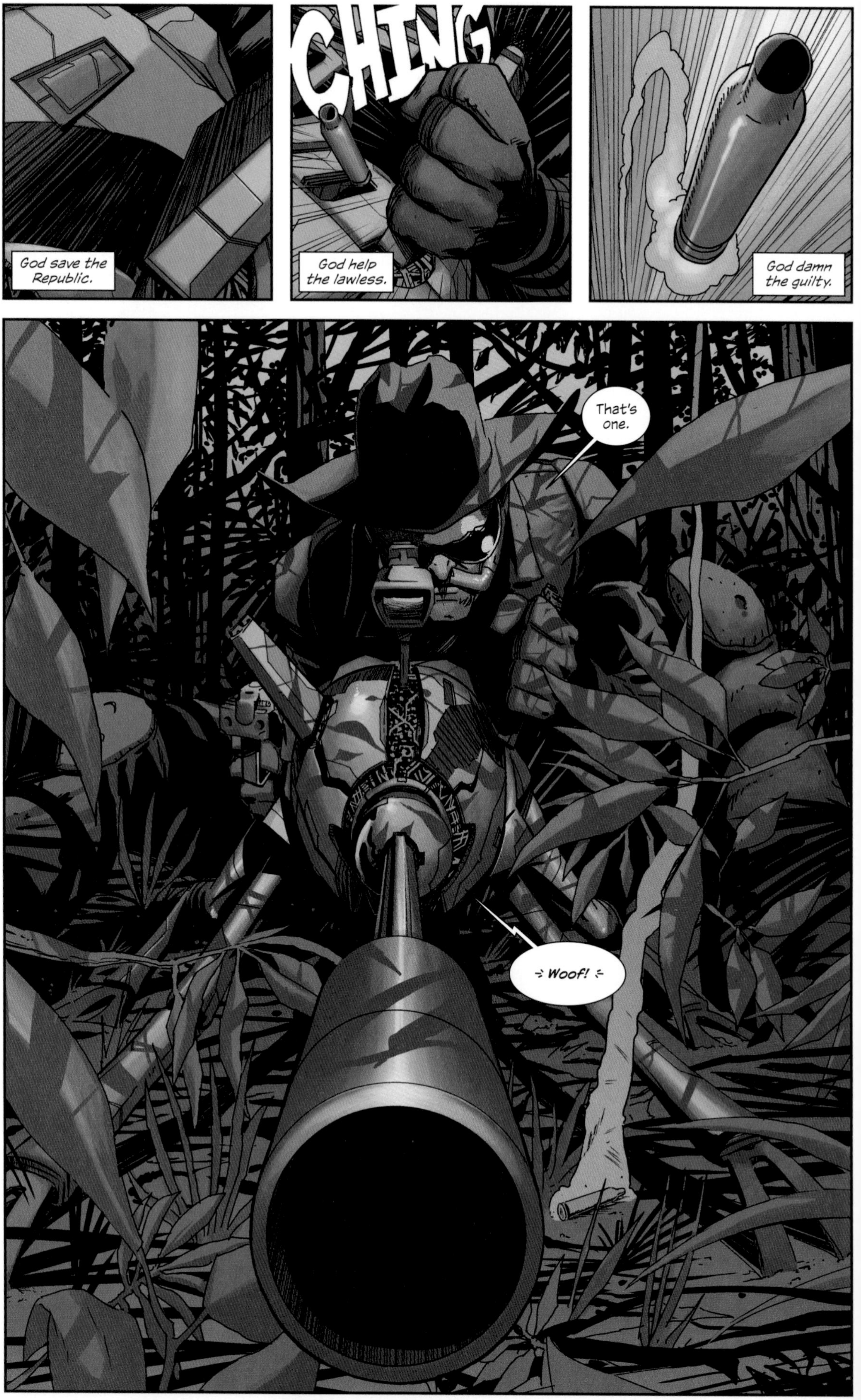
God save the Republic.
CHING
God help the lawless.
God damn the guilty.
That's one.
Woof!

ALL MEN TELL **LIES.**
THESE ARE A **FEW** OF
THEM.

Jonathan Hickman is the visionary talent behind such works as the Eisner-nominated **NIGHTLY NEWS, THE MANHATTAN PROJECTS** and **PAX ROMANA.** He also plies his trade at MARVEL working on books like **FANTASTIC FOUR** and **THE AVENGERS.**

His twin brother, Marc, is who really wrote this. Jonathan doesn't even get out of bed anymore.

Jonathan lives in South Carolina surrounded by immediate family and in-laws, which he plans on leaving unless they start showering him with the love and affection he deserves.

This includes his wife.

You can visit his website:***www.pronea.com***, or email him at:***jonathan@pronea.com.***

.

Nick Dragotta's career began at Marvel Comics working on titles as varied as **X-STATIX, THE AGE OF THE SENTRY, X-MEN: FIRST CLASS, CAPTAIN AMERICA: FOREVER ALLIES,** and **VENGEANCE.**

FANTASTIC FOUR #588 was the first time he collaborated with Jonathan Hickman, which lead to their successful run on **FF.**

In addition, Nick is the co-creator of **HOWTOONS,** a comic series teaching kids how to build things and explore the world around them. **EAST OF WEST** is Nick's first creator-owned project at Image.